INVENTORY 1995

THE NEW DEAL:

A DOCUMENTARY HISTORY

THE NEW DEAL

A
DOCUMENTARY HISTORY

edited by
William E. Leuchtenburg

UNIVERSITY OF SOUTH CAROLINA PRESS
COLUMBIA, S. C.

THE NEW DEAL

First HARPER TORCHBOOK edition published 1968 by Harper
& Row, Publishers, Incorporated, 49 East 33rd Street,
New York, N.Y. 10016.

This edition published by the University of South Carolina Press, Columbia, S.C., 1968, by arrangement with
Harper Torchbooks from whom a paperback edition is
available (TB/1354).

Library of Congress Catalog Card Number: 68-63014.

Contents

III. TOWARD THE WELFARE STATE

IV. UNIONIZING INDUSTRIAL AMERICA

V. ILL FARES THE LAND

VI. THE ROOSEVELT COALITION

VII. THUNDER ON THE LEFT

Preface

This collection is divided into nine parts organized topically but with an attempt to maintain a chronological pattern as well, for it begins with "The Crisis" that Roosevelt confronted when he took office and ends with "The Approach of War" which preoccupied the final years of his second term. The introductory essay establishes the historical context for these selections, and a collective headnote precedes each of the nine sections.

I am indebted to Esther Liberman and Rita Werner for help in photocopying and proofreading many of these selections.

W.E.L.

Introduction

No event in the twentieth century has had so great an impact on American society as the Great Depression. It struck precisely at the point when the Old Order of individualism and business leadership was scoring its greatest successes. Abruptly, with little warning, the stock market cracked, businesses folded, banks closed their doors, and more than one-third of the working force lost their jobs. One writer observed: "We seem to have stepped Alice-like through an economic looking-glass into a world where everything shrivels. Bond prices, stock prices, commodity prices, employment—they all dwindle." The suddenness and the ferocity of the collapse left the country bewildered; as Harvey Swados has written, "the American people were as absolutely unprepared for the Great Depression as if it had been a volcanic eruption in Kansas or Nebraska, pouring red-hot lava from coast to coast and border to border." By the time Franklin D. Roosevelt took office in March 1933, bewilderment had turned to anger—at the person of Herbert Hoover, at business leadership, at the slogans and values of the Old Order.

Roosevelt and the New Dealers responded to the unique opportunity they were given by pushing through an unprecedented program of legislation. As two sections of these documents make clear, some critics thought the New Deal was impairing traditional American values, while others believed that the Administration was not going nearly far enough. Yet even critics could agree that the changes wrought in the 1930's— the growth in power of the national government, the advance toward a Welfare State, the unionizing of industrial America, the subsidization of the farmer, the Supreme Court "revolution," the upheaval in political alignments—make the decade one of the most significant periods in American history.

I. The Crisis

The anthology begins with a poem in which Stephen Vincent Benét imagines a conversation with Walt Whitman. When in Selection 1

Whitman asks, "Is it well with these States?" Benét temporizes for a
moment, then confides to the good gray poet the desolation and terror
of the thirties: mass unemployment, want in the midst of plenty, homeless boys, dust storms, bitterness at businessmen, fear that democracy
may give way to a tyranny of right or left. When Whitman inquires,
"My tan-faced children?" Benét responds:

> "These are your tan-faced children.
> These skilled men, idle, with the holes in their shoes.
> These drifters from State to State, these wolvish, bewildered
>   boys . . .
> These are your tan-faced children, the parched young,
> The old man rooting in waste-heaps, the family rotting
> In the flat, before eviction . . .
> These are your tan-faced children."

Much of the rancor toward business and the Hoover Administration
arose from resentment at fatuous assurances that the situation was really
not so bad. Vice President Charles Curtis asserted that A.D. 1932 meant
"After Depression," and government spokesmen even argued that the
depression was a beneficent event, for the nation's health had never
been better. The ironically entitled article, "No One Has Starved," appearing in the business magazine *Fortune* two months before the 1932
election, was a milestone in national acceptance of the reality of the depression. In Selection 2, *Fortune* finds millions unemployed, the mechanism of local relief and private charity breaking down, and, contrary to
the bland assertions of the Hoover circle, that some people had, in fact,
died of starvation.

The ensuing documents in this section portray the growing sense of
crisis in Hoover's last year in office. The *Fortune* essay had disclosed
people scavenging food from garbage cans in St. Louis; Charles R.
Walker's article in *Forum* (Selection 3) describes another "Hooverville" in Youngstown, a pitiful collection of excrescences blotching a
noisome public dump. In Pennsylvania, he met a Slav who had come
to America thirty years before; reduced to living in a Hooverville hovel,
he cried: "If you had told me when I come to this country that now I
live here like dis, I shot you dead." By 1932, even Iowa farmers, regarded
as the mainstays of the Old Order, had startled the country by adopting
revolutionary tactics; yet, as Mary Heaton Vorse reveals in Selection 4,
they insisted that, like their forebears in the American Revolution, they
were patriots. Desperately afraid of being reduced to a peasantry, they
called for a moratorium on mortgage debts and crop prices that would
ensure them "cost of production." In the November elections, Iowa,

Hoover's native state, would join forty-one others in repudiating the Republican President, who, as Selection 5 indicates, had become a symbol
for deprivation and misery. In the final document in this section, Ruth
McKenney details in diary form (Selection 6) the rapid erosion of faith
in local government and business leadership in Akron in the weeks before Roosevelt took office. As savings vanished, as businesses went bankrupt, the community turned desperately to Washington for help.

II. The New Deal Response

Section II opens with a Washington correspondent's breathless account of the Hundred Days Congress of the spring of 1933. His report
in Selection 7 conveys the stunning impression made by the greatest
spate of legislation in the history of the republic, all crammed into less
than four months. In noting the vast expansion of the presidential
power, he observes that Franklin D. Roosevelt seemed to have been
"transfigured" from the amiable campaigner of 1932 to the resolute man
of action of 1933. Like many other Americans, the correspondent is uncertain how it will all turn out, but he is convinced that the pernicious
Old Order is finished, and that the United States is "moving along a
new path of social control and planned economy."

In Selection 8, Adolf A. Berle, Jr., one of the members of Roosevelt's
original Brain Trust, explicates the theory of the New Deal. In em-
phasizing the inadequacy of the Old Order, Berle asks: "Why is it that
with more food, more clothing, more housing, more luxuries, than we
know what to do with, there are some 25,000,000 people in the United
States who are hungry, naked, living most precariously, and with little
more than the bare necessities of subsistence?" The aim of the New
Deal, Berle stresses, is to introduce "a power of organization into the
economic system which can be used to counterbalance the effects of organization gone wrong; and to make sure that the burdens of readjustment are equitably distributed, and that no group of individuals will be
ground to powder in order to satisfy the needs of an economic balance."
Not all readers will find Berle's explanation of why the United States
should prefer the New Deal to a Socialist society fully satisfactory. More
compelling is the account by Roosevelt's Secretary of Labor, Frances
Perkins, in Selection 9, which makes clear that a society which lacks
an established administrative class and has only a limited sense of a
"State" is hardly prepared to adopt a Socialist solution.

The remaining documents in Section II illustrate some of the more
important aspects of the New Deal response to the crisis. In Selection
10, General Hugh Johnson, the swashbuckling head of the National In-

dustrial Recovery Administration, defends the use of martial propaganda to win popular support for NIRA. Historians who accept some of Johnson's claims for the achievements of the Recovery Administration would be more critical than the General is of its restrictionist economics and coercive rhetoric. Selection 11 recounts the impression made by the influx of intellectuals into Washington. In Selection 12, David E. Lilienthal, one of the three directors of the Tennessee Valley Authority, recapitulates the efforts of the TVA to revive a depressed region. The sports writer Rud Rennie notes in Selection 13 the visible signs of revived morale in the South as early as 1934. The *New York Times* correspondent Anne O'Hare McCormick, who was in Europe during the birth of the New Deal, is also struck by the changes wrought in a single year. She is especially impressed by "the steady aggrandizement of Washington" with the shift of the nation's financial capital from Wall Street to Washington. Wall Street, she writes in Selection 14, "is a kind of deserted village, deprived of its chief attractions. All the audacity in the country has been cornered by Washington . . . easily the most animated city in the world."

III. Toward the Welfare State

The United States in the 1930's took the first steps toward creating a national framework for a Welfare State. In Selection 15, Martha Gellhorn, who had served on the staff of the Federal Emergency Relief Administration, depicts the demoralization of the unemployed and the sense of desperation many felt in a world that no longer had a future. For the jobless man, the acceptance of relief appeared to be a forfeit of manhood, especially when his home was invaded by a woman social worker, no matter how well intentioned she might be. Roosevelt's decision to set up a vast works program in 1935 was an attempt, only partially successful, to wipe out the stigma of relief by creating the opportunity for federal employment on useful projects. In Selection 16, Hallie Flanagan, director of the Vassar Experimental Theatre and subsequently of the Federal Theatre Project, remembers a trip in the summer of 1935 with Harry Hopkins, a former social worker who had headed Roosevelt's relief organizations in both Albany and Washington and who had just been appointed director of the Works Progress Administration (WPA). On their way from Washington to Iowa City to attend a National Theatre Conference, Hopkins explains why work relief is superior to direct relief and asks her a searching question: "Can you spend money?" Some of the funds granted by the Emergency Relief Appropriation Act were assigned to a newly created agency, the National Youth Administration, discussed in Selection 17. The NYA aided not only college students but also high school students and vocational apprentices.

The New Dealers knew that relief was only a stopgap; of much greater long-run significance was the Social Security Act, adopted toward the close of the turbulent Second Hundred Days of 1935. In Selection 18, President Roosevelt asserts: "If the Senate and House of Representatives in this long and arduous session had done nothing more than pass this Bill, this session would be regarded as historic for all time." A week later, in a Labor Day address (Selection 19), Frances Perkins spells out the provisions of the law: old age pensions, unemployment insurance, and aid to the disabled. The new law, she concludes, "will make this great Republic a better and a happier place in which to live—for us, our children and our children's children."

IV. Unionizing Industrial America

At the outset of the New Deal, very few workers in American factories belonged to unions. In industries like steel, attempts at unionization at different times over a half century had been crushed by employers, sometimes with overt or covert support from the government. Most union members were concentrated in the American Federation of Labor, in which almost all constituent unions were organized on a craft basis. The outstanding exception was the United Mine Workers, an industrial union headed by John L. Lewis.

Lewis quickly seized upon the opportunity offered by the New Deal to recruit members for the UMW and to encourage the creation of industrial unions in industries like rubber which had long resisted organization. But when factory workers flocked into the A.F. of L. by the tens of thousands, the Federation discouraged the new unionists by breaking up their organizations into separate craft unions. Lewis and his associates insisted on a more militant policy to organize the unorganized; at the San Francisco convention of the A.F. of L. in 1934 they compelled the craft leaders to compromise, but the Federation's chieftains nullified the effect of the agreement.

At Atlantic City in October 1935, the rival forces met for a return engagement. When the craft unionists prevailed in the Resolutions Committee, Charles P. Howard, head of the typographical union, filed a minority report on behalf of the industrial unionists, and Lewis spoke in support of the minority report. Selection 20 is representative of Lewis' arrogant grandiloquence. In an address studded with archaisms like "Methinks," Lewis stormed at his opponents: "A year ago at San Francisco I was a year younger and naturally I had more faith in the Executive

Council. I was beguiled into believing. . . . At San Francisco they seduced me with fair words. Now, of course, having learned that I was seduced, I am enraged and I am ready to rend my seducers limb from limb, including Delegate Woll. In that sense, of course, I speak figuratively." His assault on the leadership of the Federation and the obdurate reply by Daniel Tobin, leader of the Teamsters, demonstrated that differences between the two factions had almost reached the breaking point. Before the convention ended, Lewis had exchanged blows with "Big Bill" Hutcheson of the Carpenters and on the following day the Lewis cadre met to plan the creation of the Committee for Industrial Organization (CIO). Started as a committee within the A.F. of L., the CIO soon became a separate rival organization.

When the CIO began the difficult task of organizing plants, it frequently encountered violence. In Selection 21, the sociologist Alfred Winslow Jones sums up the experience of the rubber workers as revealed before a hearing of the La Follette Civil Liberties Committee. The first victory for the young CIO came early in 1936 in the rubber worker capital of Akron, which set a precedent for the General Motors sit-down strike, narrated by Mary Heaton Vorse in Selection 22. When the United Automobile Workers cracked GM, their success was assured; in one year, UAW membership soared from 30,000 to 400,000. Mrs. Vorse writes: "The joy of victory tore through Flint. It was more than the joy of war ceasing, it was the joy of creation. The workers were creating a new life. The wind of Freedom had roared down Flint's streets."

In the 1930's, the national government, which had often obstructed unionization in the past, became the helpmeet of the labor movement. The same Congress which enacted the Social Security law also passed the National Labor Relations Act, excerpted in Selection 23, which gave legal sanction to labor's attempts to organize and bargain collectively. However, employers believed that the Supreme Court would invalidate the law, especially in view of its opinion in the Carter case (*Carter* v. *Carter Coal Company*, 298 U. S. 238 [1936]) which denied the power of the federal government to regulate labor conditions in coal mines. Frustrated by a series of adverse decisions by the Court, President Roosevelt, on February 5, 1937, startled the country by proposing to "pack" the Supreme Court by adding as many as six new justices. Two months later, the Court in a series of 5–4 decisions greatly expanded its earlier interpretation of the commerce clause in upholding the constitutionality of the Wagner Act. In the case chosen for Selection 24, Chief Justice Charles Evans Hughes states: "When industries organize themselves on a national scale, making their relation to interstate commerce the domi-

nant factor in their activities, how can it be maintained that their industrial labor relations constitute a forbidden field into which Congress
may not enter when it is necessary to protect interstate commerce from
nant factor in their activities, how can it be maintained that their in-
the paralyzing consequences of industrial war?" Partly as a consequence
of having government sanction for their activities, the CIO by the end
of the Roosevelt era had organized unions in all America's major industries.

V. Ill Fares the Land

When Franklin Roosevelt took office, the American farmer had his
back to the wall. Cotton prices had tumbled from 17½ cents to 4½
cents and, as one writer noted, "Wheat on the Liverpool market fetched
the lowest price since the reign of Charles II." At sheriffs' sales, farmers
lost their lands under the auctioneer's hammer. Hoover's attempt to aid
the farmer without curbing production had ended in a fiasco as mounting surpluses drove prices down. By the summer of 1931 even the chairman of Hoover's own farm board was urging "immediate plowing under
of every third row of cotton now growing."

In the Hundred Days of 1933, Congress created a program of government subsidies for farmers who would restrict output; it would be financed by a processing tax, and administered by an Agricultural Adjustment Administration (AAA). It also adopted a Farm Credit Act to
aid the mortgage-burdened farmer. Before the year was out, both Roosevelt and his Secretary of Agriculture, Henry Agard Wallace, had run
into a fire of criticism when the government plowed up cotton and
slaughtered six million little pigs. Yet, as Roosevelt explains in Selection 25, these were only temporary expedients confined to 1933. The
principle of scarcity, however, continued to characterize the New Deal
farm program down until World War II.

Secretary Wallace felt deeply troubled by the quest for scarcity at a
time when many in the world were in want, but in Selection 26 he offers a justification for curbing production. He also refers to "the old
New England town-meeting idea in the county production control associations." To some, such local controls over farm policy represented
surrender of a national program to powerful parochial interests. Yet,
when millions of farmers cast ballots in crop referenda and received
monthly checks from the government, the New Deal had clearly made
a radical departure, even if it fell short of "economic self-government."
One Russian visitor to the Department of Agriculture, where 80,000
checks a day were being sent to American farmers, exclaimed: "Good
Lord! This is a revolution!"

On January 6, 1936, the U. S. Supreme Court, in a 6–3 decision in the Butler (or Hoosac Mills) case invalidated the AAA's processing tax (*U. S. v. Butler et al.*, 297 U. S. 61 [1936]). Justice Owen Roberts delivered the majority opinion, which affirmed a judgment by a Circuit Court of Appeals, and Justice Harlan Fiske Stone filed a biting dissent. Selection 27 is an excerpt from a production of Hallie Flanagan's Federal Theatre Project, employing the "Living Newspaper" technique which combined the methods of the drama and the newsreel.

The Court's decision, which compelled the Administration to find a different device to subsidize the farmer, pushed the government further in a direction in which it was already heading: a large-scale program for soil conservation. The experience of the Plains States, where a prolonged drought had created a vast dust bowl, emphasized the perils of improper cultivation. In Selection 28, one drought victim, Caroline A. Henderson, who had lived on a homestead in Oklahoma for almost thirty years, points the moral. She views the dust bowl as, in part, a consequence of the canons of the Old Order when she writes of "the smothering silt from the fields of rugged individualists who persist in their right to do nothing." Selection 29, which also emphasizes soil depletion, presents the words spoken in the government-made documentary film, *The River*, which one writer called "a story of sin, unfolding with the relentless inevitability of Greek tragedy." Pare Lorentz's work reflects the cultural nationalism of the New Deal with its poetry of the commonplace and its rejoicing in the lovely sounds of American names.

Lorentz writes, too, of the New Deal agencies which had been attempting to cope with the problem: the Tennessee Valley Authority, the Farm Security Administration, and Roosevelt's "tree army," the Civilian Conservation Corps (CCC). In Selection 30, the novelist and short story writer Sherwood Anderson, author of *Winesburg, Ohio*, ponders the meaning of a CCC camp in the TVA country of the southern Appalachians. Anderson, who had written eloquently of the affliction of hard times, suggests in this essay that the depression also offered exhilarating opportunities. Speaking of foresters who were directing the work of the CCC'ers, he observes: "The depression has given them their chance. 'Hurrah for the depression,' one of them said to me. They are making a new kind of American man out of the city boy in the woods, and they are planning at least to begin to make a new land with the help of such boys."

If some in rural America found the depression inspiriting, for others the 1930's was a time of almost unrelieved misfortune. The drought and the drop in crop prices drove farm families from states like Caroline Henderson's Oklahoma westward to California in search of jobs as migrant workers. John Steinbeck's novel, *The Grapes of Wrath*, from which Selection 31 is taken, is the classic account of the trek of a family of "Okies," the Joads. After an arduous odyssey, they are greeted in California by hostile deputies and vigilantes who serve the interests of the huge corporation farms. In the midst of their travail, they come unexpectedly on an FSA camp, one of the very few that Congress has authorized. Tom's final question directs a pointed query at the inadequacy of the New Deal farm program: "Why ain't they more places like this?" Yet the New Deal at least made a beginning at recognizing the claims of the mudsills and the bottom dogs.

VI. The Roosevelt Coalition

The Great Depression and the New Deal produced an upheaval in American politics. For the first time since before the Civil War, a Democratic nominee entered the White House with a majority of the popular votes. A country which had been predominantly Republican now became overwhelmingly Democratic. Class replaced section as the most important determinant of political alignments.

In Selection 32, the Scripps-Howard columnist Thomas Stokes emphasizes the class cleavages which marked the 1936 campaign. Selection 33 is the speech President Roosevelt delivered at the Forbes Field rally, described by Stokes in the previous selection. Roosevelt had also come to Forbes Field in the 1932 campaign to give an address in which he stated: "I regard reduction in Federal spending as one of the most important issues of this campaign. In my opinion, it is the most direct and effective contribution that Government can make to business." Since then, the President had embarked on an unprecedented program of government spending, although he remained a believer in budget balancing.

Instead of apologizing for his departure from the promises of the 1932 campaign, Roosevelt made a bold defense of government spending. He declared:

In three years our net national debt has increased eight billions of dollars. But in two years of the recent war it increased as much as twenty-five billion dollars. National defense and the future of America were involved in 1917. National defense and the future of America were also involved in 1933. Don't you believe that the saving of America has been cheap at that price? . . .

Compare the scoreboard which you have in Pittsburgh now with the scoreboard which you had when I stood here at second base in this field four years ago. At that time, as I drove through these

great valleys, I could see mile after mile of this greatest mill and
factory area in the world, a dead panorama of silent black structures
and smokeless stacks. I saw idleness and hunger instead of the whirl
of machinery. Today as I came north from West Virginia, I saw
mines operating, I found bustle and life, the hiss of steam, the ring
of steel on steel—the roaring song of industry.

Since economic conditions were undeniably better than when FDR
had taken office, he could argue persuasively that he had rescued the
nation from a Republican depression. Yet the unemployed still num-
bered eight million in 1936, and in the next year the country would
suffer a sharp recession. Not until World War II would the country
once more enjoy full employment.

Selection 34 from Harold Ickes' diary once more enunciates the
class theme in the President's appeal. After a campaign in which the
Democrats execrated the "big financial interests," Roosevelt scored a
landslide victory over the Republican candidate, Governor Alf Landon
of Kansas. By 1936, FDR had forged an urban, lower-class coalition
which, as Samuel Lubell demonstrates in Selection 35, would be a
persistent feature of Democratic victories in later elections. Lubell
writes: "The New Deal appears to have accomplished what the Socialists, the I.W.W. and the Communists never could approach. It
has drawn a class line across the face of American politics." Roosevelt's
unprecedented string of four successive victories rested, too, on the
"politics of the deed." In explaining Roosevelt's nearly 4–1 triumph in
the working-class district of Charlestown, Massachusetts, Lubell points
out:

Hundreds got pay raises under the wage-hour law; more hundreds
of seasonal workers are having slack months cushioned by unemployment-insurance benefits. The NYA is helping from 300 to 500
youths; at the worst of the depression thousands held WPA jobs;
of 1500 persons past sixty-five in the ward, more than 600 receive
old-age assistance; another 600 cases are on direct relief and get aid
for dependent children. Charlestown is a food-stamp area; the
WPA improved its bathing beach; a new low-cost housing project
will relieve some of the ward's congestion.

VII. Thunder on the Left

It was a fundamental tenet of Marxist doctrine that an attempt such
as the New Deal to achieve reform within a capitalist framework was
doomed to failure. In the heady spring of the Hundred Days of 1933,

few paid attention to these strictures. But when in late 1933 and 1934 the move toward recovery faltered, such criticism could be made with telling effect. In Selection 36, the Marxist journalists Benjamin Stolberg and Warren Jay Vinton state: "There is nothing the New Deal has so far done that could not have been done better by an earthquake."

Radical movements often prosper not when conditions are at their worst but when they have begun to improve. In 1934, after the hopes of 1933 had been, in part, blighted by the slow pace of the next year, the country witnessed a series of eruptions, including radical-led strikes in San Francisco, Minneapolis, and Toledo. That year, the poem in Selection 37 by the Negro poet Langston Hughes was read at the annual convention of the Communist Party. It ends:

> Cause the pot's still empty,
> And the cupboard's still bare,
> And you can't build a bungalow
> Out o'air—
> > Mr. Roosevelt, listen!
> > What's the matter here?

In the same critical year of 1934, the former muckraker Lincoln Steffens, in the letter reprinted in Selection 38, writes: "Communism can solve our problem. . . . That's my muckraker's proclamation." Yet other radicals were skeptical of the claims of communism. The philosopher John Dewey, although he also reproved the New Dealers from the left, argues, in Selection 39, that the failure of the Communists to recognize the need to accommodate their ideas to the American individualistic tradition "verges to my mind on political insanity." He adds: "One of the reasons I am not a Communist is that the emotional tone and methods of discussion and dispute which seem to accompany Communism at present are extremely repugnant to me. Fair-play, elementary honesty in the representation of facts and especially of the opinions of others, are something more than 'bourgeois virtues.' "

Despite the fact that the "objective conditions" for success of a Marxist party were never more auspicious than in the 1930's, neither the Communists nor the Socialists won a sizable following, and the most effective opposition to the New Deal from the left came from such ambiguous movements as those led by Huey Long and the Reverend Charles Coughlin, both of which had decidedly "rightist" aspects as well. The leader of the Share Our Wealth movement, Senator Huey Pierce Long, advocated a redistribution of wealth the New Deal failed to achieve. Yet at the same time, his autocratic rule in Louisiana led some to fear him as an incipient fascist. Certain features of his program, such as the character of the committee he lists in Selection 40, have a conservative cast. But *My First Days in the White House*, which appeared posthumously, is written with such typically saucy arrogance that one can never be sure when Long is being serious. Roosevelt, however, viewed the Kingfish as a formidable rival, as Selection 41 suggests. He not only used the weapon of patronage but worked with Huey's opponents; denied Louisiana a share of federal spending; and dispatched revenue agents to New Orleans to ferret out evidence of tax evasion.

In Selection 41, Father Coughlin leads his organization, the National Union for Social Justice, into the newly created Union Party, an unstable amalgam of Coughlin's followers, supporters of Dr. Francis Townsend (sponsor of an old-age pension scheme), and the remnants of Long's Share Our Wealth association. Coughlin, who had won a national radio following by assaults on international bankers, had been delighted when Roosevelt, in his inaugural address on March 4, 1933, flayed the money changers. In 1933, the Michigan cleric insisted that the only choice facing the country was "Roosevelt or ruin." By 1936, he had changed his slogan to "Roosevelt and ruin," and his philippics against international financiers were increasingly coming to have anti-Semitic connotations. In 1936 the Union Party—with William Lemke, a North Dakota congressman, as its presidential candidate—polled only 882,000 votes, the Socialists 187,000, and the Communists 80,000. After 1936, Roosevelt no longer faced any significant challenge from the left.

VIII. The Conservative Opposition

Roosevelt's conservative adversaries found it difficult to mount effective opposition to the New Deal because the claims of the Republican Party and of business leaders in the 1920's had been discredited by the Great Depression. In Selection 43, Daniel O. Hastings of Delaware, chairman of the Republican Senatorial Campaign Committee in 1934, offers an indictment of the New Deal which suggests how little the party leadership recognized the changed national attitude. The Republicans, running on a platform of shibboleths, suffered an unanticipated setback in the elections that fall. Perhaps Hastings' most compelling point was his accusation that the Democrats had departed from the 1932 platform, since there could be no doubt that Roosevelt had, in fact, embarked on a number of courses either not mentioned in his 1932 campaign or diametrically opposed to some of his statements that year.

In Selection 44, the satirist H. L. Mencken strikes the same note by accusing Roosevelt of insincerity: "If he became convinced tomorrow that coming out for cannibalism would get him the votes he so sorely needs, he would begin fattening a missionary in the White House backyard come Wednesday." Mencken sneers that Roosevelt is "the greatest President since Hoover"; in Selection 45, Hoover launches his own foray on the New Deal by advancing the main claim of the Hoover school: that "the day Mr. Roosevelt was elected recovery was in progress." However, few historians would agree that the bank crisis of Hoover's last days in power resulted from anxiety about what Roosevelt would do when he took office.

Some of the conservative critique of the New Deal was well founded, but much of it seemed so far-fetched and so strident that it became a legitimate target for the kind of lampoon the humorist Frank Sullivan offers in Selection 46. Once again, Sullivan notes that antagonists of the New Deal often directed their shafts against the "dangerous" men who surrounded the President: Thomas Corcoran and Benjamin Cohen, who helped draft New Deal legislation; Felix Frankfurter of Harvard Law School, whose students manned New Deal agencies; Thurman Arnold, a critic of orthodox social doctrine whom Roosevelt appointed Assistant Attorney General in charge of trust prosecutions; the President's son, James Roosevelt, who served as his secretary for a time; and, of course, the ubiquitous Tugwell.

Conservatives, who had long viewed the courts as a bulwark of property rights, defended the judiciary even more ardently in the 1930's when the New Dealers controlled the executive and legislative branches. Roosevelt's court-packing plan of February 1937 not only outraged his Republican opponents but ruptured his own party. On June 14, the Senate Judiciary Committee, by a 10–8 vote, submitted an adverse report which rejected the President's claims that his plan would aid the poorer litigant and bring a badly needed infusion of new blood to the bench. In Selection 47, the Committee states: "It is a measure which should be so emphatically rejected that its parallel will never again be presented to the free representatives of the free people of America." A month later the Senate killed Roosevelt's Court proposal, although by then the Court, as Selection 24 demonstrates, no longer impeded government intervention in the economy. Still, for the conservatives the court-packing fracas proved to be a turning point; never thereafter did the New Dealers muster their former strength in Congress.

IX. The Approach of War

The Great Depression served to intensify isolationism and economic nationalism, and to heighten resolves not to repeat what most Americans, recalling 1917, now agreed had been an act of folly—intervention in a European war. President Roosevelt, who had been a Wilsonian internationalist, accommodated his policies to the national mood, in part because this was politically prudent and in part because he believed that in a crisis he had to give priority to domestic problems. For a brief period in the spring of 1933 he gave his backing to the forthcoming World Monetary and Economic Conference scheduled to meet in London in June. By the time the conference opened, however, the President had come to fear that an international agreement on currency stabilization might hamper his efforts to raise domestic prices. As a consequence, he dispatched his "bombshell" message of July 3 (Selection 48), which isolationists cheered as a new declaration of independence from Europe.

By 1936 the forces of isolationism and of pacifism had neared their zenith. Since it was widely believed that the United States had been trapped into World War I by developing too large an economic stake in the outcome, Congress passed a series of neutrality laws which aimed at eliminating that possibility in the future. Roosevelt's Chautauqua speech (Selection 49) in the summer of 1936 was the high point of his acquiescence in a policy of withdrawal. The President warns:

> . . . If war should break out again in another continent, let us not blink the fact that we would find in this country thousands of Americans who, seeking immediate riches—fools' gold—would attempt to break down or evade our neutrality. . . . We can keep out of war if those who watch and decide . . . make certain that the small decisions of each day do not lead toward war and if, at the same time, they possess the courage to say "no" to those who selfishly or unwisely would let us go to war.

As Hitler and Mussolini stepped up their plans for conquest in Europe and Japan launched an undeclared war on China in 1937, leaders of the peace forces redoubled their efforts to keep America out of foreign quarrels. They became especially alarmed when, in late 1937, a sense of imminent war swept the country in response to the news that Japanese planes had bombed and strafed an American gunboat moored in the Yangtse. In Selection 50, the New Republic editor Bruce Bliven expresses his anxiety that the United States might once more repeat the mistakes of World War I. Bliven writes: "It is as though I were watching for the second time the early reels of a motion picture whose story ends in tragedy. As I see the actors on the screen make again the same mistakes I have seen before, knowing what the outcome will be I am sickened by the realization of how history does in fact repeat itself—how literally true it is that we learn nothing from experience."

Yet many of the very men who dreaded the prospect of another war were appalled by the spread of fascism. Stephen Vincent Benét voices in Selection 51 the dismay of those who abhorred war but felt an outraged sympathy for the victims of totalitarianism. He notes:

> We thought we were done with these things but we were
>   wrong . . .
> We thought the long train would run to the end of Time . . .
> Now the long train stands derailed and the bandits loot it.
> Now the boar and the asp have power in our time.
> Now the night rolls back on the West and the night is solid.

In Selection 52, the young writer Irwin Shaw articulates the relentless intrusion of Hitler into the lives of a couple in love; his protagonist, with no illusions about war or those who profit from it, resigns himself to the inevitability of the coming conflict.

When war broke out in Europe in September 1939, the United States viewed the encounter indifferently, especially during the "bore war" of the winter of 1939–40. But when the Nazi forces overran Scandinavia, the Low Countries, and France in the spring of 1940, many Americans felt more directly menaced by the fascist powers. On June 10, 1940, just as he was about to leave for Charlottesville to speak to the graduating class of the University of Virginia, President Roosevelt, who had labored to keep Italy out of the war, got word that Mussolini had decided to invade France. Furious at the Duce, the President at the conclusion of his formal address (Selection 53) ad-libs: "On this tenth day of June, 1940, the hand that held the dagger has struck it into the back of its neighbor."

In his Charlottesville speech, Roosevelt announced a program of aid to the Allies. As Selection 54 from the diary of Breckinridge Long, Assistant Secretary of State, indicates, many members of Roosevelt's diplomatic corps thought FDR was taking a foolish risk and that the United States should come to terms with the fascists. Long notes that Joseph P. Kennedy, ambassador to the Court of St. James's, "does not believe in the continuing of democracy. He thinks that we will have to assume a Fascist form of government or something similar to it if we are to survive in a world of concentrated and centralized power." Roosevelt, however, persisted in efforts to aid Britain; one proposal he advanced was to barter "over-age" American destroyers for long-term leases of bases in British possessions in the Western Hemisphere. When his letter to Senator David I. Walsh (Selection 55), chairman of the Naval

Affairs Committee and a leading isolationist, failed to persuade the senator, the President went ahead on his own and negotiated the deal as an executive agreement.

While most of the country's attention was fastened on Europe, where Britain braced for an expected Nazi invasion, significant developments were also taking place in the Far East, where Japanese militants were laying plans for conquest in Southeast Asia. Throughout the 1930's, Joseph Grew, ambassador to Japan, had resisted proposals to coerce the Japanese and had put his faith in patient diplomacy. For this reason Selection 56, his "green-light" telegram, marked an important step toward war between the United States and Japan. In this document, Grew continues to warn that strong policies toward Tokyo may produce a "sudden stroke" of retaliation. Yet he now advises: "Until there is in Japan a complete regeneration of thought, a show of force, coupled with the determination that it will be used if necessary, alone can effectively contribute . . . to our own future security."

Although Roosevelt shared Grew's concern about the Japanese, he was determined not to be diverted from concentrating on aiding Britain against Germany. He still hoped that a program short of war would be successful. As he writes to Francis Sayre, high commissioner to the Philippines, in Selection 57: "We of course do not want to be drawn into a war with Japan. . . . We have no intention of being 'sucked into' a war with Germany. Whether there will come to us war with either or both of these countries will depend far more upon what they do than upon what we deliberately refrain from doing." But within a year the United States would be at war. In Selection 58, the poet Robinson Jeffers writes of the coming of war:

Foreseen for so many years: these evils, this monstrous
    violence, these massive agonies: no easier to bear.

The Roosevelt era, born of the harsh challenge of economic breakdown, would end in the throes of that new world war, so long feared, so long expected.

I
THE CRISIS

The author of Selection 1, Stephen Vincent Benét, was a distinguished American poet, best known for his epic, John Brown's Body. In Selection 2, Fortune concedes that its unemployment figures may "underestimate the real situation." No statistics on joblessness in this period are altogether reliable, but by the time Roosevelt took office, perhaps fifteen million Americans were unemployed. More than one-third of the nation had either lost jobs or were the wives or children of the unemployed. Charles R. Walker in Selection 3 refers to Father Cox of Pittsburgh, who led a "Hunger March" of a thousand men to Washington. Mary Heaton Vorse, the contributor of Selection 4, had been reporting strikes for a generation. In Selection 5, a man born in 1894, the year of the last major panic, laments l'année terrible of 1932. Ruth McKenney, who describes the Akron crisis in Selection 6, won fame not for her stark writings on social conditions but for her lighthearted play, My Sister Eileen.

1

"Is it well with these States?"

"Is it well with these States?"

"We have made many, fine new toys.
We—
There is a rust on the land.
A rust and a creeping blight and a scaled evil,
For six years eating, yet deeper than those six years,
Men labor to master it but it is not mastered.
There is the soft, grey, foul tent of the hatching worm
Shrouding the elm, the chestnut, the Southern cypress.
There is shadow in the bright sun, there is shadow upon the
    streets.
They burn the grain in the furnace while men go hungry.
They pile the cloth of the looms while men go ragged.
We walk naked in our plenty."

                    "My tan-faced children?"

"These are your tan-faced children.
These skilled men, idle, with the holes in their shoes.
These drifters from State to State, these wolvish, bewildered
    boys
Who ride the blinds and the box-cars from jail to jail,
Burnt in their youth like cinders of hot smokestacks,
Learning the thief's crouch and the cadger's whine,
Dishonored, abandoned, disinherited.

SOURCE: Stephen Vincent Benét, *Burning City* (New York, 1936),
pp. 32–5.

These, dying in the bright sunlight they cannot eat,
Or the strong men, sitting at home, their hands clasping
     nothing,
Looking at their lost hands.
These are your tan-faced children, the parched young,
The old man rooting in waste-heaps, the family rotting
In the flat, before eviction,
With the toys of plenty about them,
The shiny toys making ice and music and light,
But no price for the shiny toys and the last can empty.
The sleepers in blind corners of the night.
The women with dry breasts and phantom eyes.
The walkers upon nothing, the four million.
These are your tan-faced children."

                 "But the land?"

"Over the great plains of the buffalo-land,
The dust-storm blows, the choking, sifting, small dust.
The skin of that land is ploughed by the dry, fierce wind
And blown away, like a torrent;
It drifts foot-high above the young sprouts of grain
And the water fouls, the horses stumble and sicken,
The wash-board cattle stagger and die of drought.
We tore the buffalo's pasture with the steel blade.
We made the waste land blossom and it has blossomed.
That was our fate; now that land takes its own revenge,
And the giant dust-flower blooms above five States."

"But the gains of the years, who got them?"

                 "Many, great gains.
Many, yet few; they robbed us in the broad daylight,
Saying, 'Give us this and that; we are kings and titans;
We know the ropes; we are solid; we are hard-headed;
We will build you cities and railroads.'—as if they built
     them!
They, the preying men, the men whose hearts were like
     engines,
Gouging the hills for gold, laying waste the timber,
The men like band-saws, moving over the land.
And, after them, the others,

Soft-bodied, lacking even the pirate's candor,
Men of paper, robbing by paper, with paper faces,
Rustling like frightened paper when the storm broke.
The men with the jaws of moth and aphis and beetle,
Boring the dusty, secret hole in the corn,
Fixed, sucking the land, with neither wish nor pride
But the wish to suck and continue.
They have been sprayed, a little.
But they say they will have the land back again, these men."

"There were many such in my time.
I have seen the rich arrogant and the poor oppressed.
I have seen democracy, also. I have seen
The good man slain, the knave and the fool in power,
The democratic vista botched by the people,
Yet not despaired, loving the giant land,
Though I prophesied to these States."

"Now they say we must have one tyranny or another
And a dark bell rings in our hearts."

2

"No One Has Starved"

THE following minimal statements may be accepted as true—with the certainty that they underestimate the real situation:

1. Unemployment has steadily increased in the U. S. since the beginning of the depression and the rate of increase during the first part of 1932 was more rapid than in any other depression year.

2. The number of persons totally unemployed is now at least 10,-000,000.

3. The number of persons totally unemployed next winter will, at the present rate of increase, be 11,000,000.

4. Eleven millions unemployed means better than one man out of every four employable workers.

5. This percentage is higher than the percentage of unemployed British workers registered under the compulsory insurance laws (17.1 per cent in May, 1932, as against 17.3 per cent in April and 18.4 per cent in January) and higher than the French, the Italian, and the Canadian percentages, but lower than the German (43.9 per cent of trade unionists in April, 1932) and the Norwegian.

6. Eleven millions unemployed means 27,500,000 whose regular source of livelihood has been cut off.

7. Twenty-seven and a half millions without regular income includes the families of totally unemployed workers alone. Taking account of the numbers of workers on part time, the total of those without adequate income becomes 34,000,000 or better than a quarter of the entire population of the country.

8. Thirty-four million persons without adequate income does not mean 34,000,000 in present want. Many families have savings. But savings are eventually dissipated and the number in actual want tends to approximate the number without adequate income. How nearly it approximates it now or will next winter no man can say. But it is con-

SOURCE: "No One Has Starved," *Fortune*, VI (1932), 21–4.

servative to estimate that the problem of next winter's relief is a problem of caring for approximately 25,000,000 souls. . . .

Few if any of the industrial areas have been able to maintain a minimum decency level of life for their unemployed. Budgetary standards as set up by welfare organizations, public and private, after years of experiment have been discarded. Food only, in most cases, is provided and little enough of that. Rents are seldom paid. Shoes and clothing are given in rare instances only. Money for doctors and dentists is not to be had. And free clinics are filled to overflowing. Weekly allowances per family have fallen as low as $2.39 in New York with $3 and $4 the rule in most cities and $5 a high figure. And even on these terms funds budgeted for a twelve-month period have been exhausted in three or four. While city after city has been compelled to abandon a part of its dependent population. "We are merely trying to prevent hunger and exposure," reported a St. Paul welfare head last May. And the same sentence would be echoed by workers in other cities with such additions as were reported at the same time from Pittsburgh where a cut of 50 per cent was regarded as "inevitable," from Dallas where Mexicans and Negroes were not given relief, from Alabama where discontinuance of relief in mining and agricultural sections was foreseen, from New Orleans where no new applicants were being received and 2,500 families in need of relief were receiving none, from Omaha where two-thirds of the cases receiving relief were to be discontinued, from Colorado where the counties had suspended relief for lack of funds . . . from Scranton . . . from Cleveland . . . from Syracuse . . . But the individual localities present their own picture:

New York City

About 1,000,000 out of the city's 3,200,000 working population are unemployed. Last April 410,000 were estimated to be in dire want. Seven hundred and fifty thousand in 150,000 families were receiving emergency aid while 160,000 more in 32,000 families were waiting to receive aid not then available. Of these latter families—families which normally earn an average of $141.50 a month—the average income from all sources was $8.20. Of families receiving relief, the allowance has been anything from a box of groceries up to $60 a month. In general, New York relief, in the phrase of Mr. William Hodson, executive director of the New York Welfare Council, has been on "a disaster basis." And the effects have been disaster effects. It is impossible to estimate the number of deaths in the last year in which starvation was a contributing cause. But ninety-five persons suffering directly from starvation were admitted to the city hospitals in 1931, of whom twenty died; and 143 suffering from malnutrition, of whom twenty-five died. . . .

Philadelphia

The situation in Philadelphia was described by its Community Council in July, 1932, as one of "slow starvation and progressive disintegration of family life. . . ." "Normal" unemployment in Philadelphia is 40,000 to 50,000. . . . By May, 1932, the total of unemployed was 298,000. In the following month the Governor of the state estimated that 250,-000 persons in Philadelphia "faced actual starvation." Over the state at large the same conditions held. In June, 1931, 919,000 or 25 per cent of the normally employed in the state were unemployed, according to the "secret" report then submitted to the Governor, and the number had risen to 1,000,000 by December and to 1,250,000 in August, 1932. One hundred and fifty thousand children were in need of charity. Malnutrition had increased in forty-eight counties—27 per cent of school children being undernourished (216,000 out of a school population of 800,000). New patients in the tuberculosis clinics had doubled. . . . Outside of Philadelphia the weekly grant to a family is $3 or less in thirteen counties, and $3 to $4 in six more, while in some of the small steel towns it may be even lower. Funds in the counties are either exhausted or will be exhausted before November. . . .

Chicago

. . . Teachers in May, 1932, had had only five months cash for the last thirteen months, 3,177 of them had lost $2,367,000 in bank failures, 2,278 of them had lost $7,800,000 in lapsed policies, 805 had borrowed $232,000 from loan sharks at rates adding up to 42 per cent a year, and 759 had lost their homes. (The city at one time undertook to sell for tax default the houses of its employees unable to pay taxes because of its own default in wages.) . . .

Other urban centers

In St. Louis 125,000 of the city's 330,000 employable persons were unemployed last December, one-eighth of the population was estimated to face eviction and starvation, three-fourths of the families under care presented one or more medical problems each, and relief campaigners published full-page advertisements pointing to the number of hungry men and women rifling garbage buckets for their food. Starvation is reported as a contributory cause in several deaths. And even so the relief agencies were forced by lack of funds to drop 8,000 families on July 1 and 5,000 more on July 15. Since these cuts were made, large numbers of the destitute have been living in refuse dumps along the river where they build shacks and dig in the dump for food.

3

Hooverville

A FEW weeks ago I visited the incinerator and public dump at Youngstown, Ohio. Back of the garbage house there are at least three acres of waste land, humpy with ash heaps and junk. The area is not on the outskirts but in the middle of the steel mill district with furnaces near-by, and the tube mills and factory stacks of Youngstown. The dump is a kind of valley with a railroad embankment flanking it. As you approach from the garbage house, certain excrescences compete in vision with the ash humps and junk. They appear more organized than the rest of the place, but one is not sure. When, however, you come close, there is no doubt but the dump is inhabited.

The place is indeed a shanty town, or rather a collection of shanty hamlets, for the separate blotches are not all in one place but break out at intervals from the dump. Some of them are caves with tin roofs, but all of them blend with the place, for they are constructed out of it. From 150 to 200 men live in the shanties. The place is called by its inhabitants—Hooverville.

I went forward and talked to the men; they showed me their houses. These vary greatly from mere caves covered with a piece of tin, to weather-proof shanties built of packing boxes and equipped with a stolen window-frame or an improved door. Some have beds and one or two a kitchen stove rescued from the junk heap, though most of the men cook in communal fashion over a fire shielded by bricks in the open.

The inhabitants were not, as one might expect, outcasts or "untouchables," or even hoboes in the American sense; they were men without jobs. Life is sustained by begging, eating at the city soup kitchens, or earning a quarter by polishing an automobile—enough to bring home bacon and bread. Eating "at home" is preferred. The location of the town also has its commissary advantage; men take part of their food

SOURCE: Charles R. Walker, "Relief and Revolution," *The Forum*, LXXXVIII (1932), 73–4.

from the garbage house. This I entered; the stench of decaying food is appalling. Here I found that there were more women than men—gathering food for their families. In Hooverville there are no women.

This pitiable village would be of little significance if it existed only in Youngstown, but nearly every town in the United States has its shanty town for the unemployed, and the same instinct has named them all "Hooverville." The Pittsburgh unit has been taken under the wing of Father Cox—of Hunger March fame—who feeds the inhabitants at a soup kitchen in the cellar of his church, and who has supplied each shanty with a printed placard: "God Bless Our Home." The largest Hooverville in the United States is in St. Louis, with a hovel population of 1200. Chicago had a flourishing one, but it was felt to be an affront to municipal pride and was ordered burned. The inhabitants were summarily told to get out, and thirty minutes later the "homes" were in ashes.

In the Hooverville of Ambridge, Pennsylvania, I met a man with whom I talked a long time. He was a Slav who had come to this country thirty years ago, and who had grown sons somewhere, though he had lost touch with them. As a veteran worker, he reminisced over many jobs, skilled and unskilled, in the American mills. But he had now lost his last one. Standing in front of the huts and clasping the fist of one hand with the other, he said to me, "If you had told me, when I come to this country that now I live here like dis, I shot you dead."

He Talking about city call Hooverville
About people unemployment

4

Rebellion in the Cornbelt

THE farmers were now close to their last stand. They were witnessing the work of generations swept away before their eyes, while their government talked platitudes. They had put their faith in government, and government had failed. Then, last August, they reached a point where they could stand the strain no longer and moved toward open rebellion.

Suddenly the papers were filled with accounts of highway picketing by farmers around Sioux City. A Farmers' Holiday Association had been organized by one Milo Reno, and the farmers were to refuse to bring food to market for thirty days or "until the cost of production had been obtained.". . .

In ordinary strikes there is a concrete organization to combat. The worker is fighting the owners of a certain mine or mill. The picketing farmers have no such definite enemy. It is almost as if they were picketing the depression itself. They are organizing against ruinous prices, with foreclosure and bankruptcy as their enemies.

Highway No. 20, leading to Sioux City, has been the scene of some of the sharpest clashes between deputies and farmers. It has won itself the proud name of "Bunker Hill 20." On the night we visited No. 20 a score of men were sitting round a campfire. A boy was sprawled out on an automobile cushion asleep. Everyone was in overalls. Their sunburned faces shone red in the firelight.

A lamp in a smaller tent glowed in the darkness. A trestle table stood near at hand. The Ladies' Aid bring substantial meals to the picketers. The irregular circle round the fire, the high moonlit poplar trees, the lighted tent were like a stage set for a play. There was an air of immense earnestness about the farmers. They had been swung completely out of

SOURCE: Mary Heaton Vorse, "Rebellion in the Cornbelt," *Harper's*, CLXVI (1932), 3–9.

Talking about Farmers

their usual orbit, but they are absolutely sure of the righteousness of their cause. An old man with white mustache said:

"They say blockading the highway's illegal. I says, 'Seems to me there was a Tea-party in Boston that was illegal too. What about destroying property in Boston Harbor when our country was started?' " He sets the note of the evening.

"If we farmers go down bankrupt," says one of the younger men, "everything in this country goes down. If we get enough to live on, everybody's going to go to work again."

"When we can't buy," says another, "there can't be any prosperity. We ain't been buying nothing, not for four years."

"My binder's fallen apart so, don't know how I'm going to get through this year." The conversation moves slowly from one man to another with quiet deliberation. There is a cry:

"Truck!"

They hurry out in the roadway. All of them carry heavy stakes, some made from axe handles. None of them is armed, though a young fellow pointed to a little mound of quarter bricks.

"Plenty of Irish confetti," he said cheerily. Beside the road, handy to use, are heavy spiked logs and planks bristling with spikes to throw in front of trucks. This truck is empty. There is a short conference. The truck passes on its way.

"Good-night, boys," calls the driver. "Good luck!" He is one of them, part of the movement that is just beginning to realize its power. We go back to the fire. . . .

As we went from picket line to picket line the talk harked back continually to 1776 when other farmers blockaded the highways. Up in James they had a "battle" with deputies last Wednesday. They liken it to a revolutionary battle. Over in Stevens in South Dakota, across the Missouri to Nebraska, we find similar groups of farmers who talk of "revolution." These farmers feel that they have a historic mission. The word "revolution" occurs often among them, but what they mean is a farmers' revolt. They do not understand revolution in the communist sense. They think of themselves as fighting the banking interests of the East or the "international bankers" about whom they are perpetually talking. . . .

In the town of Fremont, Nebraska, we saw the Holiday Association in the making. The town swarmed with farmers in blue overalls. There are clots of blue coming down the street, an informal procession of farmers making for the public square, which is in the center of the town, shaded by elms like a New England common. It is hard to find parking space. The Farmers' Holiday Association is organizing the State of Nebraska.

A cattle truck has drawn up alongside the curb near the City Hall. It is decorated with homemade slogans in large black letters.

"Be Pickets Or Peasants" it advises. . . .

The Governor, who had been unable to accept the invitation to the meeting, had sent Mr. J. S. Allen, a little, nattily dressed up-state politician, to represent him. He brought the Governor's greetings and explained what the Governors' Conference might mean to the farmers. Mr. Allen said that the Governor had power to help the farmers. Under certain circumstances he could, for instance, declare a moratorium on farm debts.

As he closed, an old man got to his feet. He stood in front of the bandstand where the speakers were.

"I want to ask a question," he quavered. He turned his face up toward the Governor's representative and raised an eloquent work-gnarled hand.

"How soon," he cried, "can the Governor declare a moratorium? That is what I want to know! Can he do it right off?" He stood there, his anxious blue eyes staring at Mr. Allen, his eloquent hand lifted. You could have heard a pin drop while Mr. Allen shuffled through an apologetic answer.

Not right off, such things took time.

"You can't say *when*, you can't say *how soon?*" the old man insisted with terrifying urgency.

It was as though this old farmer represented all the hard-pressed farmers of the country, all the old people who in a short time, in a few weeks, will be driven off their farms, sold out after a lifetime of fruitful work. How soon could a governor declare a moratorium? Not in time to prevent this catastrophe? He stood there, old and frail and anxious, his arresting hand still raised. A murmur went through the crowd. They had sensed the tragedy behind the old farmer's question. All of them have felt the approach of bankruptcy and eviction. No one here but understands.

5

Beans, Bacon, and Gravy

I was born long ago, in 1894,
And I've seen many a panic, I will own;
I've been hungry, I've been cold,
And now I'm growing old,
But the worst I've seen is 1932.

REFRAIN: Oh, those beans, bacon, and gravy,
           They almost drive me crazy,
           I eat them till I see them in my dreams,
                            In my dreams;
           When I wake up in the morning,
           And another day is dawning,
           Yes, I know I'll have another mess of beans.

We congregate each morning
At the county barn at dawning,
And everyone is happy, so it seems;
But when our work is done
We file in one by one,
And thank the Lord for one more mess of beans.

We have Hooverized on butter,
For milk we've only water,
And I haven't seen a steak in many a day;
As for pies, cakes, and jellies,
We substitute sow-bellies,
For which we work the county road each day.

SOURCE: John Greenway, *American Folksongs of Protest* (Philadelphia, 1953), pp. 64-5.

If there ever comes a time
When I have more than a dime
They will have to put me under lock and key;
For they've had me broke so long
I can only sing this song,
Of the workers and their misery.

How company cut
dow on peice cuts

6

The Bank Crisis

Price Cuts   February 3, 1933

The three Akron rubber companies, Firestone, Goodrich, and Goodyear, announced another cut in tire prices.

The city was appalled. Everyone on Main Street, in East Akron, even
on West Hill, agreed that this last price cut was plain clear suicide. . . .

Regretful Robber   February 4, 1933

A lean gaunt robber who held up the Sun Oil Company gas station
at 845 Copley Road and stole $33, told the attendant, Harold Beck,
as he left, "I'm sorry to do this, but I have a wife and three children
to support. I hope you are covered with insurance."

About a Third   February 6, 1933

Trustees of the Better Akron Federation were told today by E. J. Larrick, secretary of the charitable organization, that relief costs in Akron
would probably pass the $2,000,000 mark for 1933. . . .

Mr. Larrick's somber figures showed that about a third of the 300,000
population of Greater Akron was, in early 1933, either actually on relief
or living in families where the wage earner was unemployed.

The Weather   February 9, 1933

The weather turned bitterly cold. The thermometer at the official
airport weather bureau dropped to four below and on the hills around
Akron private citizens reported readings of ten and twelve below.

Family Service headquarters were jammed with a rush of unemployed

SOURCE: Ruth McKenney, Industrial Valley (New York, 1939), pp. 61–72.

trying to get on relief. They hoped, apparently, to get fuel to keep their
families warm. . . .

Beware   February 20, 1933

Mayor C. Nelson Sparks predicted the complete disintegration of the
Akron city government unless funds were raised immediately to carry
on government functions. His "appeal" appeared without comment on
the front pages of both newspapers.

"With the closing down of the street maintenance repair department completely," Mayor Sparks wrote, "I appeal to the Chamber of
Commerce to wake up and find out what the situation really is."

"Policemen and firemen," the appeal continued, "have been fired
because of lack of funds to pay them. We have now closed down a department vital to the requirements of every person in Akron. Our streets
will crumble into holes. The building department is practically shut
down.

"The planning commission is functioning with one man. The engineering division is only a skeleton. The water bureau is losing money
every day. The garbage department is operating at such a minimum that
in certain areas farmers have been asked to take over the collection,
using the garbage for hog feed."

"I want," Mayor Sparks wound up desperately, "to impress on the
city of Akron that our government is crumbling."

The Farmer   February 21, 1933

Farmers in the country surrounding Akron made headlines today
when they rioted at two farm foreclosure sales. . . .

Tear Gas   February 25, 1933

Shots were fired and tear gas bombs exploded during another eviction
riot on Kenmore Hill today. Six persons were arrested.

Both newspapers carried small items on their back pages about the
Maryland bank holiday.

Dark Sunday   February 26, 1933

Horrible rumors spread through West Hill. Bank officials didn't show
up at church services and weren't home at one o'clock to eat the usual
big Sunday dinner with their families.

Bombshell   February 27, 1933

The Akron banks went on a "restricted withdrawal basis" this Monday morning. The . . . bulk of the 100,000 depositors of The First-Central Trust Company was completely flabbergasted. . . .

The lobby of The First-Central Trust Company was a madhouse. Bewildered grocery store owners and frantic housewives stood in line with their passbooks shrilly demanding their money. Soft-voiced clerks explained, over and over, that "everything was all right."

Wednesday   March 1, 1933

All morning and early afternoon Wednesday the Akron newspapers carried headlines such as "New Bank Accounts Growing as Akron Situation Clears."

Until three o'clock the local newspapers spread great cheer over the local banking situation. Pay rolls were said to be passing through the bank, taxes were being paid, business places were finding their operations unhampered. Of course a somewhat sinister note appeared in the back pages. Tennessee, Kentucky, West Virginia, Pennsylvania, Indiana banks were closing. Some 200 Ohio banks were on "restricted withdrawal plans." But the newspapers tush-tushed these ugly stories.

While everyone in town who had three cents was rushing out in the streets to buy early editions of the newspapers, the reporters sat stiffly outside the conference room at The First-Central Trust Company, where the frantic men who ran The First-Central Trust Company were facing facts. The bank was failing. Its cash reserve was dropping. Every hour brought nearer the moment when a clerk would say to a depositor, "We can't give you ten per cent of your account. We can't give you anything."

New York banks didn't even answer telegrams from the Akron financial wizards. The Secretary of the Treasury was not answering telephone calls. At intervals the Akron bankers received telegrams heralding new closings of banks. The long-distance operator said, "Cleveland calling." It appeared that the Cleveland banks were gradually folding up.

A little after noon, the Akron bankers were on the telephone to Columbus, arguing. They wanted the State superintendent of banks to send them a telegram ordering them to go on a straight one per cent withdrawal basis. The State superintendent was stubborn, not caring to take the onus of closing the Akron bank. Whose fault was it that the bank was failing?

The Akron bankers insisted. They couldn't just say the "Akron Plan" was a failure. They couldn't come right out in the open and say the bank was busted. The State superintendent of banks was not impressed.

Finally the telegram came. The bankers handed it over to the newspapermen with the order, "Not to appear until after three o'clock." The last editions of the newspapers, appearing an hour after the bank's business day was over, announced the practical closing of the Akron banks.

Thursday   March 2, 1933

. . . Both newspapers reported flatly that business in Akron was paralyzed.

The blight which, from Monday, had been gradually falling over the city wormed its way into every back street, into every eddy and nook of Akron. Life slowed down. The rubber companies alone had money to meet week-end pay rolls. The department stores, the grocery stores, the streetcar company, a hundred other business places had no money to pay their employees. Coal companies, unable to meet C.O.D. freight charges, predicted a fuel shortage.

The city funds were frozen in the bank. Relief funds were frozen in the bank. The county funds were frozen in the bank.

Grocery stores refused credit to old customers. Even speakeasies told favored friends, "Sales for cash only. Nobody may ever get any money again.". . .

Friday   March 3, 1933

Akron awoke to live with panic for another dreadful day. In the nearly empty streetcars, men told new scare stories. The morning papers headlined "Thirty States Now on Bank Holiday."

Throughout the unnaturally quiet city streets, the last faith in the old order of things went up in a bright fire of anger. The valley, calm on Thursday, began to seethe on Friday. Hysterical women wept on neighbors' shoulders, "Everything we had is gone. Now we go on relief."

The small merchants who had fought for months against the mounting unemployment in the city and the falling pay rolls, gave way to despair.

George Attalla, a small shoe store owner, said, "This is going to be worse. Everything is crumbling, crumbling, and the common man is left to carry the burden.". . .

Frank Brescani, a chicken shop merchant, said, "Just watch; they'll aggravate the people until there just won't be any banks. Business?

Since Monday there hasn't been any. They say this is the richest country in the world. Well, where has all the money gone to? Who took it? Where is it?"

These statements and dozens of others like them were printed in the now badly scared *Beacon Journal*. For a week the Akron newspapers had done their best to cover up for the bank. Frightened at last by the ugly spirit in the town, they suddenly shifted ground to reflect their readers' desperation.

The *Beacon Journal*, for instance, appeared with an eight-column editorial in ten-point boldface type spread all the way across the top of the front page. The editorial called for a Federal guarantee of bank deposits, and represented an amazing shift from its traditional Republican policy of keeping government out of business.

"The fact is," the *Beacon Journal* trumpeted, "the whole American business world is in a desperate situation, and it may be saved only by heroic and instant action. Either take this course [Federal guarantee of bank deposits] or confess that we are whipped, close the doors of our banks, stores and factories, and let chaos and revolution take their course, with all that these imply in the overthrow of American institutions."

"A blight," this editorial in Akron's most conservative newspaper continued, "has fallen over all American industry. A foreign invader making easy conquest of our shores could do no worse. . . ."

March 4, 1933

On Saturday morning all business came to a complete halt. The rubber shops closed. Streetcars ran on half schedules. Coal companies shut. Thousands and thousands of men, still employed despite the Depression, were sent home from work "temporarily laid off." Money nearly disappeared from circulation. Pay rolls were not met. Checks were not honored.

Early Saturday morning the telegraph editors of the two newspapers turned the power on in the wire ticker rooms. Shortly afterwards they came out with the first strips of early morning copy.

"New York," they said flatly to the news editors and the business managers and the editors, who were already standing around the city rooms at this early hour in the morning.

"New York," the telegraph editors said, holding up the long strips of wire service copy. "New York and Chicago."

"Oh, my God," the editors said. "Oh, my God."

At nine, The First-Central Trust Company opened for business. The lobby was jammed. Women swung their umbrellas wildly and bank guards rushed from one vice-president to another removing hysterical clients. Clerks paid out the one per cent allowed, under orders not to argue. The bank officials, faces drawn and harried, drank coffee at their mahogany desks and ate cheese sandwiches in full view of the depositors. Decorum disappeared.

"I haven't got a dime to feed my family on myself," clerks yelled at men who demanded, not asked for, ten dollars, anyway, please, from their accounts.

"I didn't get paid this week," men in work clothes shouted. "You got to give me some of my money."

"No!" said the clerks, signaling for the bank guards.

At noon the bank guards hustled the crowd out. "Closing time," they shouted.

The old First-Central Trust Company never opened again.

II
THE NEW DEAL RESPONSE

J. Frederick Essary, author of Selection 7, was Washington correspondent of the Baltimore Sun. In Selection 8, Adolf A. Berle, Jr., writes
about the Reconstruction Finance Corporation; created in Herbert
Hoover's Administration, the RFC did not realize its potentialities until the New Deal. Harold Ickes, mentioned in Selection 9, served as
Roosevelt's Secretary of the Interior. General Hugh Johnson, contributor
of Selection 10, developed the President's Re-employment Agreement
(PRA) to win adherence from employers to the Administration's wages
and hours stipulations. The Blue Eagle symbolized compliance with the
standards of the National Industrial Recovery Administration. Writers
often used the term "Brain Trust" loosely. The Brain Trust, subject of
Selection 11, functioned only during the 1932 campaign and was dis-
banded before Roosevelt took office; people like William C. Bullitt
never played a central rôle in it. Its most important members were Raymond Moley, Samuel I. Rosenman, Rexford G. Tugwell, and Berle.
Lilienthal sent his letter in Selection 12 to his boyhood friend, Newton
Arvin, a noted literary critic, in February 1939; Harcourt Morgan, former
president of the University of Tennessee, took charge of agricultural
affairs as a member of the TVA board. In Selection 13, Rud Rennie refers to the CWA; a temporary operation, the Civil Works Administration gave government jobs to the unemployed to tide them over the
winter of 1933–34. The amendment Anne O'Hare McCormick alludes
to in Selection 14 is the 21st Amendment, ratified on December 5, 1933;
it repealed the 18th (Prohibition) Amendment.

7

The Hundred Days

THIS is Chapter 1—in epitome—of the Roosevelt régime. And what a chapter! What a régime!

Fifteen weeks have elapsed since the New Dealers began dealing. Fifteen weeks of high-pressure activity. Fifteen weeks of whirlwind changes in the old order, of experimental panaceas, of legislative novelties and of practically unchallenged Executive domination of the colossal organism which we call the Federal Government.

More history has been made during these fifteen weeks than in any comparable peacetime period since Americans went into business for themselves on this continent. The legislation that has now been written into law, under the Roosevelt leadership, touches practically every interest in our national life. It touches some of them lightly and by indirection only. It touches others heavily and will leave a mark on them not to be erased for a generation, if at all.

Powers have been reposed in the Presidency that have made that office a virtual dictatorship. It may be looked upon both as a benevolent and a necessary dictatorship. Undoubtedly it is so looked upon in most quarters. It may not be irrevocable. But soften the phrasing as much as one may, the fact remains that the present governmental set-up amounts to temporary Executive absolutism.

These new Presidential powers, let it be recalled, extend not only to the fiscal functions of the Government—to budgetary economy, to control of gold, control of banking and to possible inflation. They extend as well to agriculture, to every branch of industry, to public works, to the railroads, to mortgaged homes and farms, to unemployment and to the relief of destitution.

Rather a large order, that!

Such sweeping powers for the most part were granted only because of the acuteness of the crisis which came to a head on the very day

SOURCE: J. Frederick Essary, "The New Deal for Nearly Four Months," *Literary Digest*, CXVI (1933), 3–4, 35.

Mr. Roosevelt took office. That day found the country in the throes of a bank depositors' panic. This panic eventually forced every banking house in the country to close, the sound and the unsound alike. It forced the commodity and securities exchanges to suspend. It caused the industrial structure of the nation to totter, and it brought on partial paralysis of the normal energies of the whole American people.

Nobody now living had ever witnessed anything like that. And instinctively we, the American people, turned to Washington for salvation. We turned there for the very good reason there was nowhere else to turn. We turned, moreover, to an untried man, just as did the people when they turned to Abraham Lincoln in 1861. We turned to an Executive who had just taken the oath, to one who had only lately concluded a campaign more marked by its amiability than by thunder and lightning, and to a man, incidentally, in whose soul the amount of iron was still an unknown quantity.

We did not have to wait long for action, however. That much is easy to remember. Untroubled by any need for additional legislation, the new President at once assumed what amounted to war powers. And assuming them, he moved with swiftness and decision to meet the emergency. On the night of March 5, twenty-four hours after his inauguration, he issued two proclamations. One of them declared a bank holiday for the nation and placed an embargo upon the withdrawal and export of gold. The other summoned Congress to meet in four days.

That was action, and action with a vengeance!

These proclamations, with their martial ring, served as a curtain-raiser for a series of dramatic steps by the Federal Government, steps that followed each other with bewildering rapidity until fourteen weeks later when Congress ended its extraordinary session (extraordinary in more senses than one), and the President packed his bags for a holiday at sea.

There are two dazzling highlights in the picture of this unparalleled period. One is Franklin D. Roosevelt the man; the other is this man's measures. Of course the two are inseparable, in a large sense. We can not think of the one, since March 4, without thinking in terms of the other. But there is something in a personality that grips one's interest far more surely than does a policy, no matter how vital that policy may be.

The mysterious way in which the President has performed his wonders, if that is the way to put it, has been something decidedly worth observing during the past four months. The way he made his campaign was an interesting thing, too. But Roosevelt the Candidate and Roosevelt the President are two different men. I assert as much, for I am well acquainted with both.

In the first rôle he was famous for his beguiling smile, famous for his soft words, famous for his punchless speeches, famous for his tenderness to his opponent and famous far above all else for his incredible majority. The smile and the soft words are still a part of his armor, but they are about all there is about him now that is suggestive of campaign days. There is plenty of punch in what he says and does in his rôle as Chief Executive. No tenderness is wasted upon those who stand in his way. The oath of office seems suddenly to have transfigured him from a man of mere charm and buoyancy to one of dynamic aggressiveness.

Also Mr. Roosevelt has proved himself to be the most adroit master of practical politics we have had in the White House in a generation. That is rather a broad statement, but I think the results of the past few weeks amply justify it.

There were two all-important phases of his job, as Mr. Roosevelt conceived it. One was to keep the public on his side by keeping it informed of his aims; the other was to play ball with the leadership of Congress. To accomplish the first end, he played and played successfully for press support, on the one hand, and on the other, he resorted with great effect to the personal use of the radio.

Most incoming Presidents have had a friendly press—for a time. All hands at the outset of a new Administration seem eager to give such officials a chance. But Mr. Roosevelt has experienced this friendliness in unusually large measure. He has had it partly because of wide-spread anxiety over what had befallen us, and partly because of the free and frank manner in which he discusses governmental problems and measures with the men whose duty it is to write about them.

For one thing, his semiweekly press conferences are in all respects conferences. Any correspondent has the privilege of questioning him, and most of us do question him, and thoroughly. Every question asked is regarded as pertinent if it deals with a governmental matter.

Naturally the President reserves the right to say upon what matters he may be directly quoted; upon what matters he will be associated with indirectly, and what matters he will discuss on a confidential basis only. None of us objects to that. The important thing is that he has abolished the old rule that press questions must be presented in writing, a one-sided rule giving the President the opportunity to ignore any question, however proper or timely, which might remotely embarrass him.

But in dealing with the press the President has been no more skillful than in dealing with the leaders of Congress. His sway over those leaders is one of the phenomena of the period. To understand it, one must again take into account the grief of the times. Without that grief he could never have brought Congress to the point of virtual abdication. He could never have driven his emergency banking bill to a vote in both

Talk About Roosevelt as President

Houses in a single day. He could never have drawn to himself unlimited power to slash veterans' compensation, or to launch the country upon the uncertain sea of inflation, or put over other schemes that have seemed revolutionary.

But the crisis only partly explains the business. His program—averaging one new bill every three days—was made possible by conference. Mr. Roosevelt drew into his circle not only his own party leaders, but the leaders of the Progressive group as well, and the leaders of the Republican minority. He talked things out with these men, convincing some, persuading others and in some mysterious manner silencing still others who were neither convinced nor persuaded.

It begins to appear that Mr. Roosevelt is at his best in conference. We have seen legislators, by groups, marching to the White House swearing as they went that they would never, never yield on this or that proposition. We have then seen them later marching away ready to vote as the President wanted, and even seeming to like it. The answer to this riddle seems to be that Mr. Roosevelt, in the first place, appears to master even the minor details of every measure that he brings up, and therefore is equipped to meet every argument. That is impressive. More important, however, is his willingness at all times to assume full responsibility before the country for the things he proposes.

If there is one thing about the President and his program more disturbing than any other, it is not his willingness to assume responsibility and let it go at that. It is his eagerness to take and champion propositions which apparently have not been suggested by him. Some of the Administration measures which fell into that category, we suspect, were evolved by his professional advisers. Such parentage in itself is not against them, I hasten to say.

But the fact that some of these measures have not been thought out and thought through—and apparently they have not—is indeed, disquieting. An example of what I mean by undigested legislation, bearing the Roosevelt brand, was cited to me by one of the ablest men in the Roosevelt group. And he is not a professor. He relates that some weeks ago he became enamored of a startlingly new governmental idea. He wrestled with it for days and slept with it for nights. Finally resolving that it was good, even though radical, he carried it to the President.

In ten minutes' time—no longer than that—he had "sold" the idea to Mr. Roosevelt. The latter leaned forward and in all earnestness assured this friend of mine that the White House would be behind the proposition 100 per cent. All this was flattering to the proposer of the plan, but just the same it caused him profound uneasiness. The President was too quick to take it.

It is far too soon to put Mr. Roosevelt down as a superman, a great statesman or a man of destiny. He still has a long way to go before achieving that eminence. But it is not too much to say that he has exhibited political sagacity and administrative efficiency to an astonishing degree. The results he has to his credit—and they are breath-taking when we try to comprehend them—can not all be charged to the "super-situation." There was the "hour," to be sure, but also there was the "man."

First to last in a session of Congress, the like of which none of us has ever seen, Mr. Roosevelt put through his program without one open break with the legislative branch. Such a break seemed imminent toward the end, upon the veterans compensation issue, after other issues a thousand times more important, moreover, had been disposed of. But a little compromise added to a great deal of firmness on the President's part, closed the breach and dissolved the rebellion.

The Roosevelt program with its fourteen major measures is now statutory law. That program smashed many of our cherished traditions, but none more ruthlessly than the American tradition of "rugged individualism." We are now moving along a new path of social control and planned economy, with the long arm of the Federal Government reaching out in a score of directions where before neither its strength nor its beneficence had been felt.

This central government of ours has now become the almoner to 12,000,000 unemployed and distressed people. It has become the guardian of middle-class investors, of the mortgaged-farm owner, of the mortgaged-home owner, of the bank depositor, and of the railway employee. It has become the partner of industry and of agriculture. And it has even become the friend of the beer maker and the beer drinker.

As a practical contribution to prosperity, the Government promises to expend $3,300,000,000 on public works. It has made an outright grant to the States of $500,000,000 to relieve the destitute, and it has agreed to subscribe a few hundred million more to the corporations which will undertake the refinancing of mortgages on farms and small homes. On top of that it will guarantee the interest on $2,000,000,000 of farm mortgage bonds and $2,000,000,000 home mortgage bonds.

The Government has gone even further. It proposes to make a gigantic experiment in the Tennessee Basin, an experiment in reforestation, soil restoration, navigation and water-power development. If the thing works, it may be given a trial in the basin of the upper Missouri, the valley of the Columbia River and wherever else there is a flood and drainage and soil erosion problem.

In order to make all these dreams come true, vast sums of money must be employed. Some of this money will be raised by increased taxation, but the most of it must be borrowed. In order to borrow, the Federal credit must be maintained through a balanced budget. Thus it is reasoned. And that is why economies in governmental operation are being enforced. These economies begin with the $350,000,000 in veterans compensation and extend to civil and military pay, to reduced departmental expenditures and to governmental reorganization. We once envisaged a saving of a billion dollars a year!

Endless pages might be written—even books—upon the legislative and executive activities of the past four months. How it will all work out, we do not know. All that we do know for a moral certainty is that the old formulas, plans, policies, programs and philosophies—the old conservatism, in a word—failed us and failed wretchedly in the depressed days of the past three years. If the New Deal wins, well and good. We will kiss the past good-by without a regret. If this Deal also fails, it can scarcely leave us any worse off than we were on March 4.

8

The New Deal as Savior
of Capitalism

AT one time the coal industry was the sickest in the United States.
By confession of the coal operators, they were in despair over their
capacity ever to revive it. The decline of purchasing power had affected
the market for transportation, the market for steel, and the market for
manufactured goods, which coal supplied. Always two or three steps
removed from consumer goods, except for the coal which went to house-
holders, this basic industry was perishing for lack of markets.

One of the most vivid memories of my first week in Washington was
the visit of a large group of coal operators to the President. It was a
visit in which they expressed their sense of defeat.

The President was extremely preoccupied with the bank closing and
fiscal policy. He had hundreds of appointments, and a host of projects,
later developed into an administrative program on the domestic front,
was under consideration. He heard them courteously, but he could not
take the time to hear all they had to say. He made a quick decision to
get them off his hands and, at the same time, get some thoughtful attention for their problem. He remembered that the Secretary of the Interior had the Bureau of Mines in his Department as well as responsibility
for the natural resources of the country. He realized that if the mines
were shut down permanently there would be problems of unemployment, and he thought of the Labor Department. Without consulting us
he turned the coal operators over to the Secretary of the Interior and
the Secretary of Labor.

We had no preliminary preparation. We had been at work only a
few days and were still getting our Departments organized and trying
to find our bearings. But we held two days of the strangest hearings that

SOURCE: Frances Perkins, *The Roosevelt I Knew* (New York, 1946),
pp. 228–31.

it has ever been my duty to sit in on. Absolutely new in the government, Harold Ickes and I sat behind a table, looking solemn as owls and representing the Government of the United States. We were so new at being "the Government" that it was really only the externals of representation.

But I suddenly got the sense of responsibility to a whole industry and to a whole nation and not merely to the President or to my special field. I had a sense of what "the Government of the United States," put into just those words, means in its influence, leadership, and conscience for all the people of the United States. In a democracy this responsibility of being "the Government," of being the individuals who, for the moment, are trusted with the duty of saying "yes" or "no" within the constitutional guarantees, is something scarcely faced by most people in advance of assuming office.

I did not ask Ickes about what went on in his mind, but certainly these ideas went through mine, and I said to myself, "Lord, I am not worthy, but I must do these things. I must give them my best thought and attention." A newly realized sense of authority is sobering.

We heard their stories. They were catastrophic stories: whole communities were practically down; local grocery stores could not operate; local schoolteachers were not being paid; local merchants and transportation systems were nearly bankrupt; everybody was in debt to somebody; soon the time would be at hand when wholesale grocers, clothing supply people, and others would no longer send goods to local merchants because their credit was almost exhausted; and all this misfortune came because the mines were down.

The miners, prime source of business in the small communities, had nothing to spend when the week was out. A whole community of middle-class folk, living out of serving the needs of the productive workers in the mines, was almost in collapse in some towns. There was practically total unemployment. The operators laid before us their reports of earnings for the last ten years. It was a story of constant decline. Surpluses were gone and stockholders hadn't been paid. Salaries to absolutely essential executives were in arrears. The operators described the plight of mine workers in terms of sympathy, which made one realize that when it comes to the facts of life there can be real understanding between owners and workers in particular industries.

The only exceptions were a few highly productive mines in the smokeless field where, because of the physical configuration of the coal seam and a favorable transportation situation, coal could be mined and go to the seaboard with a minimum of expenditure for power and transportation.

The burden of recommendations from coal operator after coal operator was that the government must take over the mines. "Will the government please take them?" they pleaded. "The operators will sell the mines to the government at any price fixed by the government. Anything so we can get out of it."

I found myself at the noon recess saying to one operator after another, "Now take courage, Mr. X. You can do it. You'll be able to run these mines. It isn't so bad as you think. I don't think you should give up. Just have courage. It's your work in the world. The government's going to do the things necessary to relieve the financial strain."

I didn't know exactly what the government was going to do, but the government had a platform pledged to do something to make it possible for the people to buy once more and for the wheels of industry to turn again. We were unable to give them any outline of what the government would do, but Mr. Ickes and I strove to encourage them to hold out a little while longer. We assured them that the government did not want to take or buy the mines; that it believed that the mines had better be operated by private ownership.

Ickes whispered to me, "What in the world would we do with the mines if we took them over? How could the Government operate them? Nobody in this Government knows how to run a coal mine. This isn't a nationalization program we have undertaken with Roosevelt."

9

The Theory of the New Deal

THERE is no mystery about the economics of the New Deal. For several generations, governments ran their affairs on the theory that natural economic forces balance themselves out. The law of supply and demand would regulate prices. When there was too little supply, the price would go up, and this would automatically increase the supply. When there was too much, the price would go down, and this would automatically decrease the supply. The efficient producer would succeed, the inefficient would fail, and this would keep the productive capacity of the country about in line with the needs for consumption. When credit was needed, bankers would supply it; when too much credit had been extended, there was a period of general inflation cutting down the debt. All this was comprehended in the governmental theory of the time which was really based on the classical economics of Adam Smith.

A tremendous force came into the world in the middle of the nineteenth century. It is usually tied up with what is called the industrial revolution and the advent of large-scale production. But we know now that the actual forces released ran further than that. The power and force of organization had come into economics. Originally this collected around great investments of capital in huge plants, such as railroads, steel companies and the like. But as the economic machinery adapted itself to the idea of great organizations to run these plants, it became possible to have great organizations only partly dependent upon such plants.

This has led to a revision in some of our economic thinking. No longer can we rely on the economics of balance to take care of human needs. The effect of organization will distort and delay the forces leading to a balance to a degree as yet unmeasured. A falling price does not mean a falling supply under an agricultural system plus a credit system so

SOURCE: A. A. Berle, Jr., "The Social Economics of the New Deal," *The New York Times Magazine*, October 29, 1933, pp. 4–9, 19.

organized that when the price went down every one tried to produce
more wheat, or more cotton or more sugar in order to get out of debt.
A big inefficient plant does not shut down because it cannot make a
profit. It reorganizes, cuts its debt to nothing, and goes right on. Then
it has no interest charges to pay, and only a small investment. It can
accordingly undersell a more efficient producer, and drive him into
bankruptcy, too. And this is repeated all through the industry.

Only after the entire industry has been bankrupted, do inefficient
plants actually begin to go out of business. This process may take
fifteen or twenty years, during which time the capital, the labor, the
customers, and the industry generally, suffer from the effects of a disorganized and unsound condition.

The old economic forces still work and they do produce a balance
after a while. But they take so long to do it and they crush so many men
in the process that the strain on the social system becomes intolerable.
Leaving economic forces to work themselves out as they now stand will
produce an economic balance, but in the course of it you may have half
of the entire country begging in the streets or starving to death.

The New Deal may be said to be merely a recognition of the fact
that human beings cannot indefinitely be sacrificed by millions to the
operation of economic forces accentuated by this factor of organization. Further, the mere process of organization which could create the
economic mechanism can be invoked to prevent the shocking toll on
life and health and happiness which readjustment under modern conditions demands.

Whatever the outcome, President Roosevelt will live in history as a
great President if only for this one fact. He not only appreciated the
situation, but had the courage to grapple with the cardinal economic
problem of modern life. And he did so not in the spirit of hatred manifested by the red revolutionary or the black Fascist abroad, but in the
typical American spirit of great generosity and great recognition that
individual life and individual homes are the precious possessions; all
else is merely machinery for the attainment of a full life.

You will find that the forces which the New Deal called into action
roughly correspond to the organized forces which economists recognize
as the senior controls of our present society. The first and the most important is the control of credit, banking and currency. This, the most
important, the most delicate and the most complex, was in obvious
collapse on March 4. Wisely, the legislation attending the banking holiday did not commit to any final solution; it is one of the problems with
which the administration has yet to deal. The reason is not far to seek.

With five countries around us managing their currency, with the whole problem of the American price level then to be worked out, with the many aspects of that problem in vivid dispute, no one in his senses would have undertaken to lay down a definitive system. What was done was to gather into the hands of the administration many of the tools which could be used on a problem of this sort. It is after all a little naïve to assume that there could be any one lever in that vast machinery which would serve as the complete solution.

A second senior control lies in the tremendously concentrated domination of certain groups over industry. Now industry heretofore has been assumed to be an enterprise conducted for private profit, providing goods and services which the country needs. But it is a great deal more than that. It is one of the principal avenues by which the national income is distributed through the form of wages, dividends, bond interest and so forth. In this item wages are distinctly the largest factor.

Now distribution of the national income is something more than a problem in social welfare. America, in a most intense form, is struggling with a problem that is common to all countries which are highly developed industrially. This is the fact that no industrial civilization can function at all unless there is a tremendous body of people able and willing to buy the products of industry.

The very process of building big factories means that there is a great output of goods which were formerly called luxuries, but which become necessities as the standard of living rises. In order to keep these plants going at all there have to be customers. Which means, when you carry it one step further, that there have to be people whose wages are high enough and steady enough to enable them to buy these goods. In the economist's jargon, it means that the national income has to be widely diffused. A national income of, say, eighty millions will not support an industrial civilization if 5 per cent of the country has most of it and 95 per cent divides the remnant. We got into exactly that position —we are there yet, for that matter—and it is one of the great obstacles to recovery.

This is, in political thinking, a new approach to the problem of wealth. The Communist has talked about having no property at all and distributing goods and services currently, because he thought of it in terms of social justice. Sociologists have talked about an evenly distributed income, on the theory that a large middle class, or rather, a nation of people of moderate means, formed the basis for a healthier national life. It remained for the hard-boiled student to work out the simple equation that unless the national income was pretty widely diffused there were not enough customers to keep the plants going; and as the plants shut down the wages shut down, too, and you became engaged in a vicious spiral in which there was less production, hence less wages, hence less income, hence still fewer customers, still less production, and so on down the scale.

We hit the bottom of that mad spiral some time last February, at which point roughly 40 per cent of all wage-earners were out of a job. At that time, as a necessary result, no factories had orders enough to carry on with; only a few railroads had traffic enough to pay their current bills, and the whole machinery threatened to fall into absolute collapse. To this problem the incoming administration addressed itself.

It was conceived that by mobilizing industry through the National Recovery Administration and requiring it to meet the responsibilities of an income distributing group, much could be done toward achieving the balance and distribution of income which is required to keep a system like ours afloat. When people talk of "creating purchasing power" what they really mean is that the national income goes not into stagnant pools of unneeded investment but into the hands of people who need goods.

Mobilization of this kind cannot be wholesale in scope; it has to be worked out industry by industry, in an intimateness of detail which can be coped with only by men thoroughly familiar with that industry. This accounts for the machinery of the National Recovery Administration. It involves, incidentally, a problem of education of a large order; for business men are not accustomed to work together, or to realize that if every one pursues his individual interest the result may be bankruptcy for all. I am not quite clear whether the hearings on national codes are not quite as important from the point of view of education as they are from the point of view of industrial organization.

The third and extremely important lever was grasped through the medium of the agricultural legislation—the first time in America that machinery has been devised to control production. We had the paradox that the more successful farming was, the more bankrupt was the farmer. And this in turn meant fewer markets for our industrial goods and ultimately unemployment in the cities. Prosperity to one section while another was in difficulties meant nothing; Mr. Roosevelt's now famous dictum that a country cannot endure "half boom and half broke" was an accurate bit of economic diagnosis as well as a brilliant phrase.

Still another of the senior controls is transportation. Through the various processes of regulation, we have held more control over railroads and transportation than over other parts of the national economy. It is plain, however, that the system was, and for that matter still is, badly askew. After conferences with the railroads themselves, the law creating a railroad coordinator was passed, with the object of setting up a nucleus of organization and at the same time providing sufficient "punch," so that the results of cooperation in railroading could be made available and could be passed on to the public either in the form of wages or in the form of lower rates or in the form of a solvent railroad; and preferably through the medium of all three.

An effective bit of machinery was the Reconstruction Finance Corporation which, properly rejuvenated, became during the early days of the administration the focus of most of the private finance of the country. Jesse Jones, the chairman of that board, took on a job the like of which has not been seen in history; for, from the beginning of the bank holiday until well through into the Summer, the Reconstruction Finance Corporation under his leadership was the principal support of our entire fabric, both of long-term and of short-term finance.

I am aware of the many criticisms leveled at the Reconstruction Finance Corporation largely arising out of its early operations, when it was conceived principally as an aid to certain great railroads and banks. Under the philosophy of a new administration, however, it became an instrument for safeguarding and making available the banking and credit structure which is the life blood of all trade. For a period the Reconstruction Finance Corporation virtually took over the great bulk of the work normally done by Wall Street and by the financial centers throughout the country; and as it has completed job after job it has turned the situation back to the respective communities in far better shape than ever before.

The overpowering burden of debt with which the country was struggling as a result of the prosperous decade threatened, and, for that matter, still threatens to engulf much of the economic activity liberated as these various great mechanisms are brought into play. That problem is by no means solved; but I merely mention the Agricultural Credit Corporation, the Home Owners Loan Corporation and other similar institutions designed to take up part of this burden and to reduce it to manageable form.

As a necessary supplement there is the program of public works designed to inject as and when necessary (and it is necessary now) additional activity into the commercial system.

There are many more similar levers and controls, but space does not permit description of them all. It is enough to say that in the aggregate they aim at introducing a power of organization into the economic system which can be used to counterbalance the effects of organization gone wrong; and to make sure that the burdens of readjustment are equitably distributed, and that no group of individuals will be ground to powder in order to satisfy the needs of an economic balance.

The overwhelming question today is, will this gigantic attempt to mold an individualist, capitalist system into a directed economic effort produce the result?

Before answering that question, it is well to look at the alternative. For myself, this alternative, drastic as it may sound, has far less terror than a general breakdown. Those of us who had the privilege of working on the original plan began with the assumption that what we needed most was a machine that worked. Whether it was rugged individualism, Fascism, Communism, Socialism, or what-not, made not the slightest bit of difference. Actually, the job was to satisfy the perfectly legitimate needs of a huge mass of people, all of whom were entitled to their right to live. If it cannot be done one way, it must be done another; but we may as well face with entire frankness what might have to be done should the present experiment fail.

A question has been asked which has not yet been answered. Every one is familiar with it. Why is it that with more food, more clothing, more housing, more luxuries, than we know what to do with, there are some 25,000,000 people in the United States who are hungry, naked, living most precariously, and with little more than the bare necessities of subsistence? Every civilized human being is asking that question; and the fact that there are millions of people to whom civilization offers nothing just now means that the question will go right on being asked until an answer is found.

Now there is an answer possible. If, let us say, the government of the United States, forgetting all about the Constitution, were to commandeer everything and every one tomorrow afternoon, it could make a program that would look something like this:

It would say to every department store, and small retailer, "You are now a government distributing office." It could say the same to every wholesaler, every jobber, every warehouse. It could say to every manufacturer of finished goods, and every supplier of raw material, "You are now a government production agency." It could say to every railroad, truckman and the like. "You are now a government transportation agency." It could say to every one working in any capacity, as president, as day laborer, or as roustabout, employed or unemployed, "You are now enrolled as a part of the government labor supply."

It could say at the same time, "All of you will now go back to work. You will produce until we tell you to stop. When we have more than enough of what you happen to be producing, we will give you a furlough, until we need some more." It could say to the miner, "You will produce copper, or coal, or iron"; to the manufacturer, "You will produce finished products and we will supply your requisitions for raw materials." It could say to the transportation agencies, "You will requisition what you need to run your railroad with, and you will transport as we direct." So far, this is very much what we do in war time.

But it would have to say something more than that. A government tackling a solution on these lines would have to say: "Nobody will be paid anything. Debts and interest are canceled. Instead of that, we will give to every one a red card entitling him to go to the nearest government distributing agency (for which you can read the department store, the little shop on the corner of Third Avenue, the drug store in the little town, the grocery shop you habitually deal with), and can get your share of the goods produced. You can use this for a small motor car, or you can use it for a barrel of flour, or for a loaf of bread. We shall have difficulties in distribution, and there may be shortages. We shall have to have regulations—you cannot step up to an automobile store (now a government distributing agency), and ask for ten big cars. But we can arrange things, as organization proceeds, so that everybody gets his share."

If such a method of distribution were arranged, and it was carefully and thoroughly done, and industry maintained its efficiency, pretty much every one in the United States would have, in terms of goods and of services, an income equivalent to somewhere in the vicinity of $5,000 a year—or rather, equivalent to what $5,000 a year income will buy now.

There are two great difficulties with this kind of solution. One of them is that no one knows whether the industrial efficiency we now have would keep up—that is, whether our productive capacity would be great enough to meet the demand, once the incentive of private profit is taken out. I do not regard this objection as very serious. We know enough about production for private profit today to know that it is as often inefficient as efficient; that while private profit in a small enterprise makes for efficiency, in a large enterprise it is quite as likely to make for wholesale plunder. Also, in time we could expect efficiency at least as great as that which we now get out of the United States Postoffice— and that is, on the whole, in season and out, a pretty dependable institution.

The other objection is, however, infinitely more serious. Supposing some one happened to be living on a scale of life which assumed that he had a cook. There are people who serve civilization best by having cooks. Perhaps they are artists, authors, musicians, college professors even; perhaps they are the kind of men and women who have to manage these various enterprises, and it is sheer waste for them to be sweeping the front entry when we need them to see that the industrial program and the esthetic needs of the country are taken care of.

How is any government to say to me that I have to be a cook, and
to you, that you can be manager of a plant or a leader of a symphony
orchestra! Will not the cook say, "This is all very well; but I have no
particular interest in being a servant in your house, while you have a
position of importance. Your red card looks exactly the same as mine;
it is good for the same thing at the local department store."

A government could, of course, maintain discipline by saying to me,
"Unless you go on cooking, you get no food cards." But that is substantially the same as imposing sentence of death by starvation unless I
go on working at a job which perhaps I may not like. Consequently, the
government would have to begin working out classifications—giving the
manager of a plant a food card which entitled him to have a cook, on
the ground that he was more highly trained and more highly valuable,
while the day laborer had a food card merely entitling him to a decent
house, an adequate supply of food and clothing, a small motor car and
a reasonable allowance of moving pictures and beer.

I can imagine an American Government doing this if it had to—but
only if it had to. If there is a general break-down, it will have to do,
temporarily at least, something very like this; but it is the last resort;
a counsel of despair; an indication that we cannot run our private lives
effectively enough to solve the situation. Moreover, under the stress of
that kind of experiment, a great deal of the grace of life and human
values, which we all of us hold dear, might very easily go out. Complicated and difficult as it may seem to manipulate private industry and
private economic processes, this is still preferable to attempting a wholesale solution, so long as there is any hope of success.

This is why the experiment of the Roosevelt administration not only
is historic, but why it must succeed. This is why the only intelligent
attitude to take is one of cooperation. This is why, though all of us
will undoubtedly have moments of discouragement at the slowness of
it, we build more strongly than we might were we either to attempt a
wholesale revolution, or to plunge back into the chaos which was failing
dismally only a few months ago.

I have perhaps less fear of the sweeping solution than most people,
because I have perhaps more faith than most people in the ability of
the United States to take almost any scheme of society and manipulate
it into a satisfactory solution. People do not change their habits easily;
and the kind of economic system people want is the kind which, in
the long run, they are likely to get.

If, for example, we were to adopt the Russian Soviet system entire,
it would look a good deal more like the Rotary Club or the four railway
brotherhoods than like the Moscow Soviet; the skyline of New York

and life in Peoria, Ill., or St. Louis, Mo., would be a good deal more like life as it is now in New York, or Peoria, or St. Louis, than like life in Petrograd, or Kieff, or Odessa.

But it is one thing not to be afraid of a change, and quite another to abandon the civilization which, by and large, has served us well, modifying it only enough to meet changed conditions. In a world in which revolutions just now are coming easily, the New Deal chose the more difficult course of moderation and rebuilding. This, in a word, is the social economics—the political economics, in the old phrase—of the New Deal.

10

NRA Ballyhoo

"BALLYHOO" is what a circus barker does to get people to spend their money for tickets to a side-show which isn't worth the money. It is the constant repetition of lies, incitements, or exaggerations and I was accused by nearly all of them of being the "biggest and most blatant ballyhoo artist in the whole New Deal."

It is true that I believed zealously and earnestly in what I was doing. When I had decided to take my job, I said to Bernie Baruch, "Chief, I wish I had your faculty for getting things done through charm and astuteness and polish and your genius for saying things very positively but so gently that nobody ever takes offense." Then he told me the story of Paul Berlenbach who was a slugger of the Dempsey type before whom nobody could stand. "But then," he said, "*somebody came along to teach him to box*. He didn't last six months. Somebody with a wallop got in the ring with him and, when he began dancing around and delivering fairy taps, they carried him through the ropes feet first. Go in there and be yourself and not Bernie Baruch, nor Jim Ham Lewis, nor Lord Chesterfield, nor anybody else but just yourself."

This I tried to do and if sometimes the verbal result savored of a cavalry barrack, my only excuse is that I spent the formative period of my life in that environment. I talked as I had always talked and in carefully re-reading all of it, I still can't see the "Ballyhoo." Out of the whole lot I have picked what is generally said to have been the worst example. . . .

It was delivered at St. Louis to a visible audience of 26,000 and over both radio chains.

There is one reason to expect success. This is a move to bring happiness back to homes, and homes are the peculiar province of wives and mothers. It is they who have borne the brunt of the four

SOURCE: Hugh Johnson, *The Blue Eagle from Egg to Earth* (Garden City, N.Y., 1935), pp. 262–8.

years' blight on decency in living. They are the purchasing agents of America. Women do 80% of our buying. It is more accurate to say that they, in some measure, control 100% of our buying. It is they who can put the Blue Eagle on everything that moves in trade or commerce. The cause could not be in surer hands. Men might argue about how many business angels could stand for the point of an economic needle—and let the chance go by, but a woman in support of her home is about as safe for triflers as a Royal Bengal Tigress at the door of a den full of cubs. When every American housewife understands that the Blue Eagle on everything that she permits to come into her home is a symbol of its restoration to security, may God have mercy on the man or group of men who attempt to trifle with this bird.

The only thing to make the President's plan effective is to understand the President's plan. And all that is necessary to understand the President's plan is to know that every employer who can show the Blue Eagle has already raised wages and made new jobs and that he cannot keep it up unless everybody acts right now to support him and buy his goods.

That simple but necessary program depends on just one thing for its success—the instant and intensive activity and support of the mothers and wives and sisters and sweethearts of this country and on nobody else in the world.

Our men had the leading part in the Revolution which made the nation—and in the Civil War which united it, and in the World War which glorified it. But, this time, it is the women who must carry the whole fight of President Roosevelt's war against depression, perhaps the most dangerous war of all. It is women in homes —and not soldiers in uniform—who will this time save our country from misery and discord and unhappiness. They will go over the top to as great a victory as the Argonne. It is zero hour for housewives. Their battle cry is "Buy now under the Blue Eagle!" and the bird is blazoned on the banners in their van.

Those who are not with us are against us, and the way to show that you are a part of this great army of the New Deal is to insist on this symbol of solidarity exactly as Peter of the Keys drew a fish on the sand as a countersign and Peter the Hermit exacted the cross on the baldric of every good man and true. This campaign is a frank dependence on the power and the willingness of the American people to act together as one person in an hour of great danger. And that brings us to the critical point of the program which I must make with all the emphasis at my command.

This thing won't last three months unless all men who now have employment and all who are now to be put back on the payroll—or to have their part-time work increased—*turn right around and pour the entire benefit back into the channels of trade.*

Our people have smiled their way through this hell—there is not one who has not made his sacrifice. If he kept his job he gave something to somebody. He helped some friend or some member of his family—too proud to ask for public help—too much up against it to refuse what we kindly call a loan. No use harping on that. . . . It is the most sublime chapter in our story . . . the secret of every decent person, which, to every decent person—is no secret at all. The blundering silent sentiment of this self-styled, hard boiled people of ours is enough to bring tears to the brazen eyes of a squatting Buddha.

To preserve a hostage to future fortune, people who have a little left have adopted a non-buying policy that is fatal to recovery. It is an unemployment psychology that sends us shabby to our work. Unpainted houses—cracked shoes, many times half-soled—shiny pants—rattling automobiles—dyed dresses—refurbished wardrobes —all these badges of unselfish husbandry must now be replaced if this plan is to have a fair chance to do what we hope for it. We must shake ourselves out of this four-year-old idea of doing without against a rainy day and we must do that overnight. . . . Buy! Buy now! Buy within prudence everything you need and have so long denied yourselves. It is the key to the whole situation.

The President said in his inaugural that he believed in putting first things first and the first thing in this great program is to get *Blue Eagles* in every window. The time for dealing with the chiseling fringe will come as soon as that is done.

We all know the possibility of an Iscariot in every Twelve. Even Judas survived for a season—and then hanged himself for shame. As soon as this great modern legion is marshaled, it will be time enough to look about us for Judas. . . . At this time, we ask only that you visualize the rare case of a man who has betrayed the confidence of the President and the people of this nation and, behind the outspread wings of the Blue Eagle, has inveigled the women of this community to support his business, and then imagine that, after just complaint and fair and patient hearing, he is at last found out as one who would prong pennies in violation of a spontaneous confidence of his government and his neighbors.

Guilty as Charged. Guilty of trifling with this great chance to lift this country out of economic hell. Guilty of a practice as cheap as stealing pennies out of the cup of a blind beggar. What should be done with such a man? . . . As happened to Danny Deever, NRA will have to remove from him his badge of public faith and business honor and "takin of his buttons off an' cut his stripes away" break the bright sword of his commercial honor in the eyes of his neighbors—and throw the fragments—in scorn—in the dust at his feet. It is a sentence of economic death. It will never happen. The threat of it transcends any puny penal provision in this law.

The Blue Eagle is a symbol of industrial solidarity and self-government. If people who are willing to cooperate for a great national purpose are not permitted to wear a badge to distinguish friend from foe, then soldiers ought not to be permitted to wear a uniform or carry a flag. Warfare should decline to guerilla sniping. The chivalry of men in battle ought to give place to well-poisoning and assassination and it was well that Richard of the Lion Heart, unvanquished in every field from Palestine to the English Channel, should die, as legend has it, from an arrow poisoned in the Caucasus by the Old Man of the Mountain to be discharged in Normandy.

I made many such speeches but this one marks the nadir of all my sinning. I can't think it was sinning. I believed these things. I still believe them. I believe them so hard that I feel that unless they are kept alive NRA will fail. I think it is failing now because people who do not understand the fundamentals of NRA are neglecting them.

Of course, the country had to be told about NRA. Some districts lagged and some forged ahead. Enemy propaganda was stronger in some places than in others. These were perilous moments. In spite of the work in Washington which was so great that sometimes for days at a time— 6 hours out of 24 was all I could spare from work—it was absolutely necessary to go all over the United States to confer with local leaders and to make speeches—sometimes three a day. Fortunately, we had the army air service to help us—a big fast Condor plane, with a desk in it. The speeches were written on hops from city to city. We visited every important town in the country except New Orleans, and flew a distance considerably greater than the earth's circumference.

Within a few weeks doubt about the first great step was over. This country was astir from coast to coast. Along the line of march were such men as stood on the banks of the Hudson while Fulton's steamboat got up steam and cried, "She'll never run—she'll never run!" We also heard a similar complaint in Washington for a month. We liked to remember that when the *Clermont* began chunking up the Hudson River, men ran alongside crying: "She'll never stop—she'll never stop." We soon heard that also. "Beware—What is the government going to do with this dangerous weapon?". . .

The climax was a Blue Eagle parade in New York, in the early part of September, 1933, arranged by Grover Whalen who had been doing the job there. I think it was one of the greatest parades ever held in the country. It proceeded in columns of masses all one day and most of the next night. It was just a jammed river of humanity flowing up Fifth Avenue and its distinctive feature was color and cheer—cheer such as I had not observed in my four years' previous residence there. These people were convinced that they had seen the worst. Hope and confidence had returned.

I stood in the reviewing stand in that parade and there were hundreds of people I knew who waved as they went past. Down below were massed batteries of cameras and I knew if I raised my hand higher than my shoulders, it would seem and be publicized as a "Fascist salute." So I never did raise it higher, I just stuck my arm out straight and wiggled my hand around. But that didn't help me—*Time* came out saying I had constantly saluted *au Mussolini* and even had a photograph to prove it, but it wasn't my arm on that photograph. It wore the taped cuff sleeve of a cut-away coat and a stiff round cuff with an old fashioned cuff button and I never wore either in my whole life. I think it was the arm of Mayor O'Brien who stood beside me which had been faked onto my body.

That was a high point in NRA history. Within four months PRA and the Blue Eagle had:

(a) Brought 96% of Commerce and Industry voluntarily under NIRA.
(b) Abolished sweatshops and child labor.
(c) Obtained an agreement from 96% of employers under it to recognize the rights of labor under 7a.
(d) Put 2,785,000 bread-winners back on pay-rolls and increased annual purchasing power by $3,000,000,000, and that is several times the aggregate result accomplished by all the other Recovery Administrations put together.
(e) Established 40 hours as the maximum work week and $12.00 as the minimum weekly pay for the lowest paid type of common labor in the United States, and practically took the wages of labor out of the field of industrial competition.
(f) Changed desperation into hopefulness not only among employees but among employers throughout the country.
(g) Acted as the greatest single educational force in homely economics in our history.

(h) Created, for the first time, an economic government throughout the United States imposed upon the political government and nearly as wide in extent.

(i) Awakened the conscience of the country to its best interest and its duty to erase these old iniquities.

11

The Brain Trust

THEY'RE a little dizzy down in Washington trying to keep up with the "brain trust."

What will it do next?

That's the big question as the Capital, shaken out of its apathy by the concussion of tremendous events, waits to see what new legislative explosion will be set off by Mr. Roosevelt's professors. . . .

Is it true that the "brain trust" is ruling the country behind the White House throne? Has it really changed our form of government to a constitutional dictatorship? Does it aim at Fascism, Communism, or what?

Those questions are making Washingtonians a bit balmy, as Arthur Sears Henning tells us in one of his dispatches to the Chicago *Tribune*—

> Official Washington has been rent asunder by the advent of the professoriat. Sides have been taken, and disputation has become feverish in Capitol cloak-rooms, in locker-rooms, at teas, and other cocktail parties.
>
> Either you are for the "brain trust" or against it. Either you point with pride to the new deal that has sprung full panoplied from the brain of the professoriat or you view with alarm the dictatorship, the farm commodity allotment, the inflation of the currency, the devaluation of the dollar, the minimum wage, the maximum price, the shorter work day, planned economic controlled capitalism, and other features of the new dispensation from on high.
>
> The "brain trust" completely overshadows the Cabinet. It is reputed to have more influence with the President, to know what he is thinking, if not inspiring the thought, to be able to swing appointments to fat jobs, and to be "in the know" generally of what is going on beneath the surface of official life.

SOURCE: "The Hullabaloo Over the 'Brain Trust,'" *Literary Digest,* CXVI (1933), 8–9.

It has taken the professors from various colleges to put the Cabinet members in their places at last—merely department heads, chief clerks. On a routine administration matter you go to a Cabinet member, but on matters of policy and the higher statesmanship you consult the professoriat.

Everybody, it seems, "wants to know the professors who are guiding our destinies." Office-seekers dog their footsteps. Hostesses vie to land them as guests of honor. Professors are the fad. In fact—

All Washington is going to school to the professors, learning all about political science and economics. Debutantes hang on their exposition of the quantitative theory of money, the law of diminishing returns, and the intricacies of foreign exchange.

Bookstores are selling their books like hot cakes. Their works are not available at the Library of Congress, the volumes having been withdrawn by the Senators and Congressmen for perusal in an effort to plumb this new force in the scheme of government which has put Congress also in its place.

Who are the members of the "brain trust"? What are they like? How do they work?

The chief, of course, is Prof. Raymond Moley of Columbia University, who, as described by Mr. Henning, is "a square-shouldered, pinkish-cheeked man, just turned forty-six, with graying brown hair lightly thatching a high-domed head." And—

He occupies a suite of offices at the State Department surrounded by a bevy of attractive young women secretaries, including honor students of one of his political science classes at Barnard College.

Altho he is vested with the title of Assistant Secretary of State, an administrative office, State Department administration is the least of his duties. He is concerned with the whole reach of governmental policies from foreign relations to fiscal affairs, from industrial integration to the incidence of taxation.

He is reputed to be the closest adviser of the President. . . .

Next Mr. Henning introduces us to Prof. Rexford G. Tugwell, instructor in economics at Columbia University, whom he ranks as second only to Mr. Moley in the "brain trust." He is nominally Assistant Secretary of Agriculture, but actually adviser to the President on economic questions—

Tall, slender, looking more youthful even than his forty-one years, Dr. Tugwell contributes a distinct flavor of scholarship to the political scene. Altho an accomplished expositor of the theory of planned economy as embodied in the industry control bill, the young professor is far prouder of his critique of the works of Thomas Hardy.

A liberal but not a radical is the self-classification of Dr. Tugwell. The liberal, he explains, is content to experiment in the reconstruction of economic institutions, while the radical prefers the "revolutionary tactics," with which, he says, "I have never found myself greatly in sympathy." Capitalism he regards as in process of evolution into "socialized industry."

Dr. Tugwell also had a hand in the preparation of the farm-relief act which has just gone into effect, tho the principal authors of that novel plan for boosting farm products prices are two other members of the "brain trust," Prof. Milburn L. Wilson of Montana Agricultural College, who is to assist George Peek in administering the law, and Prof. Mordecai Ezekiel, economic adviser to Secretary of Agriculture Wallace.

Prof. A. A. Berle is attached to the Reconstruction Finance Corporation as an expert on railroads and other corporations. Prof. John Dickinson, serving as assistant Secretary of Commerce, helped to evolve the industry control bill. Then there is youthful Lewis Douglas, director of the budget, who used to be professor of history at Amherst before he went into politics and got himself elected to Congress.

Another member of the "brain trust" is William C. Bullitt, who was Mr. Roosevelt's scout in Europe before the inauguration, and is now special assistant Secretary of State with the principal duty of advising the President on foreign affairs.

Then there are brilliant young James P. Warburg, son of Paul Warburg, who mixes finance with the composition of revue lyrics set to music by his wife, and thirty-six-year-old Charles W. Taussig, molasses magnate, who dispenses advice on trade and tariff questions.

These, then, are members of the "brain trust," or "academic Cabinet," which is producing an abundance of fears and cheers, chills and thrills.

As for the misgivings held in some quarters, Mark Sullivan tells us about them in an article copyrighted by the New York *Herald Tribune*. "Professor Tugwell," he notes in conclusion, "calls himself a 'liberal.'" And—

So do all the planners and controllers. Are they not misusing that word, and by the way they use it misleading us? Most of us think of the word "liberal" as implying the maximum of individual liberty. These self-designated liberals propose a system in which constraint, "control," is a first principle. A pregnant sentence in Professor Tugwell's book reads: "It becomes more and more clear that these freedoms have to be restricted." Does restriction of freedom mark a liberal?

Use of the word "liberal" to describe a "control" which is the opposite of liberal seems indirect, an attempt to do something to America without letting America become aware of it until after the thing is done.

This is precisely what troubles some of us in Washington. We think that in a spirit of sportsmanship and good faith the professor controllers ought to tell us plainly just where they propose to carry us, and give us a chance to say in advance whether or not we wish to be carried there. . . .

In view of all this it may be surprising to read that members of the "brain trust" itself say, "there is no such thing." They "are a little resentful of the extent to which the alleged myth has taken root in the public mind." So we are told by Frederic William Wile, writing in the Washington *Evening Star*—

What seems mainly to be objected to is the theory that the President has a private coterie of professor-advisers accustomed to assemble in more or less secret sessions whereat, amid an atmosphere of profundity and mystery, the great problems of State are pondered and miraculously solved.

One of the shining lights of the constellation commonly called the "brain trust" assures this observer that the country has got Mr. Roosevelt's professors all wrong. They never pool their minds en bloc. They seldom meet one another, and, when they do, it's usually by accident.

Each and all of these experts have been assigned their jobs, it is declared, for special and specific purposes. They have no mandate, jointly or severally, to run or to save the country.

Accepting the "brain trust" as an actuality, the Boston *Herald* says it is not hard to find the reason for this innovation since "no President, except Mr. Hoover during the last part of his Administration, has been confronted with such a diversity of intricate, far-reaching problems."

To Frank R. Kent of the Baltimore *Sun*, "the bringing by Mr. Roosevelt of these students of economics and public questions into the Government and utilizing their brains to supplement his own practical political knowledge, is an ideal combination if it can be made to work. So far it has."

12

The TVA's Mission

THE first steps seemed to me (this was back in the hectic days of
the fall of 1933) to revive Southern *morale*, almost shattered by
generations of defeat and then self-pity; and to hammer home the basic
primary need of increased income, by demonstrations, as many demonstrations as possible, but always ones that the average man who had to
carry the job ahead could see and understand—if possible, those that he
could not only see, but that he could touch and handle himself, so that
his deep-seated skepticism would disappear.

I did all I could, as our program got under way, to see that it was so
managed and publicized that these things would be always in the fore-
front. The power program, for example. Electricity is something people
understand and respond to; the fact that a fight is often involved doesn't
hurt a damn bit either, for it dramatizes the point. We kept talking
about how money is drained out of the community by these remote-
control power setups, and as the figures for community-owned distribution agencies (either public or cooperative) came in, those figures, about
people and towns everyone knew about, came alive. Rural electrification,
too, was a popular kind of demonstration, for not only increased income
but also comfort and relief from ancient drudgeries are involved.

I used to make speeches before country crowds with a lot of farm
machinery gadgets (grinders for feed, brooders, etc.) set up on a big
table in front of me, and would work these into the talk, indicating
how much some particular farmer somewhere had added to his net income when he had these machines (most of which we designed ourselves, to meet the problems of these poor farmers, poor compared to
the farmers of the North for whom the big manufacturers had previously
done all their work).

Well, it was undignified as hell, like an Indian root doctor, but those
farmers listened to every darned word, and came up afterward—and

SOURCE: *The Journals of David E. Lilienthal* (2 vols., New York, 1964),
I, 80–2.

handled the gadgets and watched the electric motor grind feed, etc. And then a cooperative would be formed and the power lines would reach them; but they got more than power; they got a lift to their dragging morale, they got a bit of economic education the only way they could, by a demonstration; and it now appears they got an experience in working together that in time will be helpful no matter what happens to this country. In one county where a cooperative association bought all the power facilities, town and country, they hold an annual meeting of all members, and one of these meetings was photographed by a paper: farmers in their best overalls and their grave faces, and over the picture the paper put this heading: The Power Trust of Alcorn County.

The same with fertilizer: you probably don't know we have built and operate a huge fertilizer plant at Muscle Shoals and elsewhere, producing the most concentrated plant food ever made, by a wonderful process discovered by our Chief Chemical Engineer and his crew. Well, in the distribution of this element absolutely essential to restoration of Southern land and Southern farm income, the same demonstration technique has been carried on, in some ways the very best of them all. Thousands of farms all over the South (and more latterly in many out-South states) act as the damndest schoolroom for the most conservative and cautious group of humans in the country, the poor farmers. That is a whole story in itself. It was this program, the inspired contribution of Dr. Harcourt Morgan out of a lifetime of devotion to the land, that brought H.A. and me together in a relationship that is the best thing I have got out of the job—and as strange and incredible as it is precious, for he is temperamentally about as far from your volatile friend as you can imagine. And that, too, is a strange tale.

Transportation was another issue: the rank discrimination against the South that exists through higher levels of freight rates, a bar against a normal expansion of manufacturing activity, and insurance to the East that the South will continue to act as a colonial region, from which to mine raw materials to be shipped out for processing elsewhere. This issue is easy to demonstrate to the average businessman, and cuts across lines of natural opposition, such as the small vested interests who have done most of the New York utility holding company's fighting for them. It took almost three years before I could get the board to take on this freight rate fight, and the delay may have been all to the good. It looks now as if the first victory is in sight. And that, too, is a story in itself, though less significant.

So much for the kind of issues on which to "demonstrate." The problem of morale is of another kind, and very hard. My notion about that was to seek to raise a feeling of regional pride, in place of the too prevalent feeling of injury, self-pity, and, of course, downright discouragement, a kind of regional nervous breakdown. I planned a series of speeches before college groups, and I think you have read some of them: the first was the commencement speech in 1936 at the University of Alabama. The reverberations have been really encouraging. The time was ripe, and without that nothing would have happened. Many others, some of them much more eloquent and better equipped by reason of being Southerners, took up the story. After a period of caution in editing my remarks, the President took it up boldly, and in his speeches and in the Report on Economic Conditions in the South, his help on the transportation matter, and on Southern wage levels, education, etc., he has set the thing going nationally. He was induced to use, or permit to be used, some of the words that get folks into trouble in the South (I don't mean the War of the Rebellion, either!) and that has led to some unnecessary cross currents. But things have certainly gone a long way.

With the power program on its feet, and fortified by thousand-year dams and 20-year contracts not subject to change by Congress, I hope to be able to devote more and more time to this job. Of course the South can't go far unless the whole national picture is changed—of course that is true. But a demonstration in the South certainly won't retard the national changes, and I think we may all learn something of method out of it.

13

How people regain their

The Revival of Confidence

WANDERING around the country with one or the other of New York's baseball teams, I find that the National Road to Ruin now is a thriving thoroughfare. It has been redecorated. People have come out of the shell-holes into which they were blown by the explosions of finance and industry. They are working and playing and seem perfectly content to let a busy tribe of professional worriers do their worrying for them. By this happy arrangement, a lot of people seem to be themselves and there is much singing of a song called "Sweet Ad-o-line."

Now, as everyone knows, "Sweet Ad-o-line" is not a song to be sung in the daytime, alone, to relieve a melancholy mood. It is a choric song to be sung with feeling in the early hours of morning. It costs money to get around to singing "Sweet Ad-o-line." One works up to it. It is a melodic expression of brotherly love, good-will, and peace. . . .

A year ago few sang "Sweet Ad-o-line." When they did it sounded sad. It lacked warmth and sincerity. It is no good unless it is warm and sincere. In fact, it is sour.

A year ago, however, everyone was a worrier. I was in Florida with the Yankees when the banks closed and left me with $8.75. (It is difficult to believe that was only about a year ago; so much has happened since then.) I debated for a while the advisability of taking a long walk on a short pier; but I couldn't find a short pier. Instead, I developed a fine second-tenor moan and joined the National Wailers' and Moaners' Association, membership free.

We came home that year through Southern cities which looked as tho they had been ravaged by an invisible enemy. People seemed to be hiding. They even would not come out to see Babe Ruth and Lou Gehrig. They simply did not have the money to waste on baseball games or amusements.

Birmingham, a once-thriving, bright metropolis, looked as if it had

SOURCE: Rud Rennie, "Changing the Tune from Gloom to Cheer," *Literary Digest*, CXVII (1934), 25.

been swept by a plague and was expecting an air-raid. The factories and many stores were shut. Few people were abroad on the streets, and they looked as tho they had just been invited to have tea with the Borgias. The streets at night were almost dark, because only a few of the street lamps were lighted.

All over the major-league baseball circuits, one saw stores for rent, silent shops, idle factories, half-empty hotels, and slim crowds in the ball-parks, night-clubs, and places of amusement. The Wailers and Moaners still were in good voice.

I went again to Florida this year to the Yankee camp in Saint Petersburg and to the Giants' camp on Miami Beach. If the ball-club had not arranged transportation for me in advance, I would have had difficulty buying space on a train. People were going to Florida in car-loads.

It costs money to go to Florida, and no one lingers under those palm-trees for any length of time free of charge. Yet, hotels were jammed, dog-tracks and race-tracks flourished, night-clubs thrived. Miami Beach guaranteed the Giants $10,000 to train in its sunshine. It was a boom year.

Railroad men and representatives of Chambers of Commerce shook their heads. They could not understand it. Maybe it was because people were not going to Europe, or to Cuba. None could explain why so many people were able to leave their homes to play for a while in Florida.

"They must have money," said a passenger agent for the Seaboard Air Line. "They can't do it for nothing."

I came home this year with the Giants, through Southern cities which a year ago had been gasping and about to die. The change was bewildering. Brass bands met the team at the railroad station. The players were paraded through the streets in automobiles. People elbowed and shoved to get into the ball-parks. There had not been anything like this since the Yankees made their triumphal tour of Texas, Oklahoma, and Arkansas in 1929.

The players looked at one another and asked: "What do you make of it?"

New Orleans was gay again. Men in spotless white coats shook up Ramos gin fizzes. Crowds went places for work and fun.

The landscape, as we moved along, was dotted with CWA signs and men were hammering and digging. Smoke issued from chimneys long unused. Stores which had been closed were open and making sales.

When the Giants came home they played to 73,087 more customers in their first nine games than they had in the same number of games the year before.

The Boston Red Sox drew 145,000 more customers in the first six days.

Betting on horse-races was made legal in New York. People flocked to the tracks.

Cocktail bars blossomed in fantastic forms in every State in which liquor is legal. Restaurants perked up. Hotels dusted entire floors of rooms long unoccupied. Head waiters stopped scowling. Musicians attacked their instruments with renewed vigor. Everywhere I go—Boston, Cincinnati, Philadelphia (no more Sunday Blue Laws), Pittsburgh (ditto), Saint Louis, Cleveland, Detroit, Chicago (enjoying a bigger and better whirl at the Fair)—crowds of people seem to be enjoying themselves. They may not be rolling in wealth, but evidently they have a few "bucks" to spend on amusements. That's something they did not have last year.

All this may mean nothing to a chronic investigator who locks himself in a roomful of reports and can prove with a chart and figures that conditions are rapidly growing worse. But when Florida has a boom season; when the South meets the Giants with a brass band; when 232,-000 baseball fans pay to see eight major-league double-headers on Memorial Day; when more than $1,000,000 changes hands at the race-tracks; when golf and tennis tournaments have funds to utilize; when one sees new automobiles on the roads and new clothes on the natives; when Ross and McLarnin box before 40,000 persons who must have had anywhere from $1 to $10 each to get in; when you have to fight your way into the fancy cocktail bars and restaurants which have sprung to life all over the country; and when the people again are singing "Sweet Ad-o-line" with feeling—then one knows, at least, that a lot of people no longer are hiding and hoarding.

14

Rediscovering America

New York

BEHIND the fog shrouding the harbor lay New York, lay America, lay all the changes of an eventful year. From the other side of the ocean the United States had looked turbulent and strange, its large, erratic movements, more startling than anything that was happening in Europe. Only a year, and in some headlong, haphazard American fashion industry had been codified, agriculture regulated, the Stock Exchange subdued almost to a standstill, banks thawed out into liquid reservoirs. The Federal Government had grown to Olympian size, the Constitution had sloughed off an amendment without a struggle, the financial capital had moved from Wall Street to Washington. The dollar sign itself had become an index of shifting values. Only a year, and nothing was as it had been.

Superficially, the New World seemed closer to the Old. As the process called the Americanization of Europe halted, there were plenty of signs to suggest that the Europeanization of America had begun. We were slowed down by the shortened hours and relaxed tempo of coded industry. After nearly five years in low, and the constant drag of unemployment, the levels of life had dropped nearer to the European plane. We had more time, less money, fewer illusions.

In mood and appearance, New York was more like a Continental city, the speakeasy streets come to life, the sidewalks brightened with outdoor cafés, boxwood hedges, bursts of convivial laughter; music in the Stadium; fountains playing under the midtown towers. Washington was more like a European capital, no longer merely a political encampment but general headquarters of all the interests of the nation. And beyond New York and Washington, beer gardens, aperitif hours, government supervision and an economic vocabulary long current in Europe spread over the land as easily as a new fashion in berets.

SOURCE: Anne O'Hare McCormick, *The World at Home*, ed. Marion Turner Sheehan (New York, 1956), pp. 227–36.

Really, however, the continents were further apart than ever. The new resemblances served only to bring into sharper relief the essential differences between the two sides of the Atlantic. Never as now, contrasting crisis with crisis, narrow margin with narrower, restricted choice with no choice, had the returning American been so struck by the comparative abundance, the comparative exuberance, the comparative security of his country. The commonest American sights moved him to wonder; the plenty and variety that filled the shops, the automatic speed and tireless banter of the soda-slingers in drug stores, the up-to-the-minute style of the crowds in the streets, the free-and-easy talk of strangers in any sort of casual encounter. This was surface, too, of course, but at its worst the smoothest, shiniest surface left in the world.

Nothing of this was visible as the incoming ship inched up the bay in a Summer fog as smothering as a steam bath. Nothing at all was visible until the thick curtain suddenly ripped open at the top and through the high peephole we had one of those trick views which make the magic of New York.

The fog banks formed a hill and in a patch of light the upper stories of the tallest buildings of lower Broadway seemed to stand on the summit, a cluster of little towers on a hill. A Florentine lawyer straining at the rail for his first glimpse of the famous skyline gazed up in astonishment. "San Gimignano!" he exclaimed, and so for a moment it was an apparition like Dante's City of the Beautiful Towers, or what remains of it six hundred years after, seen across the gray Tuscan valley.

As the mists lowered and the craning turrets lengthened, some one explained to the Florentine that this hill town was the greatest of American villages—the powerful citadel called Wall Street. Rising out of the sea that morning, it looked like a citadel, like something bold and adventurous and splendid, a monumental gesture expressing the audacity and extravagance of the system that developed America.

"The capital of capitalism!" murmured the Italian. But the American, his eyes long filled with other images, recognized something else in the familiar view. He saw that what he came back to was like nothing he had known abroad. This was a separate world, participant in the universal drama of change and crisis, but at its own pace and in its own frame. Wherever it was moving it would make its own pattern at last, distinctive and immeasurable by other standards as were the profile and the stature of its towns.

Take what has happened in Wall Street as the high sign of what has happened everywhere. Perhaps no other place has altered quite so much and no other change illustrates so handily the peculiar character of the American movement. Nothing in Wall Street soars today except the silhouette. All its haughtiness is in its towers. The bold buccaneering of capitalism, the daring and audacity which impel it to great risks and great wastes, which make it a constructive force, give way now to a caution and reserve as thick as fog. Ask why, and you receive a confounding answer, one that could not be valid, if it is, anywhere else in the world. "Capital can no longer take risks," says Wall Street, "because it is too widely distributed."

But that is not the explanation of the almost rural quiet that has settled on downtown New York. In the first months of the regime of regulation by government commission the financial district has a little of the atmosphere of an occupied town, guarded, watchful, frightened and docile. The Stock Exchange, reduced to an investment market, has lost its old excitement. The Curb is a mere echo of what it used to be.

The shadowy streets are crowded still at noon and evening, but the populace is diminished and subdued. The picturesque figures are gone, the big gamblers on margins, the motley assortment of customers' men, running from grand dukes to jockeys. The college boys, jaunty and debonair, are fewer every year; nowadays they begin their careers in conservation camps and building public roads more often than in brokers' offices and bankers' lobbies.

The mind of money has lost assurance and authority. Never a unanimous or an integrated mind, it accepts the new regulations as a defeat in a contest with what it calls the political mind and submits with what grace it can for the same reason that citizens all over the land take orders from Washington; they are afraid to oppose any policy of recovery lest by some miracle it might turn out to be the right one! Wall Street does not know the answers to the universal questions any more than do other villages. Its critics of the New Deal are more numerous, but also more restrained, than those of Middletown. Labels do not mean much in the present confusion, when radicals and conservatives so often act alike, but one hears as much revolutionary talk here as in any typical American community.

It is a fairly typical American community, in fact. It yearns for definitions, for new grooves in place of the old, as who does not? All it asks of the President at the present stage is a clear declaration of where he's going, where he'll stop, and you can listen in on that kind of talk at any corner drug store or any golf course. Its economic experts studying trends and analyzing statistics are as far apart in their conclusions as like advisers in Washington and their laborious reports are as often skipped or disregarded.

What explains the timidity, the humility and the deflation of Wall Street is that it is a kind of deserted village, deprived of its chief attractions. All the audacity in the country has been cornered by Washington. A good part of the national energy, once bent on money-making, animates the headquarters of the New Deal.

Washington today, even though the peak of nervous tension and activity is passed, is easily the most animated city in the world. It feels as if the adventurousness, the gambling spirit, of America were diverted there, or at least as if the tremendous public wagers and ventures we are making exhaust the national capacity for speculation. No private gamble can compete in interest with the vast enterprises on which we are collectively embarked and no figures Wall Street can again pile up will equal the fabulous and fascinating sums dispensed in Washington.

This transfer of power and interest began in the first months of the Roosevelt administration, perhaps before, with the organization of the RFC by Mr. Hoover. I doubt if those who have watched the process month by month get the full effect of the steady aggrandizement of Washington, but viewed as fait accompli, after a year's absence, it is as startling as if it had been accomplished by force. It wasn't, and the point is that in no other country on earth could so really radical a shift of authority have been made so quickly, so easily, and with so little alteration in the skyline that all the citadels appear as proud as ever.

All other changes one notes in rediscovering America are somehow related to this change. Undoubtedly the story would be different if the New Deal were otherwise headed and personified. Americans have found a hero. That should not be strange to one returning from lands where leaders are a cult, where pictures of kings and dictators paper every wall, yet it is surprising, even disturbing, to see some such cult at home.

When before in this country, except during campaigns, have photographs of a living President been hung in shops and homes, restaurants and gas stations? How often has a President evoked such emotion from a hard-pressed people as greeted Mr. Roosevelt in his recent trip across the continent? This mass emotion is a development; it did not appear when the President was a candidate or during his early days in the White House. Like such hero worship elsewhere, it has little to do with policies or reason. The President is more widely questioned and criticized than he was a year ago—and also more popular!

This is not peculiar to the United States. Neither is the zest for experiment which creates the atmosphere of Washington. Characteristically American, however, are the reactions of many of the men from other walks of life who find themselves for the first time participating in the business of government. . . .

They constitute the huge new bureaucracy that worries so many overburdened citizens. These new bureaucrats will hang on to their jobs as long as no other occupation is available. For the most part they are not doing the work they were trained to do, and that involves a shaking out of grooves and a readjustment of habits and standards bound to have important social effects.

Still more important, they are seeing government from the inside; two or three million hitherto passive citizens are experiencing how it works. Almost invariably they are critical of government methods, impatient of delays and red tape, appalled at the wastes of public administration. In Washington the difference in tempo between regular service people and the newcomers is a constant irritation to both. So far, at any rate, government employment does not develop in Americans the bureaucratic mind.

What it does develop, what the uncertainties of the crisis and the experiments in recovery have accentuated, is the temporizing mind. We used to live in the future, by the year or the decade; now we live in the immediate present, by the day. And no one can doubt that the zest of the experimenters in Washington is matched by a hearty appetite for change in the country at large. Evidently the New Deal still satisfies something restless in the American spirit, always ready to go, to take a chance, to try anything once.

For years this spirit has been in ferment, stirred by vague but painful dissatisfactions. America is not a happy country, though by contrast with others just now it seems buoyant and gay. It is befuddled to its depths by new ideas, tormented by doubts, worried by the debts piling up and even more by the economic philosophy of extravagance—"spending your way out." Nevertheless, no one can honestly believe that we are more unhappy now than during the feverish, straining years of the last decade. Perhaps we are happier.

In spite of everything—the midsummer slump, the great desert made by drought, multiplying strikes, the ache of a thousand fears—the whole picture is decidedly brighter than it was last year. Washington is incomparably more important and more interesting as a capital. New York is pleasanter, mellower, than it has been for years; it offers more variety, stimulation and ease than any other metropolis. In every city, on a smaller scale, there appears the same impulse to make urban life urban —more music, more public gardens, more open-air shows and open-air dining. Except for the drought area, reports an Englishman who has just crossed the continent, in ten years he has not seen American towns so relaxed or the countryside so well cared for.

My own impression is that people are so weary of the confusion of the world, growing with each year, that they are creating, or striving to create, some semblance of order in their own lives. The general effect of the industrial codes is to lift the level of the low-wage earners and lower the higher levels, with the result that the average living standard is lower than last year.

The adjustment to another plane is still felt to be temporary, as unemployment is still regarded as a temporary condition, but one striking fact emerges: no longer does everybody in America expect to grow rich. The young, especially, are deliberately facing a future in which they count on making no more than a living. Many do not even aspire to be rich. A lot of "front" has disappeared, and with it some stiffening ambition. In the strange America of today one hears the people apologizing for prosperity but not for poverty.

Beyond the material changes is a new mental attitude, even among those in whom dependence on government aid, of one kind or another, produces the passivity of the English on the dole. Perhaps by contrast with the walled-in mind in most countries of Europe, American talk seems livelier, more critical, better informed than it was. It does not take so much for granted and at the same time it accepts as a matter of course brand-new conceptions of social responsibility. In casual conversation we bandy terms we have but lately learned; whether or not the professors of the New Deal have altered our thinking, they have transformed our political and economic vocabulary.

As the result of a revolutionary agricultural program and the daily controversies on NRA codes there has been a year of national debate on searching economic issues. In the field of capital-and-labor relations we are far behind most industrial States, where the principle of collective bargaining has long been beyond discussion, but the difference between American club-car talk today and that of 1932 is really astonishing. We have come a long way since "Babbitt." In the public library of an Ohio town the librarian told me that the change in the reading habits of a typical community in the past two years indicated a rise of about eight grades in age and intelligence.

Business, according to President Roosevelt, is slowest to learn, and I suppose nothing he has said or done is more widely resented than his aspersions on the intelligence of business or his putting it in the same bracket with "gangsters and bankers." "We are going through a process which should be called the civilization of business," admits a business man. "I never realized until lately how savage and illiterate it is; you'd be surprised to know the depth of its backwardness and also how it's brushing up lately on the rules of etiquette and the three Rs. We are at the beginning, I think, of the era of the education of the economic man.

"And if government is to become increasingly powerful, as appears too probable," he added, "then the personnel of government will have to be much more thoroughly educated. Probably that is why my friends in the universities tell me that more and more boys and girls request courses to fit them for public service. It's all part of the new conviction, dawning on everybody, that there'll be fewer opportunities for what we used to call making money."

These are but straws in the wind blowing from Wall Street to the Golden Gate. I suspect that they do not indicate any very profound movement of the national spirit. Something is stirring in America, no doubt, and to greater purpose in the past year than in any ten before. But it hasn't "jelled." But if one could sum up one's first impression of change, what they would most significantly amount to is this: In the diverse struggles of today the individual and family readjustments, the industrial conflicts, the economic and political experiments, the search for moral and spiritual certainties, there is a consciousness of America as something other than a nation, as a special environment, a distinct civilization, as that separate world which every American feels it to be when he comes back from other worlds.

Mr. Hopkins expressed it the other day when he returned from studies of relief methods abroad. The answers of other nations, he said, are not the answers for us. "There is an American way which we must find for ourselves." That is what one discovers America engaged in—groping for her own way out, certain of nothing except that she must seek until she finds, or recovers, her own principle of growth and stability.

III
TOWARD THE
WELFARE STATE

Selection 15 is an excerpt from a story in Martha Gellhorn's The Trouble I've Seen, which appeared with a preface by H. G. Wells, who wrote: "Parallels to these stories could be found in the industrial regions of South Wales and England, in France, Germany, Leningrad, the Volga, the river valleys of China, Bombay, Calcutta." Selection 16 refers to E. C. Mabie, who became regional director of the Federal Theatre Project in the Midwest. The authors of Selection 17 are the newspaperman Ernest K. Lindley, who wrote the best early studies of FDR, and his wife. Both Franklin D. Roosevelt in Selection 18 and Frances Perkins in Selection 19 justify social security not simply as a humanitarian measure but as an economic stabilizer.

15

The Relief Lady Calls

PETE pushed the door open and both of the women stared at him. Mabel had not expected him to come home so soon. Usually he was out all day, looking for work. She had an idea, now, that he didn't often go to a factory or a store and apply for a job. She imagined that he was more likely just walking about the city in that new way he had, dragging his feet. Every once in a while he would stand and stare at a shop window or read the signs in front of an employment agency. She had seen him once, when he didn't know she was there watching. Perhaps he even stopped people on the street and said: "Could I clean your front steps? Could I wash your car . . . ?" She didn't want to think of that. And when he came home, nights, there was no use asking him what luck he'd had. The way he held himself told enough, and the empty unfixed look in his eyes.

When she had used up the last coffee, when the lard pail was empty and there were no more potatoes or flour in the house, she had gone alone to Relief headquarters in the City Hall and made an application, marked urgent. Now the lady had come to visit, the social worker. Some part of Mabel had stopped thinking or feeling, and she was only glad that Miss Merton was being so polite about it. She had already accepted the idea that Miss Merton should be here, asking what questions the Relief thought necessary. And she was answering them, in a flat, unmoved voice. It would be all right. They'd get Relief. And Pete wouldn't be home until after Miss Merton had gone.

She looked at him feeling frightened; she couldn't remember when she had done anything important without asking him about it first. And she knew he did not want Relief: he had said he was able to work and no one was going to make charity out of him. Miss Merton inspected him uncertainly. He hadn't shaved for some days, his shoes were muddy and wet and he looked at once exhausted and desperate: as if

SOURCE: Martha Gellhorn, *The Trouble I've Seen* (New York, 1936), pp. 122–8.

anything would send him off into a raving anger against what he had become.

"This is Miss Merton, Pete."

"Pleased ta meetcha." He didn't gather who she was, or why she was there. He was tired. He wanted to lie down, rest, close his eyes, perhaps sleep a while and not think about anything.

He went past them into the bedroom and shut the door. Mabel sighed. "We'll just talk low so's he can't hear," she explained. "He takes all this awful hard."

"Yes, I know. It is hard. Now would you mind telling me, Mrs. Hines, have you any life insurance, you or your husband?"

"No."

"Have you any relatives who could help you now?"

"No."

"Would you mind giving me a list of your nearest living relatives and their addresses?"

Mabel pulled from her memory some ignored cousins and an aunt. People died or moved away. One was very alone. She felt tired, too. She knew this only had to happen once and she hoped that it would be quickly over.

"May I look?" Miss Merton said, jotting things down in a little black note-book. She went towards the kitchen. Had to make a more or less complete inventory of what these people owned: to see if any of it could be sold, if there were any resources they hadn't yet used up. Mabel misunderstood. She made a despairing gesture and she did it quietly. She opened the bread box and the ice box and the kitchen closet. "Nothing in them," she said.

"Oh, yes. Yes, of course. By the way, here's your Relief order for the week, Mrs. Hines. For food. You can take it to your regular grocer, he'll accept it as if it were money." This was always the most nervous part: Miss Merton looked at Mabel anxiously through her glasses. Sometimes the clients got very upset about these orders. They were dreadfully small.

But Mabel didn't look at the amount; she held the slip of paper in her hand and said: "Do I take that to Mr. Burg? This piece of paper?"

"Yes."

"But then, he'll know I'm on Relief."

"Well."

"But I been buying there for over ten years regular. He knows me. He knows Pete, too; and the way we always lived and everything. I don't see how I can . . ." Her voice trailed off into miserable silence. She saw herself sneaking into Mr. Burg's store and waiting until everyone else had been served; she, who was an old and favoured customer. Mr. Burg always came out cheerfully wiping his hands on his apron and said: "Well, Mrs. Hines, and what will it be today? Fine weather we're having." He always waited on her himself. She wasn't like some that went to the store in any old clothes. She always wore a hat and fixed up before she went, as a decent woman should. A woman who was buying properly for her husband; and had a nice house and a bright clean kitchen to cook in. For years she'd been doing this. Always. And now. She looked at the grocery order and saw that it was for $3 and raised her eyes to Miss Merton, blankly.

"For a week," she said, "three dollars?"

"Yes, I'm afraid so," Miss Merton said quickly. "That's the budget for families of two, now. Of course, your coal and rent and medicine and all that is extra. It's only for food."

Mabel folded the green slip. There wasn't anything more to say. There was nothing even to think or understand or be sure of.

"What is the rent here?" Miss Merton asked.

"Twenty."

"Oh, dear."

"Why?"

"Well, I'm afraid that's more than Relief allows for rents. I'm afraid you'll have to find a cheaper place; unless your landlord would accept our usual rates or just give you credit until Mr. Hines gets a job."

"We'll have to move?"

"Well, I don't know. We'll have to work out something. That's more rent than we allow, you see."

"But we can't," Mabel said, and now she had forgotten Pete and her voice rose. "We can't. It's our home. We been here since we're married. It's our place, it belongs to us. What would we do if we had to go somewheres else? Give it up," she said, the tears sticky on her face. "Give it up."

"Who says we're gonna give it up." Pete stood in the doorway of the bedroom in stocking feet, looking strangely thin and pale.

"What's that about our house?" he said.

."We were just discussing the rent," Miss Merton said, and Mabel wiped at the tears with the back of her hand.

"Why?"

"Well, I'm from Relief, you see."

"Get out," Pete said. It was just a statement.

Miss Merton looked perplexed and a little hurt.

"Get out," Pete said. "This is my house. I don't want nothing from the Relief."

Miss Merton walked towards the front door. Mabel went with her. "He'll get over it," Mabel whispered. "He'll hafta. I don't see what else. I'll come and see you at City Hall. But you better go."

"Yes. Well, good-night, Mrs. Hines."

"Did you get her here?" Pete said.

"What else could I do? There's nothing to eat in this house, Pete Hines, and no more coal. We can't starve, can we? We can't lock up the house and die, can we?"

"Maybe not and maybe so," Pete said darkly, "but I won't have strangers coming in my house poking around. I can work," Pete said. And then suddenly he shouted it, waving his arms crazily over his head. "I can work! I can work!"

Mabel sat down in a rocker. She was too tired now to argue this thing. What did it matter, anyhow? There were only a certain number of reasons for living, and when you didn't have them any more. "What's the difference?" she said slowly, and Pete stared at her, frightened by the dead quiet of her voice. "We haven't got the baby, so it don't matter. We don't have to do all this. We don't have to."

"What're you talking about, Mabel?" he was whispering to her, but he didn't know it.

"What've we got anyhow, now? We'll be old soon."

"But I been working all my life," Pete protested. "It oughtn't to be like this. I can still work. For a long time yet. I don't see," he said.

"We had some good times anyhow, Pete."

"It's not all over yet, Mabel." But he was begging her to comfort and reassure him, to promise him a future he couldn't see.

"We had fun that year we went to the beach for a week."

"Mabel, it isn't over. Don't act like that. Oh, Mabel, Mabel." Suddenly he was down on his knees by her chair, with his head on her lap, crying awkwardly and trying to stop himself. He wept in terror and she stroked his hair, saying to him dimly: "There, there, Petie, it'll be all right." He had his arms around her, and her hands were gentle. They stayed there as it grew dark, not talking, because neither of them could think of a comforting lie for the other to believe.

16

WPA Spending

SINCE Mr. Hopkins was anxious from the first to stress the fact that the government enterprise was to be national in scope, he decided that the logical place to announce my appointment was the National Theatre Conference to be held at Iowa City on the occasion of the laying of the cornerstone of Mr. Mabie's University Theatre. On July 24, Mr. Hopkins telephoned me to meet him in Washington on the following day and go with him to Iowa City.

It was an exciting trip. Mr. Hopkins talked about everything—about engineering, about the building of airports, about the cities and countryside through which we were passing; but no matter what we started to talk about, it ended up with what was at that time the core and center of his thinking—the relationship of government to the individual. Hadn't our government always acknowledged direct responsibility to the people? Hadn't it given away the national domain in free land to veterans and other settlers? Hadn't it given away vast lands to railroad companies to help them build their systems? Hadn't the government spent fortunes on internal improvements, subsidizing the building of roads and canals, waterways, and harbors? Hadn't the government subsidized infant industries by a protective tariff? Hadn't the government also given away other intangible parts of the public domain, such as franchises to public utilities, the power to issue currency and create credit to banks, patent rights to inventors? In all of these ways, government enlarged industries, put men to work and increased buying power.

The new work program, Mr. Hopkins believed, would accomplish these same ends by giving of the nation's resources in wages to the unemployed, in return for which they would help build and improve America.

At every stop, there were newspapermen and cameramen and men with briefcases who got on for conferences. Almost all of these men

SOURCE: Hallie Flanagan, Arena (New York, 1940), pp. 24–7.

seemed to have certain characteristics in common: they were young, thin, overworked-looking, and tremendously alive. . . .

It was on this trip that Mr. Hopkins asked me a searching question. It is a question which is bound to be jeered at by critics of New Deal philosophy, but it is one of the questions at the core of that philosophy. The train through Chicago out to the midwest plains passed through the slums, and Mr. Hopkins, looking out over the abscessed gray tenements mercilessly exposed under the blinding sun, suddenly asked:

"Can you spend money?"

I said that inability to spend money was not one of my faults, but Mr. Hopkins continued seriously: "It's not easy. It takes a lot of nerve to put your signature down on a piece of paper when it means that the government of the United States is going to pay out a million dollars to the unemployed in Chicago. It takes decision, because you'll have to decide whether Chicago needs that money more than New York City or Los Angeles. You can't care very much what people are going to say because when you're handling other people's money whatever you do is always wrong. If you try to hold down wages, you'll be accused of union-busting and of grinding down the poor; if you pay a decent wage, you'll be competing with private industry and pampering a lot of no-accounts; if you scrimp on production costs, they'll say your shows are lousy and if you spend enough to get a good show on, they'll say you're wasting the taxpayers' money. Don't forget that whatever happens you'll be wrong."

With that reassuring preface, Mr. Hopkins launched into the reasons why, in spite of jeers, in spite of attacks, in spite of vituperation, we must spend money. These slums through which we were riding, these ramshackle, vermin-infested buildings housing our fellow citizens were one reason. These pale children sitting listlessly on fire-escapes were another. Sullen youths hanging around our street corners were another. Worried-looking men, gathered in silent knots before employment agencies, were still another. Houses for these people to live in, parks and playgrounds, fresh air, fresh milk and medical care for these children, schools and recreation places for youth to go to, jobs for men to do. Above all—jobs for men to do. *Danger: Men Not Working.* These were some of the reasons why we had to be able to spend money.

"It costs money to put a man to work and that's why a lot of people prefer direct relief. These people say that if we make the working conditions decent and give people a reasonable minimum to live on, people will get to like their jobs. They suggest that we make relief as degrading and shameful as possible so that people will want to get 'off.' Well—I've been dealing with unemployed people for years in one way and another and they *do* want to get off—but they can't, apparently, get 'off' into private industry. Well—if they can't get off into private industry, where can they turn if they can't turn to their government? What's a government for? And these people can be useful to America; they can do jobs no one else can afford to do—these slums, for instance. No private concern can afford to make houses for poor people to live in, because any private concern has got to show a profit. Why, we've got enough work to do right here in America, work that needs to be done and that no private concern can afford to touch, to lay out a program for twenty years and to employ every unemployed person in this country to carry it out."

What part could art play in this program? Could we, through the power of the theatre, spotlight the tenements and thus help in the plan to build decent houses for all people? Could we, through actors and artists who had themselves known privation, carry music and plays to children in city parks, and art galleries to little towns? Were not happy people at work the greatest bulwark of democracy?

17

NYA on the Campus

NYA has brought a college education within the reach not only of many superior students but of some whose abilities may properly be called exceptional. In February 1938 institutions forming a cross-section of all those participating were asked: "Are there any instances . . . where NYA has enabled a student of exceptional ability in some line to attend your institution?" Of the 52 institutions replying, 43 replied in the affirmative. . . .

Fifty of these institutions sent in information concerning individual students who were receiving or had received NYA college aid. Here are a few examples of NYA-aided students of superior or exceptional ability:

James R———, 23 years of age, had neither parents nor other close relatives to help him. Ambitious to become a criminologist, he is now enrolled in the College of Law of the University of Illinois and works on an NYA project in the Sociology Department. "It is known that he spent about the first two weeks of the semester (and before school started) sleeping in the park, in an empty house, and in one of the school buildings, with nothing to keep him warm except a dog which is his constant companion. We were finally able to locate a room job for this boy and with the aid of the NYA he has been able to pay his fees, buy his books, and pay incidental expenses. There is no doubt that he would not have been able even to start the semester if he had not had some assurance that he would receive the job which he held last year and upon which he is doing excellent work." His scholastic record for his university career is "about a 5.00 average" (5.00 being the highest grade attainable).

Kay Wilson was the winner of the national poultry judging contest

SOURCE: Betty and Ernest K. Lindley, *A New Deal for Youth* (New York, 1938), pp. 171–6.

at the Chicago Livestock Exposition, 1937, winner of the 4-H Club State oratorical contest, runner-up in the American Legion State oratorical contest, and an excellent high school student. His parents, farmers in the drought section, were unable to give him any financial help. He worked in the harvest field during the summer months, without a shirt—so intent on saving his earnings in order to go to college that he would not spend the money for one. An NYA work-scholarship for the maximum of $20 a month enabled him to attend Oklahoma Agricultural and Mechanical College, where he has become an "outstanding leader.". . .

Benito S—— came to the United States in 1929, acquiring American citizenship by virtue of the fact that his father, who was already here, was a citizen. While working as a shoemaker in Trenton he gained a high school education in a night school. He worked his way through Rutgers through NYA, work in a local shoe repair shop, waiting on tables, and other odd jobs. He completed his college course in three instead of the usual four years and was prominent in many undergraduate activities. His objective is a university professorship in Romance languages. "Truly a man of rare promise."

Henry H—— is going through Rutgers with the aid of a State scholarship, an NYA job in the ceramics department, and money saved from his previous employment as a color matcher in a large chemical concern. "His experiments with a new ceramic green are likely to add much to the knowledge of ceramic colors."

Joseph ————, a Polish-American boy from Duluth, whose father earned about $80 a month, showed exceptional ability in mathematics in high school and junior college. Federal aid enabled him to continue his studies at the University of Minnesota. On his own initiative he had read in the field of mathematics far beyond the level of the ordinary college graduate majoring in mathematics. He was assigned as an NYA research assistant to a professor of mathematics. His work was described as "astonishing." On graduation, he was awarded a fellowship at Princeton.

Leigh Gerdin was entirely dependent on his own earning capacity to obtain a college education. (His mother was a widow with a small income and two younger children in school.) At the age of 17, he entered the University of North Dakota. For four years he paid all his expenses by working for board and room and for NYA. Carrying a scholastic load heavier than average, he made A grades (except for eight semester hours of B) throughout his college course. In addition, he practiced on the piano two hours a day and composed several numbers which have been used by orchestras and choirs. In the spring of 1938 he was elected to a Rhodes Scholarship in competition with youth from six States. . . .

Mabel J——'s father was on WPA. With NYA aid she was able to enter Butler University, in Indianapolis, her home city. She completed the requirements for the two-year teacher's certificate and, after a short trial, was assigned as a regular teacher in the city schools. As a result of her earnings, the family is now off relief. "A talented young woman, gifted as a teacher, who would never have had her worth brought to light had it not been for NYA."

Mary H—— was chosen for a $400 scholarship at Connecticut College. As her father could give her little help, she had to earn money to take advantage of the scholarship. She worked as a waitress in the college dining hall, made $200 last year as a correspondent for a metropolitan newspaper, and was employed on an NYA project, while carrying full-time academic work. Scholastically she stands at the head of her class.

18

The President Signs
the Social Security Act

TODAY a hope of many years' standing is in large part fulfilled. The civilization of the past hundred years, with its startling industrial changes, has tended more and more to make life insecure. Young people have come to wonder what would be their lot when they came to old age. The man with a job has wondered how long the job would last.

This social security measure gives at least some protection to thirty millions of our citizens who will reap direct benefits through unemployment compensation, through old-age pensions and through increased services for the protection of children and the prevention of ill health.

We can never insure one hundred percent of the population against one hundred percent of the hazards and vicissitudes of life, but we have tried to frame a law which will give some measure of protection to the average citizen and to his family against the loss of a job and against poverty-ridden old age.

This law, too, represents a cornerstone in a structure which is being built but is by no means complete. It is a structure intended to lessen the force of possible future depressions. It will act as a protection to future Administrations against the necessity of going deeply into debt to furnish relief to the needy. The law will flatten out the peaks and valleys of deflation and of inflation. It is, in short, a law that will take care of human needs and at the same time provide for the United States an economic structure of vastly greater soundness.

I congratulate all of you ladies and gentlemen, all of you in the

SOURCE: Franklin D. Roosevelt, "Presidential Statement upon Signing the Social Security Act," August 14, 1935, in Samuel Rosenman (ed.), *The Public Papers and Addresses of Franklin D. Roosevelt* (13 vols., New York, 1938–1950), IV, 324–5.

Congress, in the executive departments and all of you who come from private life, and I thank you for your splendid efforts in behalf of this sound, needed and patriotic legislation.

If the Senate and the House of Representatives in this long and arduous session had done nothing more than pass this Bill, the session would be regarded as historic for all time.

19

The Significance
of Social Security

PEOPLE who work for a living in the United States of America
can join with all other good citizens on this forty-eighth anniversary of Labor Day in satisfaction that the Congress has passed the
Social Security Act. This act establishes unemployment insurance as a
substitute for haphazard methods of assistance in periods when men
and women willing and able to work are without jobs. It provides for
old age pensions which mark great progress over the measures upon
which we have hitherto depended in caring for those who have been
unable to provide for the years when they no longer can work. It also
provides security for dependent and crippled children, mothers, the
indigent disabled and the blind.

Old people who are in need, unemployables, children, mothers and
the sightless, will find systematic regular provisions for needs. The Act
limits the Federal aid to not more than $15 per month for the indi-
vidual, provided the State in which he resides appropriates a like
amount. There is nothing to prevent a State from contributing more
than $15 per month in special cases and there is no requirement to
allow as much as $15 from either State or Federal funds when a par-
ticular case has some personal provision and needs less than the total
allowed.

Following essentially the same procedure, the Act as passed provides for Federal assistance to the States in caring for the blind, a contribution by the State of up to $15 a month to be matched in turn by
a like contribution by the Federal Government. The Act also contains
provision for assistance to the States in providing payments to dependent children under sixteen years of age. There also is provision in the

SOURCE: Frances Perkins, "The Social Security Act," *Vital Speeches*,
I (1935), 792–4.

Act for cooperation with medical and health organizations charged with rehabilitation of physically handicapped children. The necessity for adequate service in the fields of public and maternal health and child welfare calls for the extension of these services to meet individual community needs.

Consider for a moment those portions of the Act which, while they will not be effective this present year, yet will exert a profound and far-reaching effect upon millions of citizens. I refer to the provision for a system of old-age benefits supported by the contributions of employer and employees, and to the section which sets up the initial machinery for unemployment insurance.

Old-age benefits in the form of monthly payments are to be paid to individuals who have worked and contributed to the insurance fund in direct proportion to the total wages earned by such individuals in the course of their employment subsequent to 1936. The minimum monthly payment is to be $10, the maximum $85. These payments will begin in the year 1942 and will be to those who have worked and contributed.

Because of difficulty of administration not all employments are covered in this plan at this time so that the law is not entirely complete in coverage, but it is sufficiently broad to cover all normally employed industrial workers.

As an example of the practical operation of the old-age benefit system, consider for a moment a typical young man of thirty-five years of age, and let us compute the benefits which will accrue to him. Assuming that his income will average $100 per month over the period of thirty years until he reaches the age of sixty-five, the benefit payments due him from the insurance fund will provide him with $42.50 per month for the remainder of his life. If he has been fortunate enough to have an income of $200 per month, his income will subsequently be $61.25 per month. In the event that death occurs prior to the age of sixty-five, 3½% of the total wages earned by him subsequent to 1936 will be returned to his dependents. If death occurs after the age of sixty-five, his dependents receive the same amount, less any benefits paid to him during his lifetime.

This vast system of old-age benefits requires contributions both by employer and employee, each to contribute 3% of the total wage paid to the employee. This tax, collected by the Bureau of Internal Revenue, will be graduated, ranging from 1% in 1937 to the maximum 3% in 1939 and thereafter. That is, on this man's average income of $100 a month he will pay to the usual fund $3 a month and his employer will also pay the same amount over his working years.

In conjunction with the system of old-age benefits, the Act recognizes that unemployment insurance is an integral part of any plan for the economic security of millions of gainfully employed workers. It provides for a plan of cooperative Federal-State action by which a State may enact an insurance system, compatible with Federal requirements and best suited to its individual needs.

The Federal Government attempts to promote and effectuate these State systems, by levying a uniform Federal pay-roll tax of 3% on employers employing eight or more workers, with the proviso that an employer who contributes to a State unemployment compensation system will receive a credit of 90% of this Federal tax. After 1937, additional credit is also allowable to any employer who, because of favorable employment experience or adequate reserves, is permitted by the State to reduce his payments.

In addition, the Act provides that after the current fiscal year the Federal Government allocate annually to the States $49,000,000 solely for the administration of their respective insurance systems, thus assuring that all money paid for State unemployment compensation will be reserved for the purpose of compensation to the worker. It has been necessary, at the present time, to eliminate essentially the same groups from participation under the unemployment insurance plan as in the old-age benefit plan, though it is possible that at some future time a more complete coverage will be formulated.

The State of New York, at the present time, has a system of unemployment compensation which might well illustrate the salient factors desired in such a plan; in the event of unemployment, the worker is paid 50% of his wages weekly for a period not exceeding 16 weeks in any 52 weeks. This payment begins within three weeks after the advent of actual unemployment. California, Washington, Utah and New Hampshire have passed unemployment insurance laws in recent months and Wisconsin's law is already in effect. Thirty-five States have old-age pension statutes and mothers' pension acts are in force in all but three States.

With the States rests now the responsibility of devising and enacting measures which will result in the maximum benefits to the Amercan workman in the field of unemployment compensation. I am confident that impending State action will not fail to take cognizance of this responsibility. The people of the different States favor the program designed to bring them greater security in the future and their legislatures will speedily pass appropriate laws so that all may help to promote the general welfare.

Federal legislation was framed in the thought that the attack upon the problems of insecurity should be a cooperative venture participated in by both the Federal and State Governments, preserving the benefits of local administration and national leadership. It was thought unwise to have the Federal Government decide all questions of policy and dictate completely what the States should do. Only very necessary minimum standards are included in the Federal measure leaving wide latitude to the States.

While the different State laws on unemployment insurance must make all contributions compulsory, the States, in addition to deciding how these contributions shall be levied, have freedom in determining their own waiting periods, benefit rates, maximum benefit periods and the like. Care should be taken that these laws do not contain benefit provisions in excess of collections. While unemployment varies greatly in different States, there is no certainty that States which have had less normal unemployment heretofore will in the future have a more favorable experience than the average for the country.

It is obvious that in the best interests of the worker, industry and society, there must be a certain uniformity of standards. It is obvious, too, that we must prevent the penalizing of competitive industry in any State which plans the early adoption of a sound system of unemployment insurance, and provide effective guarantees against the possibility of industry in one State having an advantage over that of another. This the uniform Federal tax does, as it costs the employer the same whether he pays the levy to the Federal Government or makes a contribution to a State unemployment insurance fund. The amount of the tax itself is a relative assurance that benefits will be standardized in all States, since under the law the entire collection must be spent on benefits to unemployed.

The social security measure looks primarily to the future and is only a part of the administration's plan to promote sound and stable economic life. We cannot think of it as disassociated from the Government's program to save the homes, the farms, the businesses and banks of the Nation, and especially must we consider it a companion measure to the Works Relief Act which does undertake to provide immediate increase in employment and corresponding stimulation to private industry by purchase of supplies.

While it is not anticipated as a complete remedy for the abnormal conditions confronting us at the present time, it is designed to afford protection for the individual against future major economic vicissitudes. It is a sound and reasonable plan and framed with due regard for the present state of economic recovery. It does not represent a complete solution of the problems of economic security, but it does represent a substantial, necessary beginning. . . .

This is truly legislation in the interest of the national welfare. We must recognize that if we are to maintain a healthy economy and thriving production, we need to maintain the standard of living of the lower income groups of our population who constitute ninety per cent of our purchasing power. The President's Committee on Economic Security, of which I had the honor to be chairman, in drawing up the plan, was convinced that its enactment into law would not only carry us a long way toward the goal of economic security for the individual, but also a long way toward the promotion and stabilization of mass purchasing power without which the present economic system cannot endure.

That this intimate connection between the maintenance of mass purchasing power through a system of protection of the individual against major economic hazards is not theoretical is evidenced by the fact that England has been able to withstand the effects of the world-wide depression, even though her prosperity depends so largely upon foreign trade. English economists agree with employers and workers that this ability to weather adverse conditions has been due in no small part to social insurance benefits and regular payments which have served to maintain necessary purchasing power.

Our social security program will be a vital force working against the recurrence of severe depressions in the future. We can, as the principle of sustained purchasing power in hard times makes itself felt in every shop, store and mill, grow old without being haunted by the spectre of a poverty-ridden old age or of being a burden on our children.

The costs of unemployment compensation and old-age insurance are not actually additional costs. In some degree they have long been borne by the people, but irregularly, the burden falling much more heavily on some than on others, and none of such provisions offering an orderly or systematic assurance to those in need. The years of depression have brought home to all of us that unemployment entails huge costs to government, industry and the public alike.

Unemployment insurance will within a short time considerably lighten the public burden of caring for those unemployed. It will materially reduce relief costs in future years. In essence, it is a method by which reserves are built up during periods of employment from which compensation is paid to the unemployed in periods when work is lacking.

The passage of this act with so few dissenting votes and with so much intelligent public support is deeply significant of the progress which the American people have made in thought in the social field and awareness of methods of using cooperation through government to overcome social hazards against which the individual alone is inadequate.

During the fifteen years I have been advocating such legislation as this I have learned that the American people want such security as the law provides. It will make this great Republic a better and a happier place in which to live—for us, our children and our children's children. It is a profound and sacred satisfaction to have had some part in securing this great boon to the people of our country.

IV
UNIONIZING
INDUSTRIAL AMERICA

The dramatis personae of Selection 20 include William Green, president of the American Federation of Labor, and Matthew Woll, leader of the Photo Engravers' Union. In Selection 21, the opponent of the United Rubber Workers of America (URWA) was Clifton Slusser, vice president and factory manager of Goodyear. The Flint, Michigan sitdown strike in Selection 22 began on January 1, 1937, Governor Frank Murphy's first day in office. The only attempt to use force to dislodge the sit-downers ended in a rout of the police ("bulls") in the Battle of Bulls Run. Pengally Hall served as strike headquarters for the Auto Workers. In Selection 23, the draftsmen of the Wagner Act take special pains to stress the ways in which labor relations affect interstate commerce, a contention which the Supreme Court accepts in Selection 24.

20

The Struggle for Industrial Unionism

DELEGATE LEWIS, UNITED MINE WORKERS: Mr. Chairman and
delegates of the convention—I rise to support the minority report
as presented to this convention by Delegate Howard. I do not speak
without some background and some knowledge on this subject acquired
in the field of actual experience. I have not gained that knowledge
through delving into academic treatises or in sitting in a swivel chair
pondering upon the manner in which those upon the firing line should
meet their daily problems. I have had perhaps as much experience in organizing workers in the various industries as any member of the Executive Council of the American Federation of Labor or any officer thereof.
I served an apprenticeship of five and one-half years as a general organizer for the American Federation of Labor before I became an officer of
the United Mine Workers of America. During that period of time I
worked in the steel industry, the rubber industry, the glass industry, the
lumber industry, the copper industry and other industries in most of
the states of this Union.

Then, as now, the American Federation of Labor offered to the workers in these industries a plan of organization into Federal labor unions
or local trade unions with the understanding that when organized they
would be segregated into the various organizations of their respective
crafts. Then, as now, practically every attempt to organize those workers
broke upon the same rock that it breaks upon today—the rock of utter
futility, the lack of reasonableness in a policy that failed to take into
consideration the dreams and requirements of the workers themselves,
and failing to take into consideration the recognized power of the ad-

SOURCE: Report of the Proceedings of the Fifty-fifth Annual Convention
of the American Federation of Labor (Washington, 1936), pp. 534–8,
540–2, 653–9.

versaries of labor to destroy these feeble organizations in the great modern industries set up in the form of Federal labor unions or craft organizations functioning in a limited sphere.

For twenty-five years or more the American Federation of Labor has been following this precise policy, and surely in the absence of any other understanding of the question, a record of twenty-five years of constant, unbroken failure should be convincing to those who actually have a desire to increase the prestige of our great labor movement by expanding its membership to permit it to occupy its natural place in the sun.

What is the record? Delegate Howard expressed it when he said that we laid claim to a membership of approximately three and a half million, out of an organizable number of approximately thirty-nine million. There is the answer. If we know nothing else on the question we can at least read the results, and in reading the results we surely understand that our influence is less great, that our activities are more circumscribed, and that our power is more limited to achieve our natural and desirable and virtuous objective than it would be if we had those twenty-five million workers that President Green, in his public address of 1934, talked of organizing. Where are they? Where are those twenty-five million that in a moment of exuberance we were going to organize? Perhaps President Green's arithmetic was wrong and he meant twenty-five thousand, because the total results are nearer the twenty-five thousand than the twenty-five million. . . .

On that basis I submit it to be a reasonable statement that it will be a long time before the American Federation of Labor organizes those 25,000,000 workers that we are all so anxious to organize. There are others among us who believe that the record indicates a need for a change in policy. This convention floor is teeming with delegates from those industries where those local unions have been established and where they are now dying like the grass withering before the Autumn sun, who are ready to tell this convention of the need for that change in policy.

Those of us who have had experience in these mass production industries are ready to state our professional judgment for what it may be worth and say that it is an absolute fact that America's great modern industries cannot be successfully organized and those organizations maintained against the power of the adversaries of labor in this country under the policy which has been followed for the last quarter of a century in dealing with that subject.

There has been a change in industry, a constant daily change in its processes, a constant change in its employment conditions, a great concentration of opposition to the extension and the logical expansion of the trade union movement. Great combinations of capital have assembled great industrial plants, and they are strung across the borders of our several states from the north to the south and from the east to the west in such a manner that they have assembled to themselves tremendous power and influence, and they are almost 100 per cent effective in opposing organization of the workers under the policies of the American Federation of Labor.

What are we going to do about it? There are some of us who say, let us take council, one with the other, let us put into effect a policy in these certain specified mass production industries that will enable the workers to stand together as a unit against these great commercial units that are exploiting industry at the present time. And the great voice of the workers in those industries, as articulate as their own circumstances will permit, comes to the American Federation of Labor in the form of messages and communications and resolutions to this convention and articles in the press, and in the liberal press, encouraging attention to that subject. Why do we hesitate? We hesitate, perhaps, because there are men here representing great organizations that have rendered a splendid service to their membership formed, on craft lines, who fear that such a policy would jeopardize the interests of their members and jeopardize the interests of their own positions. Their unions are already jeopardized and their membership is already jeopardized because unless the American Federation of Labor may be successful in organizing these unorganized workers, it is extremely doubtful whether many of these organizations now so perfect, now so efficient, will long be permitted to endure and to function in a manner that is conducive to the well-being of their membership.

There are great influences abroad in the land, and the minds of men in all walks of life are disturbed. We are all disturbed by reason of the changes and the hazards in our economic situation and as regards our own political security. There are forces at work in this country that would wipe out, if they could, the labor movement of America, just as it was wiped out in Germany or just as it was wiped out in Italy.

There are those of us who believe that the best security against that menace and against that trend and against that tendency is a more comprehensive and more powerful labor movement. We believe that the way should be paved so that those millions of workers who are clamoring for admission into our councils might be made welcome upon a basis that they understand and that they believe is suited to their requirements. And in consequence of that we are assembled in this convention with the eyes of these millions of workers upon the convention to decide this momentous question. Methinks that upon this decision of this convention may rest the future of the American Federation of Labor, because upon this decision will rest the question of whether the American Federation of Labor may be forged into an instrumentality that will render service to all of the workers or whether the American Federation of Labor and its leaders will rest content in that comfortable situation that has prevailed through the years, where they are only required to render service to a paltry three or four or five million of the forty odd million wage workers of this country who, after all, want to be union men.

The average worker, however circumscribed, does not need to be told that a trade union or labor organization is of advantage to him if he is given the privilege of being a member of it under circumstances that he can accept. The average man who does not belong to a union but who works for a corporation in this country understands the contribution that the American labor movement makes toward the improvement of his standards and the well-being of his dear ones, and down in the recesses of his heart, no matter how much he may be compelled by circumstances to conceal it, there burns the feeling of warm appreciation for those forward souls, for those daring spirits who comprise the membership of organized labor in this country and who stand upon their feet four square to the world, asking for their rights as men and asking for the rights of all men.

And so out of my small experience, be it what it may, there is a profound belief on my part that there is a great reservoir of workers here numbering millions and millions of men and women, and back of them stand great numbers of millions of dependents who want the American Federation of Labor to adopt a policy that will be sufficiently flexible and sufficiently modern that it will permit them to join with us in this great fight for the maintenance of the rights of workers and for the upholding of the standards of modern democracy. . . .

I happen to know that in the rubber industry there are literally thousands of men employed who either were former members of the United Mine Workers of America or are the sons of former members of the United Mine Workers of America and who believe in the industrial form of organization because they were reared in that atmosphere. They know and understand that form of organization. They have tasted of its fruits and having tasted of its fruits they are not content in the rubber industry to be further exploited in these feeble attempts to establish collective bargaining in the haunts of the rubber barons in the same way we have been trying to establish it for twenty-five years.

I was in their rubber strike at Akron years and years and years ago—

and the years pass faster than I should like them to pass—when this question was up, the same question of organization and the same question of collective bargaining that we have had out there during the past two years, and when President Green, who sits here upon my left, was the chairman of an investigating committee sent in to that rubber industry by the Senate of Ohio to investigate conditions and to make recommendations there that might allay the confusion, restore order in the community, and yield to citizens an equality of rights under the law.

And after the lapse of all these years we find that the American Federation of Labor is still tinkering with this job in the great rubber stronghold of Akron in the same inefficient manner as was the case some twenty or more years ago, with no more result and no more hope. The men employed in these rubber plants write me gratuitously and say that the kind of organization they want in the rubber industry is the kind of organization that the United Mine Workers of America have in the mining industry. That is what they want. Why not give it to them? Theirs is the problem of opposing those corporations so firmly entrenched in the rubber industry who have never yielded to the rights of collective bargaining. If they are going to fight voluntarily for their rights and are willing to do so and are willing to assimilate the punishment that may be inflicted upon them by these corporations in that industry, why not let the rest of us, who perhaps will not shed any blood personally, let them make their rules, so that they may have a chance to win? . . .

So we find that the San Francisco convention policy has not been administered by the Executive Council of the American Federation of Labor. We find that Chairman Woll, of this committee, mildly lectures Delegate Lewis and quotes at length from a speech made in San Francisco, asking the convention to accept the report of the committee on the ground that Delegate Lewis now, after the lapse of one year, is not satisfied with the San Francisco action.

Well, a year ago at San Francisco I was a year younger and naturally I had more faith in the Executive Council. I was beguiled into believing that an enlarged Executive Council would honestly interpret and administer this policy—the policy we talked about for six days in committee, the policy of issuing charters for industrial unions in the mass production industries. But surely Delegate Woll would not hold it against me that I was so trusting at that time. I know better now. At San Francisco they seduced me with fair words. Now, of course, having learned that I was seduced, I am enraged and I am ready to rend my seducers limb from limb, including Delegate Woll. In that sense, of course, I speak figuratively. . . .

The United Mine Workers of America are calling now, and have been calling upon the American Federation of Labor, to put men and organizers and money into the iron and steel industry and to tell these arrogant steel barons to yield to the principles of collective bargaining in that industry.

If you go in there with your craft union they will mow you down like the Italian machine guns will mow down the Ethiopians in the war now going on in that country; they will mow you down and laugh while they are doing it and ridicule your lack of business acumen, ridicule your lack of ordinary business sagacity in running your own affairs, because of the caviling in your own councils and the feebleness of your methods.

There is more in this proposition than a mere academic discussion of the modus operandi of organization; there is more to this proposition than revolves around the mere acceptance or rejection of the resolution. The economic well-being and the dream of the future of millions of Americans are involved in the question of whether the American Federation of Labor will be able to devise policies that will permit it to function in a manner that will achieve its own objectives, not the objectives of some one else, but the declared objectives of the American Federation of Labor since the first day it was organized—the objectives of organizing the unorganized.

Surely I don't need to portray to the convention of the American Federation of Labor, composed as it is of its great leaders, the advantages that will come to labor and to America through the organization of the unorganized.

President Green goes down to the White House sometimes to call upon the President of this Republic to discuss the affairs of labor, and the interests of labor and the common people of this country. And sometimes he goes over to the Congressional halls, and he appears there before great committees of the two Houses to make articulate in a public way the things for which labor stands. Now, when he goes down there he goes as the representative of perhaps three and one-half million American working men. How much more powerful and influential would be the silver-tongued President Green if he were able to appear before the Congress of the United States or the President of this Republic speaking, not for three and one-half million specialized craftsmen organized in the American Federation of Labor, but speaking for five million, or ten million, or twenty million of workers in American industry who have joined the American Federation of Labor when you have given them a chance and made them welcome. . . .

Is it right, after all, that because some of us are capable of forging great and powerful organizations of skilled craftsmen in this country that we should lock ourselves up in our own domain and say, "I am merely working for those who pay me?" Isn't it right that we should contribute something of our own strength, our own virtues, our own knowledge, our own influence toward those less fortunately situated, in the knowledge that if we help them and they grow strong, in turn that we will be the beneficiary of their changed status and their strength? The strength of a strong man is a prideful thing, but the unfortunate thing in life is that strong men do not remain strong. And that is just as true of unions and labor organizations as it is true of men and individuals.

And, whereas, today the craft unions of this country may be able to stand upon their own feet and like mighty oaks stand before the gale, defy the lightning, yet the day may come when this changed scheme of things—and things are changing rapidly now—the day may come when those organizations will not be able to withstand the lightning and the gale. Now, prepare yourselves by making a contribution to your less fortunate brethren, heed this cry from Macedonia that comes from the hearts of men. Organize the unorganized and in so doing you make the American Federation of Labor the greatest instrumentality that has ever been forged in the history of modern civilization to befriend the cause of humanity and champion human rights. . . .

PRESIDENT GREEN: The Chair recognizes Delegate Tobin.

DELEGATE TOBIN, TEAMSTERS: Mr. Chairman and fellow delegates, I know the hour is getting late. I know it is difficult to ask you to exercise a little patience with me, because this is a very important question we are now discussing. . . .

I heard it said by President Lewis, said in all sincerity, that the question under discussion was not merely the adoption of the resolution. That is true, and I quite agree with him. There is more behind this thing than just what appears on the surface, in my judgment. There is an attempt being made to destroy the very foundation upon which this Federation has been builded and upon which it has succeeded for years. . . .

Industrial trade unionism is not new. It has been tried in nearly every country in Europe and it was tried in this country under the guise of the Knights of Labor. There are men in this convention who were pioneers and fighters in the Knights of Labor. They know its history, with machinists and musicians sitting beside the laborers and teamsters, all mixed up in one muddle, trying to make a wage scale, and those who had the greatest number of votes controlled the minority. Such destruction and demoralization took place that the old Knights of Labor, which gave us so many pioneers in the American Federation of Labor, died on account of dissension and distrust and jealousy.

Who are the men who formed the American Federation of Labor? Every one of them were members of the Knights of Labor, a form of industrial trade unionism. One of the founders, Pete McGuire, a carpenter of Philadelphia, and one of the greatest fighters we ever had then or now in the trade union movement, Jim Duncan, of the Granite cutters—do you think he did not know the trade union movement and its philosophies? Gompers, the Jew, who was driven from London, the greatest American citizen that this labor movement has ever produced. He struggled in the Knights of Labor for recognition and decided it was a failure, and he laid the foundation for this Federation of Labor. And so on down the line, with Frank Foster, the printer of Boston, and with innumerable others whose spirits must writhe in persecution and misery listening to the charges and counter-charges that have been made that this Federation of Labor has twenty-five years of continuous failure. . . .

Mr. Chairman, one of the greatest organizers the world ever produced since the beginning of Christianity was the lowly Nazarene, and He said to one of His people, "Upon this rock I will build My Church and the gates of hell shall not prevail against it."

To us was given a charter—a charter from the American Federation of Labor, and Gompers, McGuire, Duncan, Foster, and the other men said: "Upon the rock of trades autonomy, craft trades, you shall build the church of the labor movement, and the gates of hell nor trade industrialism shall not prevail against it."

21

Violence at Goodyear

AT the same hearings, William H. Ricketts, one of the leaders of the Goodyear local of the United Rubber Workers in Akron, reported the conversation that took place at a meeting of the heads of the local with Mr. Slusser. . . .

MR. RICKETTS. . . . I asked him where he would move production that the labor organization would not follow. He replied that they were moving a lot of production to Gadsden. And I said, "I would like to go to Gadsden and help organize the Gadsden plant."
SENATOR LA FOLLETTE. Did Mr. Slusser make any comment on your statement?
MR. RICKETTS. He did. He offered to bet me a hundred dollars I could not get off the train at Gadsden, Ala., and that, if I did, I would leave there on a stretcher.

Mr. Slusser himself commented on this conversation at another point in the testimony.

SENATOR LA FOLLETTE. Do you recall stating words to this effect, that if an organizer did get off the train he would have to come back on a stretcher?
MR. SLUSSER. No: I told him he might get his head knocked off. [Laughter.]

About a month after this conference, President Sherman H. Dalrymple of the U.R.W.A. went to Gadsden to help in the organizing of the union and to address a meeting on June 6, 1936. Mr. Dalrymple testified as to how the meeting had been broken up.

MR. DALRYMPLE. Someone raised up behind me, and pulled my glasses off, and they fell on the floor. And when I reached down to

SOURCE: Alfred Winslow Jones, Life, Liberty, and Property (Philadelphia, 1941), pp. 119–22.

get my glasses a fellow hit me in the jaw. The plain-clothes man shoved me out of the way.

The sheriff came up, and he said, "Better break up this meeting." I said, "It is already broken up, Sheriff." He said, "Come on and go with me." I said, "My wife is here with me." He said, "Your wife will be taken care of." I said, "My wife came here with me and she is going out with me." So he called my wife over to me.

When I was going down the steps people grabbed me by the hair, and I was kicked a couple of times. I said, "Sheriff, I am afraid you are leading me out here into a mob." He said, "Never mind; I'll take care of you."

When we got into the street I was kicked a couple of times, and just as we were going on the sidewalk on the far side they grabbed my hands from behind and shoved them up between my shoulders, and someone grabbed me by the hair of the head and pulled my head back over my shoulders and began to pound me in the face, both sides.

I worked my way down toward the hotel. And by that time I got my hands loose and got hold of a wire that was across the hotel door. And someone grabbed me by the hair of the head again and jerked me back and tore the wire off the door. I worked my way down to the corner and back to the door, and finally worked my way through the door.

SENATOR LA FOLLETTE. What was the sheriff doing in the meantime?

MR. DALRYMPLE. The Sheriff was alongside of me saying, "Never mind, boys, we will take care of him. Never mind, boys."

.   .   .

MR. DALRYMPLE. I returned home on Monday, if I remember rightly, and on Tuesday morning when I went to get up I knew there was something badly wrong with me. We called the doctor, Dr. Kretsky, and he said I had concussion of the brain, and they sent me to the hospital for a week. . . .

Further affidavits and testimony made it perfectly clear that the company had organized this action and others like it. Power was shut off so that the special deputies could be in town for the fighting, and the workers who supported the company in its various actions were paid full time at the regular rate for the vigilante work. In some cases it was made clear that their promotion would depend on what they did for the company against the union organizers.

22

Sit-down at General Motors

THE Chevrolet plant covers eight acres and has nine divisions and a power house. Plant No. 4 is the key plant which makes the motors. Without Plant No. 4, Chevrolet cannot make cars. This plant is set in a hollow. A little hill about five hundred feet long leads to it.

It was around Chevy 4 that the company guards had been stationed but now they were all concentrated in Plant No. 9, with tear gas and clubs, and all fighting occurred within the plant. There was no disorder anywhere else.

Every step was timed. The sound car appeared in front of No. 9. Word was sent to the meeting going on in Pengally Hall. The workers hurried to picket Chevrolet 9 headed by the Women's Emergency Brigade with their red caps.

Behind the windows were dimly seen figures fighting. There was something terrifying in that shadowy battle.

The women went up and started breaking windows. Someone called out: "We mustn't break windows, we mustn't destroy anything." Others answered, "We've got to let air in—they've gassed our boys inside." Nobody wanted to break windows, but it was necessary.

Word came from the sound car calling to the men to stand fast. Finally the sound car recalled the women, and sent them to rest at headquarters. They left reluctantly. Not even they knew that at this very moment, the real sit-down was taking place in Chevrolet 4, blocks away.

At headquarters casualties were coming in. The Women's Auxiliary room was crowded with men getting minor injuries dressed. There were eighteen casualties in all. Two of them had to be taken to the hospital. The room was soon full of bleeding men, the table heaped high with crimson gauze. None of the casualties happened outside the plant.

One of the men was badly cut about the face. They bandaged his

SOURCE: Mary Heaton Vorse, *Labor's New Millions* (New York, 1938), pp. 74–90.

head until he looked as though he were gazing out of a nun's head-dress. As he was being bandaged, he told his story:

"One hundred of us started walking to Plant No. 9. When the company guards sprang out at us the first thing I knew I saw a big company policeman about to crack down on a fellow near me. I grabbed for his club. He was so big he swung me around and I got the club on the tip of my chin. That is how I got my chin cut.

"Next I was knocked down by a policeman, and that's how I got my head cut. I was bleeding all over. A couple of the company cops were standing over me when I opened my eyes—as much as I could, for blood—and said: 'You want some more—you S. O. B.?' Boy, they were tough. But we were stronger than they were. Men were fighting every-where. They let off the tear gas, but we fought our way out.". . .

The women had come back from No. 9 where they had let air in to the gassed men. One of the women was standing wiping her eyes which were smarting with tear gas. Around her clung the acid smell of gas. Around the room were red-capped members of the Emergency Brigade, that was formed after the Battle of Bulls Run. . . .

I went down to the Chevrolet plant with two members of the Emer-gency Brigade. The workers had now captured plant No. 4. The street was full of people—there were about twenty policemen between the bridge and the high gate of the plant. They were quiet and unprovoca-tive, so the crowd of pickets was good-natured. The sound car was di-recting operations.

The use of the sound truck is new in strike procedure and it is hard to know how a strike was ever conducted without it. As we came down past the policemen a great voice, calm and benign, proclaimed that everything was in hand—the plant was under control.

Next the great disembodied voice, really the voice of auburn-haired young Roy Reuther, urged the men in the plant to barricade themselves from tear gas. Every now and then the voice boomed:

"Protection squad. Attention! Guard your sound car. Protection squad. Attention!"

Then the voice addressed the workers who crowded the windows of the lower levels. At the top of the steep flight of steps were the workers of the plant, lunch buckets under their arms, waving at the pickets in the street. A crowd of workers fringed the roof. The sound car inquired if they were union men. They shouted, "Yes." The crowd cheered.

The measured soothing voice of the sound car boomed:

"Word has come to us that there are men in the crowd anxious to join the union. Go to the last car, you will find the cards ready to sign. If you have no money for dues with you you can come to Pengally Hall later." The sound car struck up "Solidarity" and the men at the top of the steps, on top of the plant, in the street, all sang.

A woman's voice next—Genora Johnson. She told the crowd that the women had gone to the hall to wipe their eyes clear of tear gas and would soon be back. "We don't want any violence; we don't want any trouble. We are going to do everything we can to keep from trouble, but we are going to protect our husbands."

Down the hill presently came a procession, preceded by an American flag. The women's bright red caps showed dramatically in the dark crowd. They were singing, "Hold the Fort."

To all the crowd there was something moving about seeing the women return to the picket line after having been gassed in front of plant No. 9. A cheer went up; the crowd took up the song. The line of bright-capped women spread itself out in front of the high gate. Clasping hands, they struck up the song, "We Shall Not Be Moved." Some of the men who had jumped over the gate went back, amid the cheers of the crowd.

I went to the top of the little hill and a file of men were coming out of the back of the building.

"Are you going home?"

"Home—Hell no! We're going back to picket the plant. Half of us are sitting down inside, and half of us are coming out to picket from the street."

"How many of you are for the sit-down?"

"Ninety per cent," a group of them chorused.

It was getting dark, the crowd had grown denser. A black fringe of pickets and spectators was silhouetted against the brilliant green lights of the plant windows. . . .

[On February 11, 1937, the strike ended with a settlement in which General Motors granted in writing a partial, but significant, recognition to the union and promised not to discriminate against union members. As Edward Levinson has written: "The agreement constituted a monumental advance for unionism in the automobile industry."]

What happened that day in Flint was something that no one who ever saw it could possibly forget. Never since Armistice Day has anything been seen comparable to its intensity. A mighty emotion shook the working people of that town. Joy and freedom dominated Flint's commonplace streets.

It was as if Flint had been under a spell for a long time, perhaps always. Fear and suspicion had walked through Flint's streets. People didn't dare to join unions. They'd get fired, they'd lose their jobs. Your next door neighbor might be a spy. No one knew who the stool pigeons were. The people who had got used to living that way didn't know how maimed they were.

General Motors had come into Flint and made a city out of a crossroads. General Motors had dominated the town. It had ruled its political life and it had set its face against unions. Men had organized on their peril. Unions were kept out by fear. And now that fear was over. No wonder that the people marching in the line stretched out their hands to their friends on the sidewalk and said:

"You can join now, you can join now, we are free!". . .

When the men from Fisher No. 1 had accepted the agreement they marched in a parade to the plants at the other end of the town which were still guarded by the militia. The barrier of soldiers drew aside.

The crowd with flags marched cheering into the guarded zone.

The strikers were coming out of Chevrolet No. 4, flags preceding them. There were flags on the steps and flags on the street. Flares lighted up the scene. Cheers for Governor Murphy filled the air. Strikers' wives were waving to husbands they had not seen for days. A woman held up a baby. The procession marched down the street. Another roar filled all space.

The Fisher No. 2 boys marched out. They marched out in military formation from the quiet of the empty, waiting plant, carrying neat bundles of their things. They became part of the crowd that was now bright with confetti. People carried toy balloons. The whole scene was lit up by the burst of glory of the photographers' flares. The big flags punctuated the crowd with color.

They shouted to the rhythm of "Freedom, Freedom, Freedom!"

Chevrolet Avenue was packed from bridge to bridge. People swarmed over the murky little Flint River with its new barbed wire fences. They came past Chevrolet No. 4 and they came up the street past Fisher No. 2. They came, flags at their head, singing. They marched from the plants back to union headquarters. The streets were lined all the way with cheering people. Men and women from the cars and marchers shouted to the groups of other working people who lined the streets, "Join the union! We are free!"

The marchers arrived in front of Pengally Hall. They gathered in increasing thousands. The hall itself was jammed. They no longer let people into the building. Inside and outside, the loud speakers were going. Homer Martin, Wyndham Mortimer, Bob Travis and the other strike leaders addressed the roaring crowds.

The joy of victory tore through Flint. It was more than the joy of war ceasing, it was the joy of creation. The workers were creating a new life. The wind of Freedom had roared down Flint's streets. The strike had ended! The working people of Flint had begun to forge a new life out of their historic victory.

23

The National Labor
Relations Act

Be it enacted by the Senate and House of Representatives of the United States of America in Congress assembled,

SEC. 1. The denial by employers of the right of employees to organize and the refusal by employers to accept the procedure of collective bargaining lead to strikes and other forms of industrial strife or unrest, which have the intent or the necessary effect of burdening or obstructing commerce by (a) impairing the efficiency, safety, or operation of the instrumentalities of commerce; (b) occurring in the current of commerce; (c) materially affecting, restraining, or controlling the flow of raw materials or manufactured or processed goods from or into the channels of commerce or the prices of such materials or goods in commerce; or (d) causing diminution of employment and wages in such volume as substantially to impair or disrupt the market for goods flowing from or into the channels of commerce. . . .

It is hereby declared to be the policy of the United States to eliminate the causes of certain substantial obstructions to the free flow of commerce and to mitigate and eliminate these obstructions when they have occurred by encouraging the practice and procedure of collective bargaining and by protecting the exercise by workers of full freedom of association, self-organization, and designation of representatives of their own choosing, for the purpose of negotiating the terms and conditions of their employment or other mutual aid or protection. . . .

SEC. 7. Employees shall have the right to self-organization, to form, join, or assist labor organizations, to bargain collectively through representatives of their own choosing, and to engage in concerted activities, for the purpose of collective bargaining or other mutual aid or protection.

SOURCE: 49 U. S. Statutes at Large 449 (1935).

SEC. 8. It shall be an unfair labor practice for an employer—

(1) To interfere with, restrain, or coerce employees in the exercise of the rights guaranteed in section 7.

(2) To dominate or interfere with the formation or administration of any labor organization or contribute financial or other support to it. . . .

(3) By discrimination in regard to hire or tenure of employment or any term or condition of employment to encourage or discourage membership in any labor organization. . . .

(4) To discharge or otherwise discriminate against an employee because he has filed charges or given testimony under this Act.

(5) To refuse to bargain collectively with the representatives of his employees, subject to the provisions of Section 9(a).

SEC. 9. (a) Representatives designated or selected for the purposes of collective bargaining by the majority of the employees in a unit appropriate for such purposes, shall be the exclusive representatives of all the employees in such unit for the purposes of collective bargaining in respect to rates of pay, wages, hours of employment, or other conditions of employment. . . .

SEC. 10. (a) The Board is empowered . . . to prevent any person from engaging in any unfair labor practice (listed in section 8) affecting commerce. This power shall be exclusive, and shall not be affected by any other means of adjustment or prevention that has been or may be established by agreement, code, law, or otherwise. . . .

24

The Supreme Court Sustains the Wagner Act

IN a proceeding under the National Labor Relations Act of 1935, the National Labor Relations Board found that the respondent, Jones & Laughlin Steel Corporation, had violated the Act by engaging in unfair labor practices affecting commerce. The proceeding was instituted by the Beaver Valley Lodge No. 200, affiliated with the Amalgamated Association of Iron, Steel and Tin Workers of America, a labor organization. The unfair labor practices charged were that the corporation was discriminating against members of the union with regard to hire and tenure of employment, and was coercing and intimidating its employees in order to interfere with their self-organization. The discriminatory and coercive action alleged was the discharge of certain employees.

The National Labor Relations Board, sustaining the charge, ordered the corporation to cease and desist from such discrimination and coercion, to offer reinstatement to ten of the employees named, to make good their losses in pay, and to post for thirty days notices that the corporation would not discharge or discriminate against members, or those desiring to become members, of the labor union. As the corporation failed to comply, the Board petitioned the Circuit Court of Appeals to enforce the order. The court denied the petition, holding that the order lay beyond the range of federal power. . . . We granted certiorari. . . .

Contesting the ruling of the Board, the respondent argues (1) that the Act is in reality a regulation of labor relations and not of interstate commerce; (2) that the Act can have no application to the respondent's relations with its production employees because they are not subject to regulation by the federal government; and (3) that the provisions of

SOURCE: NLRB v. Jones and Laughlin Steel Corporation, 301 U.S. 1 (1937).

the Act violate § 2 of Article III and the Fifth and Seventh Amendments of the Constitution of the United States.

The facts as to the nature and scope of the business of the Jones & Laughlin Steel Corporation have been found by the Labor Board and, so far as they are essential to the determination of this controversy, they are not in dispute. The Labor Board has found: The corporation is organized under the laws of Pennsylvania and has its principal office at Pittsburgh. It is engaged in the business of manufacturing iron and steel in plants situated in Pittsburgh and nearby Aliquippa, Pennsylvania. It manufactures and distributes a widely diversified line of steel and pig iron, being the fourth largest producer of steel in the United States. With its subsidiaries—nineteen in number—it is a completely integrated enterprise, owning and operating ore, coal and limestone properties, lake and river transportation facilities and terminal railroads located at its manufacturing plants. It owns or controls mines in Michigan and Minnesota. It operates four ore steamships on the Great Lakes, used in the transportation of ore to its factories. It owns coal mines in Pennsylvania. It operates towboats and steam barges used in carrying coal to its factories. It owns limestone properties in various places in Pennsylvania and West Virginia. It owns the Monongahela connecting railroad which connects the plants of the Pittsburgh works and forms an interconnection with the Pennsylvania, New York Central and Baltimore and Ohio Railroad systems. It owns the Aliquippa and Southern Railroad Company which connects the Aliquippa works with the Pittsburgh and Lake Erie, part of the New York Central system. Much of its product is shipped to its warehouses in Chicago, Detroit, Cincinnati and Memphis,—to the last two places by means of its own barges and transportation equipment. In Long Island City, New York, and in New Orleans it operates structural steel fabricating shops in connection with the warehousing of semi-finished materials sent from its works. Through one of its wholly-owned subsidiaries it owns, leases and operates stores, warehouses and yards for the distribution of equipment and supplies for drilling and operating oil and gas wells and for pipe lines, refineries and pumping stations. It has sales offices in twenty cities in the United States and a wholly-owned subsidiary which is devoted exclusively to distributing its product in Canada. Approximately 75 per cent of its product is shipped out of Pennsylvania. . . .

While respondent criticises the evidence and the attitude of the Board, which is described as being hostile toward employers and particularly toward those who insisted upon their constitutional rights, respondent did not take advantage of its opportunity to present evidence to refute that which was offered to show discrimination and coercion. In this situation, the record presents no ground for setting aside the order of the Board so far as the facts pertaining to the circumstances and purpose of the discharge of the employees are concerned. Upon that point it is sufficient to say that the evidence supports the findings of the Board that respondent discharged these men "because of their union activity and for the purpose of discouraging membership in the union." We turn to the questions of law which respondent urges in contesting the validity and application of the Act.

First. *The scope of the Act.*—The Act is challenged in its entirety as an attempt to regulate all industry, thus invading the reserved powers of the State over their local concerns. It is asserted that the references in the Act to interstate and foreign commerce are colorable at best; that the Act is not a true regulation of such commerce or of matters which directly affect it but on the contrary has the fundamental object of placing under the compulsory supervision of the Federal government all industrial labor relations within the nation. The argument seeks support in the broad words of the preamble (section one) and in the sweep of the provisions of the Act, and it is further insisted that its legislative history shows an essential universal purpose in the light of which its scope cannot be limited by either construction or by the application of the separability clause. . . .

The grant of authority to the Board does not purport to extend to the relationship between all industrial employees and employers. Its terms do not impose collective bargaining upon all industry regardless of effects upon interstate or foreign commerce. It purports to reach only what may be deemed to burden or obstruct that commerce and, thus qualified, it must be construed as contemplating the exercise of control within constitutional bounds. . . .

Second. *The unfair labor practices in question.* . . . Employees have as clear a right to organize and select their representatives for lawful purposes as the respondent has to organize its business and select its own officers and agents. Discrimination and coercion to prevent the free exercise of the right of employees to self-organization and representation is a proper subject for condemnation by competent legislative authority. Long ago we stated the reason for labor organizations. We said that they were organized out of the necessities of the situation; that a single employee was helpless in dealing with an employer; that he was dependent ordinarily on his daily wage for the maintenance of himself and family; that if the employer refused to pay him the wages that he thought fair, he was nevertheless unable to leave the employ and resist arbitrary and unfair treatment; that union was essential to give laborers opportunity to deal on an equality with their employer. . . .

Third. *The application of the Act to employees engaged in production.—The principle involved.*—Respondent says that whatever may be said of employees engaged in interstate commerce, the industrial relations and activities in the manufacturing department of respondent's enterprise are not subject to Federal regulation. The argument rests upon the proposition that manufacturing in itself is not commerce. . . .

The congressional authority to protect interstate commerce from burdens and obstructions is not limited to transactions which can be deemed to be an essential part of a "flow" of interstate or foreign commerce. Burdens and obstructions may be due to injurious action springing from other sources. The fundamental principle is that the power to regulate commerce is the power to enact "all appropriate legislation" for "its protection and advancement". . . to adopt measures "to promote its growth and insure its safety". . . ."to foster, protect, control and restrain.". . . Although activities may be intrastate in character when separately considered, if they have such a close and substantial relation to interstate commerce that their control is essential or appropriate to protect that commerce from burdens and obstructions, Congress cannot be denied the power to exercise that control. . . .

Fourth. *Effects of the unfair labor practice in respondent's enterprise.* —Giving full weight to respondent's contention with respect to a break in the complete continuity of the "stream of commerce" by reason of respondent's manufacturing operations, the fact remains that the stoppage of those operations by industrial strife would have a most serious effect upon interstate commerce. In view of respondent's far-flung activities, it is idle to say that the effect would be indirect or remote. It is obvious that it would be immediate and might be catastrophic. We are asked to shut our eyes to the plainest facts of our national life and to deal with the question of direct and indirect effects in an intellectual vacuum. Because there may be but indirect and remote effects upon interstate commerce in connection with a host of local enterprises throughout the country, it does not follow that other industrial activities do not have such a close and intimate relation to interstate commerce as to make the presence of industrial strife a matter of the most urgent national concern. When industries organize themselves on a national scale, making their relation to interstate commerce the dominant factor in their activities, how can it be maintained that their industrial labor relations constitute a forbidden field into which Congress may not enter when it is necessary to protect interstate commerce from the paralyzing consequences of industrial war? We have often said that interstate commerce itself is a practical conception. It is equally true that interferences with that commerce must be appraised by a judgment that does not ignore actual experience.

Experience has abundantly demonstrated that the recognition of the right of employees to self-organization and to have representatives of their own choosing for the purpose of collective bargaining is often an essential condition of industrial peace. Refusal to confer and negotiate has been one of the most prolific causes of strife. This is such an outstanding fact in the history of labor disturbances that it is a proper subject of judicial notice and requires no citation of instances. . . . But with respect to the appropriateness of the recognition of self-organization and representation in the promotion of peace, the question is not essentially different in the case of employees in industries of such a character that interstate commerce is put in jeopardy from the case of employees of transportation companies. And of what avail is it to protect the facility of transportation, if interstate commerce is throttled with respect to the commodities to be transported! . . .

V
ILL FARES THE LAND

Franklin Roosevelt's speech in Selection 25, delivered from the White House portico to a delegation of farmers in the spring of 1935, is a good example of the personal "you and me" style of his informal talks. In speaking to farmers, he assumed the guise of a tiller of the soil in New York and Georgia: "I know that I got only four and a half cents for my cotton." To illustrate a point, he would often invent people; the prominent banker and the newspaper editor he mentions in this speech may both be mythical characters. Henry Wallace, who defends restrictionism in Selection 26, continued to probe for ways to plan for abundance; by World War II he would be arguing that America had a mission to feed the world. In Selection 27, Daniel O. Hastings was the Republican senator from Delaware, Alfred E. Smith the former Democratic presidential nominee who had become a severe critic of the New Deal, and Earl Browder the Communist Party leader. The prominence given Browder is one indication of the communist influence within the Federal Theatre that caused such uneasiness in Congress. Shortly before Caroline Henderson's letters in Selection 28 were published, she wrote to an editor: "As you doubtless know from newspaper accounts, conditions here are immensely worse than when the final letters were sent to the Atlantic. Nothing that we hoped for has happened; all that we dreaded has come to pass." Pare Lorentz's reference, "ill-clad, ill-housed, and ill-fed," misquotes Roosevelt's Second Inaugural Address in which the President spoke of "one-third of a nation ill-housed, ill-clad, ill-nourished." In Selection 30, Sherwood Anderson refers to Tobacco Road, a play by Erskine Caldwell which drew crowds on Broadway largely because of the loose sexual mores of his characters, but which also signalized the discovery of Southern rural poverty in the 1930's. "Pinchot of Pennsylvania" was Gifford Pinchot, chief forester under Theodore Roosevelt and subsequently governor of Pennsylvania. Critics called John Steinbeck's The Grapes of Wrath, excerpted in Selection 31, the Uncle Tom's Cabin of the Great Depression.

wondered about Winter wheat. What I don't understand is how they are able to cut it when it gets all covered up with snow."

The other was the editor of a great metropolitan paper. He visited me down in Georgia when the cotton was nearly grown but before the bolls had formed. Looking out over the cotton fields, he said to me:

"What a great number of raspberries they grow down here!"

Raspberries was right. At 4½ cents a pound for cotton, his mistake was, perhaps, a natural one.

I was speaking of adjustment. It is your duty and mine to continue to educate the people of this country to the fact that adjustment means not only adjustment downward, but adjustment upward.

If you and I agree on a correct figure for a normal carry-over it means that if we have a bumper crop one year we will, by mutual consent, reduce the next year's crop in order to even up that carry-over.

At the same time, if we get a short crop in a given year, you and I agree to increase the next year's crop to make up the shortage. That is exactly what we are doing today in the case of wheat.

It is high time for you and for me to carry, by education, knowledge of the fact that not a single program of the AAA contemplated the destruction of an acre of food crops in the United States, in spite of what you may read or be told by people who have special axes to grind.

It is high time for you and me to make clear that we are not plowing under cotton this year—that we did not plow it under in 1934 and that we only plowed some of it under in 1933 because the Agricultural Adjustment Act was passed after a huge crop of cotton was already in the ground.

It is high time for us to repeat on every occasion that we have not wastefully destroyed food in any form. It is true that the relief administrator has purchased hundreds of thousands of tons of foodstuffs to feed the needy and hungry who are on the relief rolls in every part of the United States.

The crocodile tears shed by the professional mourners of an old and obsolete order over the slaughter of little pigs and other measures to reduce surplus agricultural inventories deceive very few thinking people, and least of all the farmers themselves.

The acknowledged destiny of a pig is sausage, or ham, or bacon or pork. In these forms millions of pigs were consumed by vast numbers of needy people who otherwise would have had to do without.

Let me make one other point clear for the benefit of the millions in cities who have to buy meats.

Last year the nation suffered a drought of unparalleled intensity. If there had been no government program—if the old order had obtained in 1933 and 1934—that drought on the cattle ranges of America, and in the Corn Belt would have resulted in the marketing of thin cattle, immature hogs and in the death of these animals on the range and on the farm.

Then we would have had a vastly greater shortage than we face today.

Our program saved the lives of millions of head of livestock. They are still on the range. Other millions are today canned and ready for this country to eat.

I think that you and I are agreed in seeking a continuance of a national policy which on the whole is proving successful. The memory of old conditions under which the product of a whole year's work often would not bring you the cost of transporting it to market is too fresh in your minds to let you be led astray by the solemn admonitions and specious lies of those who in the past profited most when your distress was greatest.

You remember, and I remember, that not so long ago the poor had less food to eat and less clothes to wear, and that was at a time when you had to practically give away your products. Then the surpluses were greater and yet the poor were poorer than they are today when you farmers are getting a reasonable, although still an insufficient price.

I have not the time to talk with you about many other policies of your government which affect the farm population of the country. I have not the time to go into the practical work of the Farm Credit Administration which, in all of its ramifications, has saved a million farms from foreclosure and has accomplished the first great reduction in exorbitant interest rates that this country has ever known.

Because your cause is so just no one has the temerity to question the motives of your "march on Washington." It is a good omen for government, for business, for bankers and for the city dwellers that the nation's farmers are becoming articulate and that they know whereof they speak.

I hope you have enjoyed your stay in Washington. Seeing your government at first hand, you may have a better idea why its efforts at times seem lumbering and slow and complicated.

On the other hand, you may have seen that we are moving faster and accomplishing more practical results than you have been led to believe by the high and mighty gentlemen I have spoken of.

I want to thank you for your patience with us. I want to pledge our whole-hearted cooperation as you go forward.

26

The Paradox of Scarcity and Abundance

THOUGH abundance is at hand, we still live by old standards of denial. The situation is confusing. There are those who say that there cannot be a surplus so long as there is a single hungry Chinaman. Fundamentally and eventually this may be true; but these standpat sentimentalists who weep that farmers should practice controlled production do not suggest that clothing factories go on producing *ad infinitum*, regardless of effective demand for their merchandise, until every naked Chinaman is clad. Nor do they feel that plow factories should abandon production control until every hungry Chinaman has a plow. We must play with the cards that are dealt. Agriculture cannot survive in a capitalistic society as a philanthropic enterprise. If the cry of those who bid our farmers think of all those hungry Chinamen, and plant more land, were heeded, it would mean that long before the last hungry Chinamen were taken care of, hundreds of thousands of American farm families would be destroyed.

The feeling that man should live by providing goods for his neighbors, not by withholding goods, goes very deep; and I believe that it is spreading. But the condition of greater balance and justice we now seek, in a capitalistic structure hastily mended, can certainly not be obtained by arranging that everybody work under the profit system except the farmer. The farmer's instinct has always been to be decent and unbusinesslike, to provide to the uttermost, never to deny. This instinct, obeyed by millions of scattered individuals in a society seeking profits and setting prices on a scarcity basis, took our farmers up the long hill to the poorhouse; and killed them as customers. Their death as consumers closed thousands of factories and helped to throw millions out

SOURCE: Henry A. Wallace, *New Frontiers* (New York, 1934), pp. 138–9, 180–1, 187–8.

of work. Now we are trying to give our farmers their rightful place in a more decent and balanced system, a system that will work democratically and make for neighborliness and a shared abundance. The people who raise the cry about the last hungry Chinamen are not really criticising the farmers or the AAA, but the profit system, as we have inherited it from our past. . . .

It was a foregone conclusion that the public would not like the idea of slaughtering baby pigs. Doubtless it is just as inhumane to kill a big hog as a little one, but few people would appreciate that. They contended that every little pig has the right to attain before slaughter the full pigginess of his pigness. To hear them talk, you would have thought that pigs are raised for pets. Nor would they realize that the slaughter of little pigs might make more tolerable the lives of a good many human beings dependent on hog prices. We simply had to make up our minds to face an unfavorable public reaction, despite the diversion of 100,000,-000 pounds of baby pork to relief channels. . . .

The most important consideration of all, to my mind, was the understanding that this program was superficial, and that it must be followed in 1934 by something much more fundamental. So in announcing the emergency slaughter program, in the course of an address August 18 at the Chicago fair, I said we were proceeding on the assumption that this program would be followed by a program in 1934 and perhaps 1935 involving both corn acreage and hog numbers. The slaughter program was to be financed later on by a processing tax on hog products, which could also finance the program to be adopted for 1934.

I was terribly concerned lest the Corn Belt fail to see how dangerous this drastic slaughter program could be, if not tied up to a reduction in corn acreage in 1934. The after-effects could be disastrous to hog prices in 1934–35. Not one farmer in a hundred, it seemed, realized what a terrible mess the Corn Belt would be in, unless it promptly dug deep both in thinking and action. . . .

Necessarily we could not be sure how all our plans would work. Along an "untrod path" there is no telling what dangers and obstacles you will meet. But we were beginning to have the comfortable feeling that the new machinery was lumbering into effective action. Economic results could not yet be measured, but reports from the wheat States, especially, told of a genuine revival of the old New England town-meeting idea in the county production control associations. In making individual acreage allotments add up to a total that jibed with government statistics, farmers were doing a significant job of economic self-government. Though in this and all the other programs there was opportunity for disastrous friction, the human will to make the machinery function was more powerful than the friction.

Impatience with the speed of the program was to be expected, and in announcing some of the programs we were altogether too optimistic as to the date when benefit payments would go out. The tedious task of getting millions of contracts thoughtfully considered, signed, and then approved both locally and at Washington, took much longer than we thought it would. The mere physical job of handling that many contracts here at Washington, of auditing them and of getting out the checks, taxed our inventiveness to the utmost. By using the most ingenious machinery available—machinery which is uncanny in its transformation of punch-holes into names, addresses, and amounts—we were finally able to get the output of checks up to a maximum of 80,000 a day. But to do the job it required fifteen hundred people, plus a battery of comptometers and check-writing machines, working twenty-four hours a day.

The spectacle of all this going on in a room half a city block in area so impressed a Russian visitor last summer that he exclaimed, "Good Lord! This is a revolution!"

27

Triple A Plowed Under

SCENE TWENTY-THREE
(Supreme Court . . . AAA killed)

CHARACTERS

VOICE OF LIVING NEWSPAPER
VOICE OVER LOUDSPEAKER
SUPREME COURT JUSTICE ROBERTS—figure in silhouette
SUPREME COURT JUSTICE STONE—figure in silhouette
SEVEN OTHER SUPREME COURT JUSTICES—figures in silhouette
DANIEL O. HASTINGS, SENATOR FROM DELAWARE—in silhouette
ALFRED E. SMITH—in silhouette
EARL BROWDER—in silhouette
THOMAS JEFFERSON—in silhouette
FIRST MAN
SECOND MAN
THIRD MAN
A WOMAN
FOURTH MAN
FIFTH MAN

VOICE OF LIVING NEWSPAPER (over LOUDSPEAKER):
   January 6, 1936. . . . Supreme Court invalidates AAA in Hoosac
   Mills case.
VOICE (also over LOUDSPEAKER):
   The majority opinion—Justice Roberts.
(As travelers open from rear, projection of Constitution is
thrown on glass curtain. Discovered in shadow against projec-

SOURCE: "Triple A Plowed Under," by the Staff of the Living Newspaper,
Federal Theatre Plays (New York, 1938), pp. 44-7.

tion are JUSTICE STONE, THREE OTHER JUSTICES, *then* JUSTICE ROBERTS, *and the* FOUR REMAINING JUSTICES, *right.* ROBERTS *rises to one-foot platform directly in front of him.* FIVE JUSTICES *who concurred in his opinion, turn in profile as he begins to speak.)*

JUSTICE ROBERTS:

. . . Beyond cavil the sole objective of the legislation is to restore the purchasing price of agricultural products to a parity with that prevailing in an earlier day; to take money from the processor and bestow it on the farmers. The Constitution is the supreme law of the land, ordained and established by the people. All legislation must conform to the principles it lays down. The power to confer or withhold unlimited benefits is the power to coerce or destroy. This is coercion by economic pressure. The judgment is affirmed.

(He steps down; JUSTICE STONE *steps up.)*

VOICE OVER LOUDSPEAKER:

The minority opinion—Justice Stone.

(The FIVE JUSTICES *concurring with* JUSTICE ROBERTS *turn to full front. The* TWO *concurring with* STONE *turn in silhouette.)*

JUSTICE STONE:

Courts are concerned with the power to enact statutes, not with their wisdom. The only check upon their own exercise of power is our own sense of self-restraint. For the removal of unwise laws from the statute books, appeal lies not to the courts, but to the ballot, and to the processes of democratic government.

So may the judicial power be abused. "The power to tax is the power to destroy," but we do not for that reason doubt its existence. Courts are not the only agents of government which must be assumed to have the capacity to govern.

(As JUSTICE STONE *steps down,* SENATOR HASTINGS *enters, right, steps on higher platform at back, throwing his shadow into a much larger projection than that of the* JUSTICES.)*

SENATOR HASTINGS:

This re-establishes Constitutional government. It gives back to the States the power they intended to reserve when they adopted the Constitution. The chances are it will improve the condition of the country, as did the decision of the NRA.

*(HASTINGS *steps down and exits left.* ALFRED E. SMITH *enters right, steps on platform vacated by* HASTINGS.)*

ALFRED E. SMITH:

We don't want the Congress of the United States singly or severally to tell the Supreme Court what to do. We don't want any administration that takes a shot at the Constitution in the dark, and tries to put something over in contradiction of it, upon any theory that there is going to be a great public power in favor of it, and it is possible that the United States Supreme Court may be intimidated into a friendly opinion with respect to it. But I found, all during my public life, that Almighty God built this country, and he did not give us that kind of a Supreme Court.

(SMITH *steps down, and exits left.* BROWDER *enters right; steps on platform vacated by* SMITH.)

EARL BROWDER:

The reactionaries seek to turn both "Americanism" and the Constitution into instruments of reaction, but neither of these things belongs to them. Nowhere does the Constitution grant the Supreme Court power over Congress, but it does make Congress the potential master of the Supreme Court. I repeat, the Constitution of the United States does not give the Supreme Court the right to declare laws passed by Congress unconstitutional.

(BROWDER *steps down and exits left.* THOMAS JEFFERSON *enters right, steps on platform vacated by* BROWDER.)

THOMAS JEFFERSON:

There must be an arbiter somewhere. True, there must. But does that prove it is either the Congress or the Supreme Court? The ultimate arbiter is the people of the Union, assembled by their deputies in convention at the call of Congress or two-thirds of the States.

(*Travelers slowly close, with* JEFFERSON *remaining standing on platform, center.*)

VOICE OVER LOUDSPEAKER:

Farmers voted, by more than 6 to 1, for continuance of Triple-A.

(MEN *start crossing stage in front of travelers, from right to left.*)

FIRST MAN:

The AAA is dead. . . . (*Exits left.*)

SECOND MAN:

No more allotment checks. . . . (*Exits left.*)

THIRD MAN:

What the hell're we agoin' to do this winter? (*Exits left.*)

A WOMAN:

How're we goin' t' get coal? (*Exits left.*)

FOURTH MAN:

They say the people wrote the Constitution. . . . (*Exits left.*)
FIFTH MAN:
   Them people have been dead a long time. . . . (*Also exits.*)

Blackout

28

Letters from the Dust Bowl

Eva, Oklahoma
June 20, 1935

MY DEAR EVELYN:—

Your continued interest in our effort to "tie a knot in the end of the rope and hang on" is most stimulating. Our recent transition from rain-soaked eastern Kansas with its green pastures, luxuriant foliage, abundance of flowers, and promise of a generous harvest, to the dust-covered desolation of No Man's Land was a difficult change to crowd into one short day's travel. Eleanor has laid aside the medical books for a time. Wearing our shade hats, with handkerchiefs tied over our faces and vaseline in our nostrils, we have been trying to rescue our home from the accumulations of wind-blown dust which penetrates wherever air can go. It is an almost hopeless task, for there is rarely a day when at some time the dust clouds do not roll over. "Visibility" approaches zero and everything is covered again with a silt-like deposit which may vary in depth from a film to actual ripples on the kitchen floor. I keep oiled cloths on the window sills and between the upper and lower sashes. They help just a little to retard or collect the dust. Some seal the windows with the gummed-paper strips used in wrapping parcels, but no method is fully effective. We buy what appears to be red cedar sawdust with oil added to use in sweeping our floors, and do our best to avoid inhaling the irritating dust. . . .

Early in May, with no more grass or even weeds on our 640 acres than on your kitchen floor, and even the scanty remnants of dried grasses from last year cut off and blown away, we decided, like most of our neighbors, to ship our cattle to grass in the central part of the state. We sent 27 head, retaining here the heifers coming fresh this spring. . . .

The day after we shipped the cattle, the long drouth was temporarily broken by the first effective moisture in many months—about one and

SOURCE: Caroline A. Henderson, "Letters from the Dust Bowl," *Atlantic Monthly*, CLVII (1936), 540–3.

one-quarter inches in two or three gentle rains. All hope of a wheat
crop had been abandoned by March or April.

Contrary to many published reports, a good many people had left
this country either temporarily or permanently before any rains came.
And they were not merely "drifters," as is frequently alleged. In May a
friend in the southwestern county of Kansas voluntarily sent me a list
of the people who had already left their immediate neighborhood or
were packed up and ready to go. The list included 109 persons in 26
families, substantial people, most of whom had been in that locality
over ten years, and some as long as forty years. In these families there
had been two deaths from dust pneumonia. Others in the neighborhood
were ill at that time. Fewer actual residents have left our neighborhood,
but on a sixty-mile trip yesterday to procure tractor repairs we saw many
pitiful reminders of broken hopes and apparently wasted effort. Little
abandoned homes where people had drilled deep wells for the precious
water, had set trees and vines, built reservoirs, and fenced in gardens,—
with everything now walled in or half buried by banks of drifted soil,—
told a painful story of loss and disappointment. I grieved especially over
one lonely plum thicket buried to the tips of the twigs, and a garden
with a fence closely built of boards for wind protection, now enclosing
only a hillock of dust covered with the blue-flowered bull nettles which
no winds or sands discourage. . . .

The coming of the long-desired rain gave impetus to the Federal
projects for erosion control. Plans were quickly made, submitted to
groups of farmers in district gatherings, and put into operation without
delay.

The proposition was that, in order to encourage the immediate listing of abandoned wheat ground and other acreage so as to cut down
wind erosion, the Federal Government would contribute ten cents per
acre toward the expense of fuel and oil for tractors or feed for horses, if
the farmers would agree to list not less than one fourth of the acreage
on contour lines. Surveys were made promptly for all farmers signing
contracts for either contour listing or terracing. The latest report states
that within the few weeks since the programme was begun in our county 299,986 acres have been ploughed or listed on these contour lines—
that is, according to the lay of the land instead of on straight lines with
right-angled turns as has been the usual custom.

The plan has been proposed and carried through here as a matter of
public policy for the welfare of all without reproach or humiliation to
anyone. It should be remembered that 1935 is the fourth successive year
of drouth and crop failure through a great part of the high plains region,
and the hopelessly low prices for the crop of 1931 gave no chance to

build up reserves for future needs. If the severe critics of all who in any way join in government plans for the saving of homes and the restoration of farms to a productive basis could only understand how vital a human problem is here considered, possibly their censures might be less bitter and scornful.

At any rate the contour listing has been done over extensive areas. If rains come to carry forward the feed crops now just struggling up in the furrows, the value of the work can be appraised. The primary intention of the plan for contour listing is to distribute rainfall evenly over the fields and prevent its running off to one end of the field or down the road to some creek or drainage basin. It is hoped that the plan will indirectly tend to lessen wind erosion by promoting the growth of feed crops, restoration of humus to denuded surfaces, and some protection through standing stubbles and the natural coverage of weeds and unavoidable wastes. One great contributing cause of the terrible dust storms of the last two years has been the pitiful bareness of the fields resulting from the long drouth.

I am not wise enough to forecast the result. We have had two most welcome rains in June—three-quarters of an inch and one-half inch. Normally these should have been of the utmost benefit, though they by no means guarantee an abundant feed crop from our now sprouting seeds as many editorial writers have decreed, and they do nothing toward restoring subsoil moisture. Actually the helpful effects of the rains have been for us and for other people largely destroyed by the drifting soil from abandoned, unworked lands around us. It fills the air and our eyes and noses and throats, and, worst of all, our furrows, where tender shoots are coming to the surface only to be buried by the smothering silt from the fields of rugged individualists who persist in their right to do nothing.

A fairly promising piece of barley has been destroyed for us by the merciless drift from the same field whose sands have practically buried the little mulberry hedge which has long sheltered our buildings from the northwest winds. Large spaces in our pastures are entirely bare in spite of the rains. Most of the green color, where there is any grazing, is due to the pestilent Russian thistles rather than to grass. Our little locust grove which we cherished for so many years has become a small pile of fence posts. With trees and vines and flowers all around you, you can't imagine how I miss that little green shaded spot in the midst of the desert glare.

Naturally you will wonder why we stay where conditions are so extremely disheartening. Why not pick up and leave as so many others have done? It is a fair question, but a hard one to answer.

Recently I talked with a young university graduate of very superior attainments. He took the ground that in such a case sentiment could and should be disregarded. He may be right. Yet I cannot act or feel or think as if the experiences of our twenty-seven years of life together had never been. And they are all bound up with the little corner to which we have given our continued and united efforts. To leave voluntarily—to break all these closely knit ties for the sake of a possibly greater comfort elsewhere—seems like defaulting on our task. We may have to leave. We can't hold out indefinitely without some return from the land, some source of income, however small. But I think I can never go willingly or without pain that as yet seems unendurable.

There are also practical considerations that serve to hold us here, for the present. Our soil is excellent. We need only a little rain—less than in most places—to make it productive. No one who remembers the wheat crops of 1926, 1929, 1931, can possibly regard this as permanently submarginal land. The newer methods of farming suggest possibilities of better control of moisture in the future. Our entire equipment is adapted to the type of farming suitable for this country and would have to be replaced at great expense with the tools needed in some other locality. We have spent so much in trying to keep our land from blowing away that it looks foolish to walk off and leave it, when somewhat more favorable conditions seem now to "cast their shadows before." I scarcely need to tell you that there is no use in thinking of either renting or selling farm property here at present. It is just a place to stand on—if we can keep the taxes paid—and work and hope for a better day. We could realize nothing whatever from all our years of struggle with which to make a fresh start.

We long for the garden and little chickens, the trees and birds and wild flowers of the years gone by. Perhaps if we do our part these good things may return some day, for others if not for ourselves.

Will joins me in earnest hopes for your recovery. The dust has been particularly aggravating to his bronchial trouble, but he keeps working on. A great reddish-brown dust cloud is rising now from the southeast, so we must get out and do our night work before it arrives. Our thoughts go with you.

29

The River

The Body of the Nation

But the basin of the Mississippi is the Body of the Nation. All the other parts are but members, important in themselves, yet more important in their relations to this. Exclusive of the Lake basin and of 300,000 square miles in Texas and New Mexico, which in many aspects form a part of it, this basin contains about 1,250,000 square miles. In extent it is the second great valley of the world, being exceeded only by that of the Amazon. The valley of the frozen Obi approaches it in extent; that of the La Plata comes next in space, and probably in habitable capacity, having about eight-ninths of its area; then comes that of the Yenisei, with about seven-ninths; the Lena, Amoor, Hoang-ho, Yang-tse-Kiang, and Nile, five-ninths; the Ganges, less than one-half; the Indus, less than one-third; the Euphrates, one-fifth; the Rhine, one-fifteenth. It exceeds in extent the whole of Europe, exclusive of Russia, Norway, and Sweden. *It would contain Austria four times, Germany or Spain five times, France six times, the British Islands or Italy ten times.* Conceptions formed from the river-basins of Western Europe are rudely shocked when we consider the extent of the valley of the Mississippi; nor are those formed from the sterile basins of the great rivers of Siberia, the lofty plateaus of Central Asia, or the mighty sweep of the swampy Amazon more adequate. Latitude, elevation, and rainfall all combine to render every part of the Mississippi Valley capable of supporting a dense population. *As a dwelling-place for civilized man it is by far the first upon our globe.*—Mark Twain's *Life on The Mississippi.*

From as far West as Idaho,
   Down from the glacier peaks of the Rockies—
From as far East as New York,
   Down from the turkey ridges of the Alleghenies

source: Pare Lorentz, *The River* (New York, 1938).

Down from Minnesota, twenty five hundred miles,
  The Mississippi River runs to the Gulf.
Carrying every drop of water, that flows down two-thirds the con-
    tinent,
Carrying every brook and rill, rivulet and creek,
Carrying all the rivers that run down two-thirds the continent,
The Mississippi runs to the Gulf of Mexico.
Down the Yellowstone, the Milk, the White and Cheyenne;
The Cannonball, the Musselshell, the James and the Sioux;
Down the Judith, the Grand, the Osage, and the Platte,
The Skunk, the Salt, the Black, and Minnesota;
Down the Rock, the Illinois, and the Kankakee
The Allegheny, the Monongahela, Kanawha, and Muskingum;
Down the Miami, the Wabash, the Licking and the Green
The Cumberland, the Kentucky, and the Tennessee;
Down the Ouchita, the Wichita, the Red, and Yazoo—
Down the Missouri three thousand miles from the Rockies;
Down the Ohio a thousand miles from the Alleghenies;
Down the Arkansas fifteen hundred miles from the Great Divide;
Down the Red, a thousand miles from Texas;
Down the great Valley, twenty-five hundred miles from Minnesota,
  Carrying every rivulet and brook, creek and rill,
Carrying all the rivers that run down two-thirds the continent—
The Mississippi runs to the Gulf.
New Orleans to Baton Rouge,
Baton Rouge to Natchez,
Natchez to Vicksburg,
Vicksburg to Memphis,
Memphis to Cairo—
We built a dyke a thousand miles long.
Men and mules, mules and mud;
Mules and mud a thousand miles up the Mississippi.
A century before we bought the great Western River, the Spanish
    and the French built dykes to keep the Mississippi out of New
    Orleans at flood stage.
In forty years we continued the levee the entire length of the great
    alluvial Delta,
That mud plain that extends from the Gulf of Mexico clear to the
    mouth of the Ohio.
The ancient valley built up for centuries by the old river spilling
    her floods across the bottom of the continent—
A mud delta of forty thousand square miles.

Men and mules, mules and mud—
New Orleans to Baton Rouge,
Natchez to Vicksburg,
Memphis to Cairo—
A thousand miles up the river.
And we made cotton king!
We rolled a million bales down the river for Liverpool and
    Leeds . . .
1860: we rolled four million bales down the river;
Rolled them off Alabama,
Rolled them off Mississippi,
Rolled them off Louisiana,
Rolled them down the river!
We fought a war.
We fought a war and kept the west bank of the river free of slavery
    forever.
But we left the old South impoverished and stricken.
Doubly stricken, because, beyond the tragedy of war, already the
    frenzied cotton cultivation of a quarter of a century had taken
    toll of the land.
We mined the soil for cotton until it would yield no more, and
    then moved west.
We fought a war, but there was a double tragedy—the tragedy of
    land twice impoverished.
Black spruce and Norway pine,
Douglas fir and Red cedar,
Scarlet oak and Shagbark hickory,
Hemlock and aspen—
There was lumber in the North.
The war impoverished the old South, the railroads killed the steam-
    boats,
But there was lumber in the North.
Heads up!
Lumber on the upper river.
Heads up!
Lumber enough to cover all Europe.
Down from Minnesota and Wisconsin,
Down to St. Paul;
Down to St. Louis and St. Joe—
Lumber for the new continent of the West.
Lumber for the new mills.
There was lumber in the North and coal in the hills.

Iron and coal down the Monongahela.
Iron and coal down the Allegheny.
Iron and coal down the Ohio.
Down to Pittsburgh,
Down to Wheeling,
Iron and coal for the steel mills, for the railroads driving
West and South, for the new cities of the Great Valley—
We built new machinery and cleared new land in the West.
Ten million bales down to the Gulf—
Cotton for the spools of England and France.
Fifteen million bales down to the Gulf—
Cotton for the spools of Italy and Germany.
We built a hundred cities and a thousand towns:
St. Paul and Minneapolis,
Davenport and Keokuk,
Moline and Quincy,
Cincinnati and St. Louis,
Omaha and Kansas City . . .
Across to the Rockies and down from Minnesota,
Twenty-five hundred miles to New Orleans,
We built a new continent.
Black spruce and Norway pine,
Douglas fir and Red cedar,
Scarlet oak and Shagbark hickory.
We built a hundred cities and a thousand towns—
But at what a cost!
We cut the top off the Alleghenies and sent it down the river.
We cut the top off Minnesota and sent it down the river.
We cut the top off Wisconsin and sent it down the river.
We left the mountains and the hills slashed and burned,
And moved on.
The water comes downhill, spring and fall;
Down from the cut-over mountains,
Down from the plowed-off slopes,
Down every brook and rill, rivulet and creek,
Carrying every drop of water that flows down two-thirds the con-
    tinent
1903 and 1907,
1913 and 1922,
1927,
1936,
1937!

Down from Pennsylvania and Ohio,
Kentucky and West Virginia,
Missouri and Illinois,
Down from North Carolina and Tennessee—
Down the Judith, the Grand, the Osage, and the Platte,
The Rock, the Salt, the Black and Minnesota,
Down the Monongahela, the Allegheny, Kanawha and Muskingum,
The Miami, the Wabash, the Licking and the Green,
Down the White, the Wolfe, and the Cache,
Down the Kaw and Kaskaskia, the Red and Yazoo,
Down the Cumberland, Kentucky and the Tennessee—
Down to the Mississippi.
New Orleans to Baton Rouge—
Baton Rouge to Natchez—
Natchez to Vicksburg—
Vicksburg to Memphis—
Memphis to Cairo—
A thousand miles down the levee the long vigil starts.
Thirty-eight feet at Baton Rouge
River rising.
Helena: river rising.
Memphis: river rising.
Cairo: river rising.
A thousand miles to go,
A thousand miles of levee to hold—
Coastguard patrol needed at Paducah!
Coastguard patrol needed at Paducah!

200 boats—wanted at Hickman!
200 boats wanted at Hickman!

Levee patrol: men to Blytheville!
Levee patrol: men to Blytheville!

2000 men wanted at Cairo!
2000 men wanted at Cairo!

A hundred thousand men to fight the old river.
We sent armies down the river to help the engineers fight a battle
     on a two thousand mile front:
The Army and the Navy,
The Coast Guard and the Marine Corps,

The CCC and the WPA,
The Red Cross and the Health Service.
They fought night and day to hold the old river off the valley.
Food and water needed at Louisville: 500 dead, 5000 ill;
Food and water needed at Cincinnati;
Food and water and shelter and clothing needed for 750,000 flood
    victims;
Food and medicine needed at Lawrenceburg;
35,000 homeless in Evansville;
Food and medicine needed in Aurora;
Food and medicine and shelter and clothing for 750,000 down in
    the valley.
Last time we held the levees,
But the old river claimed her valley.
She backed into Tennessee and Arkansas
And Missouri and Illinois.
She left stock drowned, houses torn loose,
Farms ruined.

1903 and 1907.
1913 and 1922.
1927.
1936.
1937!
We built a hundred cities and a thousand towns—
But at what a cost!
Spring and fall the water comes down, and for years the old river
    has taken a toll from the Valley more terrible than ever she
    does in flood times.
Year in, year out, the water comes down
From a thousand hillsides, washing the top off the Valley.
For fifty years we dug for cotton and moved West when the land
    gave out.
For fifty years we plowed for corn, and moved on when the land
    gave out.
Corn and wheat; wheat and cotton—we planted and plowed with
    no thought for the future—
And four hundred million tons of top soil,
Four hundred million tons of our most valuable natural resource
    have been washed into the Gulf of Mexico every year.

And poor land makes poor people.

Poor people make poor land.

For a quarter of a century we have been forcing more and more
farmers into tenancy.

Today forty per cent of all the farmers in the great Valley are
tenants.

Ten per cent are share croppers,

Down on their knees in the valley,

A share of the crop their only security.

No home, no land of their own,

Aimless, footloose, and impoverished,

Unable to eat even from the land because their cash crop is their
only livelihood.

Credit at the store is their only reserve.

And a generation growing up with no new land in the West—

No new continent to build.

A generation whose people knew King's Mountain, and Shiloh;

A generation whose people knew Fremont and Custer;

But a generation facing a life of dirt and poverty,

Disease and drudgery;

Growing up without proper food, medical care, or schooling,

"Ill-clad, ill-housed, and ill-fed"—

And in the greatest river valley in the world.

*There is no such thing as an ideal river in Nature, but the Mississippi
is out of joint.*

Dust blowing in the West—floods raging in the East—

We have seen these problems growing to horrible extremes.

When first we found the great valley it was forty per cent forested.

Today, for every hundred acres of forests we found, we have ten left.

*Today five per cent of the entire valley is ruined forever for agri-
cultural use!*

*Twenty-five per cent of the topsoil has been shoved by the old
river into the Gulf of Mexico.*

*Today two out of five farmers in the valley are tenant farmers—ten
per cent of them share croppers, living in a state of squalor unknown to the poorest peasant in Europe*

*And we are forcing thirty thousand more into tenancy and cropping
every year.*

*Flood control of the Mississippi means controls in the great Delta
that must carry all the water brought down from two-thirds the
continent*

And control of the Delta means control of the little rivers, the

*great arms running down from the uplands. And the old river
can be controlled.*
We *had the power to take the valley apart—we have the power to
put it together again.*

In 1933 we started, down on the Tennessee River, when our
Congress created the Tennessee Valley Authority, commissioned to
develop navigation, flood control, agriculture, and industry in the
valley: a valley that carries more rainfall than any other in the
country; the valley through which the Tennessee used to roar down
to Paducah in flood times with more water than any other tributary
of the Ohio.

First came the dams.

Up on the Clinch, at the head of the river, we built Norris Dam,
a great barrier to hold water in flood times and to release water down
the river for navigation in low water season.

Next came Wheeler, first in a series of great barriers that will
transform the old Tennessee into a link of fresh water pools locked
and dammed, regulated and controlled, down six hundred fifty
miles to Paducah.

But you cannot plan for water unless you plan for land: for the
cut-over mountains—the eroded hills—the gullied fields that pour
their waters unchecked down to the river.

The CCC, working with the forest service and agricultural experts, have started to put the worn fields and hillsides back together; black walnut and pine for the worn out fields, and the gullied
hillsides; black walnut and pine for new forest preserves, roots for
the cut-over and burned-over hillsides; roots to hold the water in
the ground.

Soil conservation men have worked out crop systems with the
farmers of the Valley—crops to conserve and enrich the topsoil.

Today a million acres of land in the Tennessee Valley are being
tilled scientifically.

But you cannot plan for water and land unless you plan for
people. Down in the Valley, the Farm Security Administration
has built a model agricultural community. Living in homes they
themselves built, paying for them on long term rates, the home-
steaders will have a chance to share in the wealth of the Valley.

More important, the Farm Security Administration has lent
thousands of dollars to farmers in the Valley, farmers who were
caught by years of depression and in need of only a stake to be self-
sufficient.

But where there is water there is power.

Where there's water for flood control and water for navigation, there's water for power—

Power for the farmers of the Valley.

Power for the villages and cities and factories of the Valley.

West Virginia, North Carolina, Tennessee, Mississippi, Georgia and Alabama.

Power to give a new Tennessee Valley to a new generation.

Power enough to make the river work!

Epilogue

We got the blacks to plant the cotton and they gouged the top off the valley.

We got the Swedes to cut the forests, and they sent them down the river.

Then we moved our saws and our plows and started all over again;

And we left a hollow-eyed generation to peck at the worn-out valley;

And left the Swedes to shiver in their naked North country.

1903, 1907, 1913, 1922, 1927, 1936, 1937—

For you can't wall out and dam two-thirds the water in the country.

We built dams but the dams filled in.

We built a thousand-mile dyke but it didn't hold;

So we built it higher.

We played with a continent for fifty years.

Flood control? Of the Mississippi?

Control from Denver to Helena;

From Itasca to Paducah;

From Pittsburgh to Cairo—

Control of the wheat, the corn and the cotton land;

Control enough to put back a thousand forests;

Control enough to put the river together again before it is too late . . . before it has picked up the heart of a continent and shoved it into the Gulf of Mexico.

30

Tough Babes in the Woods

THEY have made a little town under the hill—between two hills— in a narrow valley down which flows a mountain stream. This is one of a dozen such little towns I have been in during the last week, and they are all pretty much alike. There is an army man and a forester or two in each camp. The army men have charge of the camp. They differ. Some add little home-like touches, others do not. There may be twenty or thirty or fifty houses in such a camp town, and it may have one street or two or three. They are laying down sidewalks in the one I have just been in. This is the time of mud in the valleys and in the hills. Soon the spring rains will be coming here.

The boys in this camp town, at the edge of which I am sitting—I am sitting with my notebook on a flat stone under a rhododendron bush— the boys go up the hills and bring down flat stones. They are laying side-walks along the street down which I look, making their town neat against the muddy time to come. A man goes about among them di-recting the work, a tall lean intelligent man of thirty. He is the forester of this camp—a soft-speaking Southerner—and this is Saturday, so the boys do not go to work in the woods. It is a clear quiet day and rather warm. Spring will be coming soon in this Southern Appalachian coun-try. I hear a little animal moving back of me in the woods. A hawk floats in the clear blue sky above the valley.

When I drove over to this mountain camp this morning I saw a man plowing a hillside above the next valley to the South. He was a lean, ragged, hard-bitten mountain man, and he lived in a one-room cabin at the end of the field he was plowing. I have seen as many as nineteen children in one family in such a cabin. I have seen poverty that has made me halt. I have seen a thousand such cabins perched on hills in southwestern Virginia, Pennsylvania, West Virginia, Tennessee, north Georgia, Kentucky, and westward, across the Mississippi, in the Ozark

SOURCE: Sherwood Anderson, *Puzzled America* (New York, 1935), pp. 69–83.

mountains of the Missouri, and only two weeks ago, in the city of New York, I saw just such a cabin on the stage, in a play called *Tobacco Road.*

Tobacco Road, indeed! It is a road to ruin—this Poor White hillside farming going on year after year, over millions of acres of the American hill country. As for the Poor White Georgia Cracker man of the Georgia plains, tied to his cotton and tobacco farming on poor exhausted soil, his story is a different one. We are in the hills now. This is the story of the hill man. The story here also one of wasted fine material. I know the mountain men, and when I am at home I live among them. The story of the lives they live, how they got like that, the death of the children of this fine stock by undernourishment—this is another tragic American story. How I have hated the romanticists who have thrown the cloud of romance about such lives.

But I am trying to tell now the story of the camp towns, of the CCC coming to these hills. They are scattered out over the country, hundreds, even thousands of such little temporary towns—the government putting them up. The houses of the towns are long one-story affairs built of thick building paper. They stand up high and dry above the valley bottoms on stone foundations.

There is a commissary building, a mess hall, a post office, a library, a temporary hospital. They are all temporary houses.

Suppose they shouldn't be temporary. Suppose what is going on here is but a beginning. It is an interesting idea that this thing that has now begun in America—government having a thought of the land, men in Washington, in government, daring to say—"We'll begin trying it."

Trying what?

Suppose it should come down to this, that there is a plot on foot in America—men actually serious about it—a plot, let's say, to save America from the Americans.

Actually they are serious about the plot, some of them. I have been in Washington—talked to men there, men who struck me as first-rate, serious-minded men—not at all romantic. I do not mean bankers or industrialists. I mean men of another type—scientific men, government engineers, foresters, hard-working men, most of whom have been employed for years in the Interior and the Agricultural departments.

Much of what these men told me is, as they say in Washington now —"off the record." It is still, it seems, somewhat irregular even a little dangerous to have dreams of a greater America, an America really used. You can't call names.

"What, you dream of a physical America controlled, plowing of the land controlled—this or that section of America to be permanently in forest—river flow control, floods controlled at the flood source?"

"You say that one great flood—let us say of Mother Mississippi—may cost more than ten years' constructive work back in the hills, in denuded forests where floods begin?"

"This, off the record. Some one may think I am a Socialist or a Bolshevik."

Men's minds pushing, somewhat timidly, into a new social view of physical America. How are they to tell the story to that lean mountain man? Let us say that he owns his few poor hillside acres. Who is to tell him, "Thou shalt not"? The right to go on plowing, where plowing is sheer land destruction—the traditional right of the American individualist, big or little.

"It's mine."

"It's mine."

Who is to say to me, a free American, "Thou shalt not"?

Into this camp have come boys, the greater number of them from American cities. They are young boys, most of them about high school age. But for this depression, in the natural flow of an older American life—it seems suddenly old now—as things have been running in America for the last two, three or four generations these boys, being for the most part city and town boys, would have come out of school and would have become clerks or factory hands.

Or—and this would go for a lot of them—they would have become tough city guys—the kind that make bright young gangsters—the kind you see leaning against walls near gang hangouts in cities.

"How much to kill a man?"

"How much?"

But, you see, even the rackets have become a bit thin now, clerkships have fallen away, prohibition has gone, the factories are not exactly howling for men.

So these CCC camps have gathered them in, all kinds of men.

That forester down there, directing the boys as they lay sidewalks in their new woods town, was in Montana last year. He had under him out there some two or three hundred boys, mostly from the East Side of New York—tough birds—most of them, he says. He speaks of them with an affectionate grin. "Boy, what we had to do to them—what they did to us." They have been jerked up out of that environment, hauled in fast trains across two-thirds of the United States and thrown into a forest camp some seven thousand feet up in the magnificent hills. They had to build the camps, keep themselves clean, keep their bedding and their quarters clean, learn to swing an axe— "We had to watch them like babes that they did not kill each other with the axes." The boys learned to make beds, learned the necessary sanitary laws that must govern men living in camps, the give and take of man to man, so essential to life where men live, sleep, talk, dream in one great room— rows of cots all in the open—the door at the end of the room open— sight of the wooded hills when you go to sleep at night, when you wake in the morning—

These men, the greater majority of them out of the crowded factory towns.

"It's the beginning of some kind of revolution in life—for them at least."

"Sure."

Not every man can swing an axe. Some men born in the forests, never get the knack. There are Babe Ruths among axemen too.

It is a kind of revolution in many lives that goes both backward and forward. Forward, let's say, to a possible conception of an America that shall belong essentially to all Americans—as one thoughtful, serious-minded man, who felt he owed something to the ground under his feet, might feel toward one farm—such a man as might say to himself— "I want to leave this piece of ground, on which I have lived my life and made my living, a better piece of ground than it was when I came upon it." You get the idea—at least a dream of all American farmers saying "We'll live to build, not destroy."

Something of that sort.

Let's say, a new comprehensive forward look and then also, in this CCC thing something else—a kind of movement backward to an earlier American tone of life, when life did centre about the forests and the land, when men went out and fought it out with nature and got something men can get in no other way—a kind of man-making process that factory work and clerkships haven't as yet been able to bring into men's lives.

To use the land also to make men.

To use men also to make the land.

Who in America doesn't know what, over great stretches of country, we Americans have done to the land? Soil erosion going on that is costing us each year more than the entire cost of our military and naval establishments, and all of this due to the old belief that if I own a piece of land I have the right to do as I please with it. I can tear off the forest.

"It's mine, isn't it?"

The valley down which I look as I sit writing is one of a thousand such valleys in the range of mountains that stretch across our country from East to West, separating the North from the South. It is a stream-source country. This country with the great stretches of cut-over lands in northern Michigan, Wisconsin, and Minnesota is the stream source from which comes much of the water of the Mississippi. The valley down which I look is watered by one of the little rivers that come down from the hills. There might be fifty such streams in one county in this country. The natives tell me that all were formerly good trout and bass streams. They went softly along through the deep woods. They were icy cold even in summer. They were steady year-round streams, fed by mountain springs. The valley is broken by many little side valleys. It is like an old saw with many teeth broken out. In each little side valley may be found a few under-fed mountain families, persistently plowing hillside lands that will not and cannot make them a living.

These CCC camps are a beginning. If you look at the map you will see them scattered most thickly along the Pacific Coast, north at the headwaters of the Mississippi and in these border mountains between the North and South, and on the southern side of these hills where the streams go down to the Atlantic. There are camps now everywhere in these hills along the Southern Appalachian, the Cumberland, the Blue Ridge, and westward to the Mississippi and the Ozarks. They extend eastward to where, at Lynchburg, Virginia, the big hills end and the little ones step softly down to the Tidewater country.

It may well be that all of this land, except only the valley bottoms, should be wiped out as farming lands. Let the trees again have the hills. There should be better use for the life of these hill men, starving and destroying in these hills.

The hand of government is reaching out and out. The government is acquiring all the time more and more thousands of acres of these hill lands.

They are having classes in the camps. They are teaching geography and history. As the boys work in the forests, a forester goes with them. They are learning to tell the ash from the maple and the spruce from the oak. It is a tremendous educational experiment.

The greater number of the boys are city bred. They are from the families of the poor. They are young American born—Poles, Italians, Jews, Lithuanians, and Germans—the first generation away from the old country. They are short squat figures of American men in the making, with the twang of the city speech on their lips. Nearly all of the boys in this camp town are out of the back streets of Newark, Hoboken, Jersey City, and New York. "Where are you from, buddy?" I say to one of them.

"Oh, take a look. What do you t'ink?"

"I'm from Avenue A."

The mountain men who come into the camp, to work, or just to look, stand staring at the city boys. They laugh softly. Such awkward axe-swinging. Some of these mountain men have been axe-swingers since they were babes. Some of them, the older ones, worked in the lumber camps in these hills when the first forests, the great forests, were cut away. They tell you about it. First the great companies with the big band mills came, taking the best, and these were followed by the little peckerwood mills—often a model T Ford engine and a saw, cleaning up what the big ones left.

There was destruction and waste aplenty. Who cared? Individualism. The old America. "You should have seen it before they came," an old mountain man said. A kind of awe creeps into his voice. "The forest was like a great church. Oh, the great trees. You sank to your knees in the moss under foot."

I myself remember an old man who came to my father's house when I was a boy. He was an old, old man from an Ohio River town where my own father once lived and he talked to my father of the river. "I remember when I was a boy," he said. "I swam with other boys in the Ohio. It was a clear stream then. We used to swim way out and look down. The water was so clear we could see the bottom."

There is something still to be seen in this CCC movement. It isn't just an idea of giving a certain number of men work, helping them over the depression.

The leaves of the forest trees, even the young new trees, now growing, fall and lie on the ground. Next year more leaves fall. There is a soft porous bottom made. Moss begins to grow. It is a great blotter. Pinchot of Pennsylvania, when he was making his first fight against forest destruction, used to go before control committees with a wide board in his hand. He set the board on a table at an angle of forty-five degrees and poured a glass of water down it.

Then he took the same board and tacked blotting paper on it. Again he poured water down the board, but this time it did not rush off. That told the story. It is a thing the government can do and that the individual cannot do. There are these millions of acres of water-shed land, none of it any good for farming. It should go back into forests, making future wealth.

Rains come and wash the plowed lands away and every rain takes its toll of richness. You go through these hill lands in the spring and summer, seeing the hill men at the plow, often on lands so steep you wonder that the man and bony horse do not both roll to the bottom—

men slowly and painfully plowing, planting, and hoeing—then the rains—there the fields go.

It would not have mattered so much if it were only one field, a few fields plowed and lost, great gashes in the hillsides, water rushing down pell-mell, floods in the low lands, towns destroyed. There are still millions of such fields being plowed. The whole country pays.

Multiply it. Multiply it.

The forester comes up to me along the street of the camp. He sees me sitting and writing under the rhododendron bush and hesitates. "Hello," I say.

"I do not want to disturb you."

We grin at each other. "Come on," he says.

Putting my notebook into my pocket I go and get into his truck and we begin climbing up a mountain road. It's risky going. This is one of the new roads the city boys have made. It rained last night and the car slithers about. Up and up we go, far up into the hills and the car stops. We go on afoot. We go into the brush. Climbing over fallen logs, up and up. "I wanted to show you a tree they didn't get," he says, referring to the early lumber men. We stop before a great spruce far up in the hills. "They had to leave it," he says. "They couldn't get to it."

We are sitting now on a rocky promontory and looking way over the hills. From up here the smaller hills are like the waves of the sea in a storm. The man I am with is one of the believers. He talks and talks. He is sore at the lumberman who beat him into these forests.

"The government should never have let them do it," he keeps saying. "We should have had a chance. Our men should have been here." He declares that under the foresters the lumber companies might have taken as much lumber without denuding the hills. "They could have taken out all the good timber and left the half-grown trees that in another generation would have made a second great cutting."

Now it will take us fifty years to get back what was wantonly destroyed. He stands beside me on the mountain top swearing, but it is already an old story to me, this cry of the forester. Now they are in the woods again. They are directing the work of these boys in the CCC camps.

The depression has given them their chance. "Hurrah for the depression," one of them said to me. They are making a new kind of American man out of the city boy in the woods, and they are planning at least to begin to make a new land with the help of such boys.

31

The Joads Reach a Government Camp

IT was late when Tom Joad drove along a country road looking for the Weedpatch camp. There were few lights in the countryside. Only a sky glare behind showed the direction of Bakersfield. The truck jiggled slowly along and hunting cats left the road ahead of it. At a crossroad there was a little cluster of white wooden buildings.

Ma was sleeping in the seat and Pa had been silent and withdrawn for a long time.

Tom said, "I don' know where she is. Maybe we'll wait till daylight an' ast somebody." He stopped at a boulevard signal and another car stopped at the crossing. Tom leaned out. "Hey, mister. Know where the big camp is at?"

"Straight ahead."

Tom pulled across into the opposite road. A few hundred yards, and then he stopped. A high wire fence faced the road, and a wide-gated driveway turned in. A little way inside the gate there was a small house with a light in the window. Tom turned in. The whole truck leaped into the air and crashed down again.

"Jesus!" Tom said. "I didn' even see that hump."

A watchman stood up from the porch and walked to the car. He leaned on the side. "You hit her too fast," he said. "Next time you'll take if easy."

"What is it, for God's sake?"

The watchman laughed. "Well, a lot of kids play in here. You tell folks to go slow and they're liable to forget. But let 'em hit that hump once and they don't forget."

SOURCE: John Steinbeck, *The Grapes of Wrath* (New York, 1939), pp. 389–93.

"O! Yeah. Hope I didn' break nothin'. Say—you got any room here for us?"

"Got one camp. How many of you?"

Tom counted on his fingers. "Me an' Pa an' Ma, Al an' Rosasharn an' Uncle John an' Ruthie an' Winfiel'. Them last is kids."

"Well, I guess we can fix you. Got any camping stuff?"

"Got a big tarp an' beds."

The watchman stepped up on the running board. "Drive down the end of that line an' turn right. You'll be in Number Four Sanitary Unit."

"What's that?"

"Toilets and showers and wash tubs."

Ma demanded, "You got wash tubs—running water?"

"Sure."

"Oh! Praise God," said Ma.

Tom drove down the long dark row of tents. In the sanitary building a low light burned. "Pull in here," the watchman said. "It's a nice place. Folks that had it just moved out."

Tom stopped the car. "Right there?"

"Yeah. Now you let the others unload while I sign you up. Get to sleep. The camp committee'll call on you in the morning and get you fixed up."

Tom's eyes drew down. "Cops?" he asked.

The watchman laughed. "No cops. We got our own cops. Folks here elect their own cops. Come along."

Al dropped off the truck and walked around. "Gonna stay here?"

"Yeah," said Tom. "You an' Pa unload while I go to the office."

"Be kinda quiet," the watchman said. "They's a lot of folks sleeping."

Tom followed through the dark and climbed the office steps and entered a tiny room containing an old desk and a chair. The guard sat down at the desk and took out a form.

"Name?"

"Tom Joad."

"That your father?"

"Yeah."

"His name?"

"Tom Joad, too."

The questions went on. Where from, how long in the State, what work done. The watchman looked up. "I'm not nosy. We got to have this stuff."

"Sure," said Tom.

"Now—got any money?"

"Little bit."

"You ain't destitute?"

"Got a little. Why?"

"Well, the camp site costs a dollar a week, but you can work it out, carrying garbage, keeping the camp clean—stuff like that."

"We'll work it out," said Tom.

"You'll see the committee tomorrow. They'll show you how to use the camp and tell you the rules."

Tom said, "Say—what is this? What committee is this, anyways?"

The watchman settled himself back. "Works pretty nice. There's five sanitary units. Each one elects a Central Committee man. Now that committee makes the laws. What they say goes."

"S'pose they get tough," Tom said.

"Well, you can vote 'em out jus' as quick as you vote 'em in. They've done a fine job. Tell you what they did—you know the Holy Roller preachers all the time follow the people around, preachin' an' takin' up collections? Well, they wanted to preach in this camp. And a lot of the older folks wanted them. So it was up to the Central Committee. They went into meeting and here's how they fixed it. They say, 'Any preacher can preach in this camp. Nobody can take up a collection in this camp.' And it was kinda sad for the old folks, 'cause there hasn't been a preacher in since."

Tom laughed and then he asked, "You mean to say the fellas that runs the camp is jus' fellas—campin' here?"

"Sure. And it works."

"You said about cops—"

"Central Committee keeps order an' makes rules. Then there's the ladies. They'll call on your ma. They keep care of kids an' look after the sanitary units. If your ma isn't working, she'll look after kids for the ones that is working, an' when she gets a job—why, there'll be others. They sew, and a nurse comes out an' teaches 'em. All kinds of things like that."

"You mean to say they ain't no cops?"

"No, sir. No cop can come in here without a warrant."

"Well, s'pose a fella is jus' mean, or drunk an' quarrelsome. What then?"

The watchman stabbed the blotter with a pencil. "Well, the first time the Central Committee warns him. And the second time they really warn him. The third time they kick him out of the camp."

"God Almighty, I can't hardly believe it! Tonight the deputies an' them fellas with the little caps, they burned the camp out by the river."

"They don't get in here," the watchman said. "Some nights the boys patrol the fences, 'specially dance nights."

"Dance nights? Jesus Christ!"

"We got the best dances in the county every Saturday night."

"Well, for Christ's sake! Why ain't they more places like this?"

VI
THE ROOSEVELT COALITION

Forbes Field, scene of both Selections 32 and 33, was the home of the Pittsburgh Pirates; hence the baseball analogies that Roosevelt employs. The war metaphor the President uses in his speech appeared frequently in New Deal rhetoric. The "reactionary Democrats" Ickes mentions in Selection 34 were—besides Al Smith—James A. Reed, former senator from Missouri; John W. Davis, Democratic presidential candidate in 1924; and Bainbridge Colby, who had been Secretary of State under Woodrow Wilson. Ickes' last paragraph foreshadows the Supreme Court controversy of 1937, in which Stanley Reed was Solicitor General, Homer Cummings Attorney General, and Justice James Clark McReynolds Roosevelt's implacable foe on the Court. Samuel Lubell pioneered the kind of political reporting found in Selection 35, an early example of Lubell's writing.

32

FDR's Class Coalition

THE common people were not voting party labels in 1936 as religiously as before.

They were voting a man.

To me, the whole political story of the country was epitomized in the jubilant night meeting for President Roosevelt in the baseball park, Forbes Field, at Pittsburgh on an eastern campaign swing just before his triumphal tour of the West.

As I picked my way through the mad throng which filled the grandstand and the field an hour before the President was due to arrive, I saw a plump little old woman, nearly as broad as long, run cackling and screeching merrily through the crowd. She was just buoyant with animal spirits. All by herself she was having one magnificent time.

Crushed on her head, a bit onesided in a gesture of bravado, was a red, white and blue hat. It did not stand up properly and erect, like the other souvenir hats you spotted here and there in the jostling, merry crowd. (Across the front of the hats was a picture of the President.) It looked for all the world like the tricolored cockade which other women wore once so many years ago. Gaily and nonchalantly she dashed away and was lost in the crowd.

She was the crowd.

Before the President arrived, before the convoy of motor-cycle policemen put-putted slowly through a gate in the far corner of the park, before the deliverer appeared in his open car to wave his hat and set off a great burst of human joy and delirium that swept across the field and thundered back from the grandstand—they had their Danton, one of their own.

State Senator Warren R. Roberts he was, a stern-faced, square sort of fellow, who knew the common touch.

He gave them their enemies and they spat out their names—Andy

SOURCE: Thomas Stokes, *Chip Off My Shoulder* (Princeton, N.J., 1940), pp. 458–60.

Mellon (poor, poor Andy, he said, and they tittered); Textile Joe Grundy, Pew (the oil man), Rockefeller (the still bigger oil man).

"Boo" came the swelling chorus after each name to smite their champion pleasantly in the face. He smiled with grim satisfaction. (You could almost hear the swish of the guillotine blade as it fell.)

Then, cleverly, he began to set the poor off against the rich.

"The President," he said, "has decreed that your children shall enjoy equal opportunity with the sons of the rich." He spoke of "the smug complacence of pseudo-aristocracy." He recalled how the sons of the poor and the sons of the rich shared tins of bully beef, fought side by side, died together, in the World War. But since then, he said, something had happened.

A Mirabeau appeared in the handsome presence of their governor, George H. Earle, a son of wealth who had taken up the cause of the common people. He, too, gave them their enemies:

"There are the Mellons, who have grown fabulously wealthy from the toil of the men of iron and steel, the men whose brain and brawn have made this great city; Grundy, whose sweatshop operators have been the shame and disgrace of Pennsylvania for a generation; Pew, who strives to build a political and economic empire with himself as dictator; the duPonts, whose dollars were earned with the blood of American soldiers; Morgan, financier of war."

Between each name he was forced to pause as the crowd vented its scorn on its enemies, like the whine of the hurricane before it strikes. He stood, smiling and confident, enjoying the tempest he had produced. (Again, you could almost hear the swish of the guillotine blade as it fell.)

The mob was whipped into a frenzy ready for the deliverer.

He entered in an open car. It might have been the chariot of a Roman Emperor.

They drowned him with paeans of joy.

33

Roosevelt Explains
the Box Score

Mr. Chairman, Governor Earle, my friends of Pennsylvania:

A baseball park is a good place to talk about box scores. Tonight I am going to talk to you about the box score of the Government of the United States. I am going to tell you the story of our fight to beat down the depression and win recovery. From where I stand it looks as though the game is pretty well "in the bag."

I am convinced that when Government finance or any other kind of finance is honest, and when all the cards are on the table, there is no higher mathematics about it. It is just plain, scoreboard arithmetic.

When the present management of your team took charge in 1933, the national scoreboard looked pretty bad. In fact, it looked so much like a shut-out for the team that you voted a change of management in order to give the country a chance to win the game. And today we are winning it.

When the new management came to Washington, we began to make our plans—plans to meet the immediate crisis and plans that would carry the people of the country back to decent prosperity.

You and I and everybody else saw the millions out of work, saw the business concerns running in the red, saw the banks closing. Our national income had declined over 50 per cent—and, what was worse, it showed no prospect of recuperating by itself. By national income I mean the total of all income of all the 125,000,000 people in this country—the total of all the pay envelopes, all the farm sales, all the profits of all the businesses and all the individuals and corporations in America.

During the four lean years before this Administration took office, that

SOURCE: Samuel Rosenman (ed.), *The Public Papers and Addresses of Franklin D. Roosevelt*, V, 401–8.

national income had declined from eighty-one billions a year to thirty-eight billions a year. In short, you and I, all of us together, were making forty-three billions—spelled with a "b," not an "m"—forty-three billion dollars less in 1932 than we made in 1929.

Now, the rise and fall of national income—since they tell the story of how much you and I and everybody else are making—are an index of the rise and fall of national prosperity. They are also an index of the prosperity of your Government. The money to run the Government comes from taxes; and the tax revenue in turn depends for its size on the size of the national income. When the incomes and the values and transactions of the country are on the down-grade, then tax receipts go on the down-grade too. If the national income continues to decline, then the Government cannot run without going into the red. The only way to keep the Government out of the red is to keep the people out of the red. And so we had to balance the budget of the American people before we could balance the budget of the national Government.

That makes common sense, doesn't it?

The box score when the Democratic Administration came to bat in 1933 showed a net deficit in our national accounts of about $3,000,-000,000, accumulated in the three previous years under my predecessor.

National income was in a downward spiral. Federal Government revenues were in a downward spiral. To pile on vast new taxes would get us nowhere because values were going down—and that makes sense too.

On top of having to meet the ordinary expenses of Government, I recognized the obligation of the Federal Government to feed and take care of the growing army of homeless and destitute unemployed.

Something had to be done. A national choice had to be made. We could do one of two things. Some people who sat across my desk in those days urged me to let Nature take its course and to continue a policy of doing nothing. I rejected that advice because Nature was in an angry mood.

To have accepted that advice would have meant the continued wiping out of people of small means—the continued loss of their homes and farms and small businesses into the hands of people who still had enough capital left to pick up those homes and farms and businesses at bankruptcy prices. It would have meant, in a very short time, the loss of all the resources of a multitude of individuals and families and small corporations. You would have seen, throughout the Nation, a concentration of property ownership in the hands of one or two per cent of the population, a concentration unequaled in any great Nation since the days of the later Roman Empire.

And so the program of this Administration set out to protect the small business, the small corporation, the small shop, and the small individual from the wave of deflation that threatened them. We realized then, as we do now, that the vast army of small business men and factory owners and shop owners—together with our farmers and workers—form the backbone of the industrial life of America. In our long-range plan we recognized that the prosperity of America depended upon, and would continue to depend upon, the prosperity of them all.

I rejected the advice that was given to me to do nothing for an additional reason. I had promised, and my Administration was determined, to keep the people of the United States from starvation.

I refused to leave human needs solely in the hands of local communities—local communities which themselves were almost bankrupt.

To have accepted that advice would have been to offer bread-lines again to the American people, knowing this time, however, that in many places the lines would last far longer than the bread. In those dark days, between us and a balanced budget stood millions of needy Americans, denied the promise of a decent American life.

To balance our budget in 1933 or 1934 or 1935 would have been a crime against the American people. To do so we should either have had to make a capital levy that would have been confiscatory, or we should have had to set our face against human suffering with callous indifference. When Americans suffered, we refused to pass by on the other side. Humanity came first.

No one lightly lays a burden on the income of a Nation. But this vicious tightening circle of our declining national income simply had to be broken. The bankers and the industrialists of the Nation cried aloud that private business was powerless to break it. They turned, as they had a right to turn, to the Government. We accepted the final responsibility of Government, after all else had failed, to spend money when no one else had money left to spend.

I adopted, therefore, the other alternative. I cast aside a do-nothing or a wait-and-see policy.

As a first step in our program we had to stop the quick spiral of deflation and decline in the national income. Having stopped them, we went on to restore purchasing power, to raise values, to put people back to work, and to start the national income going up again.

In 1933 we reversed the policy of the previous Administration. For the first time since the depression you had a Congress and an Administration in Washington which had the courage to provide the necessary resources which private interests no longer had or no longer dared to risk.

This cost money. We knew, and you knew, in March, 1933, that it would cost money. We knew, and you knew, that it would cost money for several years to come.

The people understood that in 1933. They understood it in 1934, when they gave the Administration a full endorsement of its policy. They knew in 1935, and they know in 1936, that the plan is working.

All right, my friends, let us look at the cost. Since we could not get the money by taxes we borrowed it, and increased the public debt.

President Hoover's Administration increased the national debt in the net amount of over three billion dollars in three depression years, and there was little to show for it. My Administration has increased the national debt in the net amount of about eight billion dollars and there is much to show for it.

Put that figure of eight billions out here on the scoreboard, and let me tell you where the dollars went.

Over a billion and a half went for payment of the World War Veterans' Bonus this year instead of in 1945. That payment is now out of the way, and is no longer a future obligation of the Government.

As for the other six and a half billions of the deficit we did not just spend money; we spent it for something. America got something for what we spent—conservation of human resources through C.C.C. camps and through work relief; conservation of natural resources of water, soil and forest; billions for security and a better life. While many who criticize today were selling America short, we were investing in the future of America.

Contrast those expenditures and what we got for them with certain other expenditures of the American people in the years between 1920 and 1930. During that period not merely eight billions but many more billions came out of American pockets and were sent abroad—to foreign countries where the money was used for increasing foreign armaments, for building foreign factories to compete with us, for building foreign dwellings, swimming pools, and slaughter houses, for giving employment to the foreign unemployed—foreign boondoggling, if you will.

Those dollars, billions of them, were just as good American money— just as hard-earned—just as much the reward of our thrift—as the dollars we have spent during these three years at home giving work to the unemployed. Most of those dollars sent abroad are gone for good. Those billions, lost to us under previous Administrations, do not, by the way, include the other billions loaned by the United States to foreign Governments during and immediately after the War.

I ask you the simple question: Has it not been a sounder investment for us during these past three years to spend eight billion dollars for

American industry, American farms, American homes and the care of American citizens?

I have used the figure of eight billion dollars as representing the net increase in our national debt. Immediately people will rush into print or run to the microphone to tell you that my arithmetic is all wrong. They will tell you that the increase in the national debt is thirteen billions instead of eight. That is technically and morally just as correct as if someone were to try to scare you about the condition of your bank by telling you all about its liabilities and not telling you about its assets.

That is technically and morally just as correct as telling you good people here in Pennsylvania that none of your bank deposits or insurance policies is sound.

When you are told that the United States Treasury has thirteen billions more of liabilities than it had in 1933, you should also be told that it has six billion dollars of increased assets to set off against these liabilities.

In three years our net national debt has increased eight billions of dollars. But in two years of the recent war it increased as much as twenty-five billion dollars. National defense and the future of America were involved in 1917. National defense and the future of America were also involved in 1933. Don't you believe that the saving of America has been cheap at that price? It was more than defense—it was more than rescue. It was an investment in the future of America.

And, incidentally, tonight is an anniversary in the affairs of our Government which I wish to celebrate with you and the American people. It is October first, and it marks the end of a whole year in which there has been not a single national bank failure in all the United States. It has been fifty-five years since that kind of record has been established. You and I can take this occasion to rejoice in that record. It is proof that the program has worked.

Compare the scoreboard which you have in Pittsburgh now with the scoreboard which you had when I stood here at second base in this field four years ago. At that time, as I drove through these great valleys, I could see mile after mile of this greatest mill and factory area in the world, a dead panorama of silent black structures and smokeless stacks. I saw idleness and hunger instead of the whirl of machinery. Today as I came north from West Virginia, I saw mines operating, I found bustle and life, the hiss of steam, the ring of steel on steel—the roaring song of industry.

And now a word as to this foolish fear about the crushing load the debt will impose upon your children and mine. This debt is not going to be paid by oppressive taxation on future generations. It is not going to be paid by taking away the hard-won savings of the present generation.

It is going to be paid out of an increased national income and increased individual incomes produced by increasing national prosperity.

The deficit of the national Government has been steadily declining for three years running, although technically this year it did not decline, because we paid the Bonus this year instead of 1945. Without the Bonus the deficit would have declined this year also.

The truth is that we are doing better than we anticipated in 1933. The national income has gone up faster than we dared then to hope. Deficits have been less than we expected. Treasury receipts are increasing. The national debt today in relation to the national income is much less than it was in 1933, when this Administration took office.

The national income was thirty-eight billions in 1932. In 1935 it was fifty-three billions and this year it will be well over sixty billions. If it keeps on rising at the present rate, as I am confident that it will, the receipts of the Government, without imposing any additional taxes, will, within a year or two, be sufficient to care for all ordinary and relief expenses of the Government—in other words, to balance the budget.

The Government of this great Nation, solvent, sound in credit, is coming through a crisis as grave as war without having sacrificed American democracy or the ideals of American life.

34

Talk about campaign

A Complete Rout

Saturday, November 7, 1936

The campaign continued in high gear until the very end. Landon made a speech in New York at Madison Square Garden Thursday night, October 29, in which he challenged the President bluntly to state his position on a number of national issues and tell what he would do as to these matters if he should be re-elected. Then Landon started back, via St. Louis, for Topeka, Kansas, making speeches all along the way, with one particularly big meeting in St. Louis.

The President meanwhile was not idle. He coursed back and forth in eastern Pennsylvania, including Philadelphia, drawing tremendous crowds wherever he went. Then he made his last big speech at Madison Square Garden on Saturday night. This was a fine climax to his speaking campaign. He completely ignored the questions that had been asked of him by Governor Landon from the same platform two evenings earlier. An immense throng turned out for this meeting. From New York he went to Hyde Park. Both Landon and the President, as well as others, were on the air for a few last gasps on Monday night.

I have felt perfectly confident of the result for the past two months or more. I went to bed Monday night believing that New York, Ohio, and Illinois would certainly be for the President. Despite the fact that the President himself was uncertain about Indiana, I believed that, lying as it does between Ohio and Illinois, it would go the same as these other two states. I also believed that Pennsylvania would be carried by the President. I had my doubts about all of New England, except Connecticut. There, during the last few days it appeared that the President would win. I did not know much about Michigan or Iowa, but I was confident of Wisconsin and Minnesota and all of the western states generally, except South Dakota. I thought that Nebraska was safe, and I had a sneaking hope that the President would carry Kansas. However,

source: *The Secret Diary of Harold L. Ickes* (3 vols., New York, 1953–1954), I, 700–5.

this was nothing more than a hope. I also felt reasonably confident of West Virginia.

But, even believing as I did that the President would carry many more states than he needed in order to win, I was not prepared for the surprising results that came over the radio Tuesday night. I had been suffering from a severe attack of lumbago since Sunday afternoon, so that I was content to stay at home and listen to my own radio. It was soon clear that the President had not only won but that he had gone over by a tremendous popular and electoral college vote.

It is all over now, but even in retrospect the result is astonishing. Landon carried only two states—Maine and Vermont, with eight electoral votes between them. Although there are still some precincts missing, the President's popular majority is well over ten million. There has been nothing like it in the history of American politics. The Democrats gained Governors and Senators and Congressmen where already they had too many Congressmen and Senators and, with respect to some states, too many Governors. The President pulled through to victory men whose defeat would have been better for the country. It was a complete rout of the Republican party and the big financial interests that had hoped through that party to regain control of the Federal Government. . . .

To my view, the outstanding thing about the campaign was the lack of influence of the newspapers. With over eighty per cent of the newspapers of the country fighting Roosevelt, it is remarkable that he should have swept everything as he did. Cook County was an outstanding example. There, only the tabloid *Times* supported the President, with the *Tribune*, the *News*, and the Hearst papers in bitter opposition. Nevertheless, the President carried Cook County by over six hundred thousand votes, and he carried downstate Illinois as well. Never have the newspapers, in my recollection, conducted a more mendacious and venomous campaign against a candidate for President, and never have they been of so little influence. Apparently the people saw through the whole tissue of deceit and lies and misrepresentation. They sensed that the great financial interests which were backing Landon and pouring money into his campaign fund had some sinister purpose. In my judgment, they voted for the President because they believed that he had some interest in and concern for the welfare of the common man. The very bitterness of the assault upon the President by the newspapers reacted in his favor. . . .

The President seemed very happy yesterday. He talked a lot about the election and its implications. He spoke of the fact that he has now an absolutely free hand without the danger of being charged with hav-

ing broken campaign promises. As a matter of fact, the political situation, from his point of view, is quite fortunate. Reactionary Democrats,
like Al Smith, Jim Reed, John W. Davis, and Bainbridge Colby, have
definitely gone off a deep end. They certainly are through as Democrats,
and I do not see how they can hope to become leaders in the Republican party, notwithstanding the almost total lack of competent leadership in that party. . . .

At Cabinet meeting there was a good deal of discussion about the
Supreme Court. I think that the President is getting ready to move
in on that issue and I hope that he will do so. Solicitor General Reed,
who attended in the absence of the Attorney General, reported that
Mr. Justice Stone is ill. The President made the remark that he expected Mr. Justice McReynolds still to be on the bench when he was
a hundred and five years old. Reed replied laughingly that McReynolds
seemed to be in the best possible health. The President instructed Reed
to go ahead as rapidly as possible with the Government cases that are
pending, involving the constitutionality of New Deal legislation. He ex-
pects this legislation to be declared unconstitutional and evidently looks
to that as a background for an appeal to the people over the head of the
Court. I am keen myself that this question should be raised and I hope
to be able to take part in that fight, if and when it comes.

35

Politics of the Deed

MUCH more than the third-term tradition was shattered when
President Roosevelt took the oath of office again on Monday.

Who elected him? As in all elections, there were many crosscurrents,
but the 1940 answer is simple and inescapable.

The little fellow elected him, because there are more of the little
fellow and because he believed Mr. Roosevelt to be his friend and protec-
tor.

Roosevelt won by the vote of Labor, unorganized as well as organized,
plus that of the foreign born and their first and second generation de-
scendants. And the Negro.

It was a class-conscious vote for the first time in American history,
and the implications are portentous. The New Deal appears to have accomplished what the Socialists, the I.W.W. and the Communists never
could approach. It has drawn a class line across the face of American
politics. . . .

Mr. Roosevelt is the first President to owe his election in such great
measure to the teeming cities. On the farms and in the towns Mr.
Willkie more than held his own. It was in the industrial centers that
the Republican hopes were blacked out in factory smoke.

The Republican campaign had virtually no effect on this vote, the
evidence argues. I doubt that anything Willkie might have done would
have affected it. The election was not decided on the issues he debated,
but on forces long at work—economic status, nationalities, birth rates.
The rise of Government as an employer on a scale rivaling the biggest
business is a fourth. And the indications are that this vote might have
gone to Roosevelt for a fourth or a fifth term as readily as for a third. . . .

The New Deal has aimed at a bloodless revolution.

In 1940 it went a long way toward accomplishing it.

In the shadow of the Bunker Hill Monument, in historic Charles-

SOURCE: Samuel Lubell, "Post-Mortem: Who Elected Roosevelt?" *Saturday Evening Post*, CCXIII (1941), 9–11, 91–6.

town, Roosevelt rolled up a plurality of nearly four to one. . . . A typical Boston working-class district, Charlestown is not a slum. Poorer sections of the city went nine to one for Roosevelt. Prevailing incomes of Charlestown families range from $1200 to $1500; about one in five own their homes. Those who do are mighty proud of it. Good-sized metal plates proclaiming the owner's name are nailed to every door like family shields.

William J. Galvin, the thirty-six-year-old councilman and Democratic ward leader, has a simple explanation for the Roosevelt vote: "Probably no section in the country gained more under the New Deal." Galvin can check off the gains against the total ward population of 30,000: Hundreds got pay raises under the wage-hour law; more hundreds of seasonal workers are having slack months cushioned by unemployment-insurance benefits. The NYA is helping from 300 to 500 youths; at the worst of the depression thousands held WPA jobs; of 1500 persons past sixty-five in the ward, more than 600 receive old-age assistance; another 600 cases are on direct relief and get aid for dependent children. Charlestown is a food-stamp area; the WPA improved its bathing beach; a new low-cost housing project will relieve some of the ward's congestion.

Nearly one half of those of voting age are under forty. The economic memories of many of these voters begin with Hoover. Galvin's two younger brothers got out of high school during the depression and went into CCC camps. They now are working as electrician's and pipefitter's helpers in the near-by Boston Navy Yard, which has more than quadrupled its employment in recent months. Galvin has two other brothers, a lawyer and a school custodian; one of his brothers-in-law works as a planner in the navy yard and the others work as bookbinder, salesman and chauffeur. Of nine Galvin breadwinners, five rely on public employment. To the two younger brothers, the New Deal has meant advancement as real as any they could have got under a private employer.

To Charlestown's Irish, the New Deal has meant an advance along other fronts too. They are the sons and daughters, the grandsons and granddaughters of the immigrants who swarmed into Boston in the last quarter of the nineteenth century. Then the "Yankee vote" ruled Massachusetts. Classified-job advertisements carried notices, "No Irish need apply."

But the immigrant Irish reared larger families than the Yankees. Through sheer numbers, they toppled the barriers in profession after profession. By the 20's they had acquired local political dominance. Being Democrats under Republican Presidents, though, they were denied Federal recognition until Roosevelt.

Reporters in the Boston Federal Building cannot recall a single Irishman on the U. S. district court before 1933. Roosevelt has made two appointments to that court, the names, Sweeney and Ford. Postmaster Peter Tague, who lives in Charlestown, is Irish, as are the collector of customs, the U. S. marshal, several assistant U. S. attorneys. In Charlestown alone, Galvin estimates, Irishmen have got more than 400 Federal jobs under the New Deal. Not only for the poor but for those better off economically, Roosevelt has become the champion of the Irish climb up the American ladder. . . .

Even more so than with the Irish in Boston, Roosevelt, to [Detroit] auto workers, is the "friend" who gave them recognition. The New Deal enabled them to build their union. It taught them the strength of their numbers, and with the feeling of power has come a growing class-consciousness. The workers themselves use the phrase. "I'm franker than you," one local official replied when I asked him why he voted for Roosevelt. "I'll say it, even though it doesn't sound nice. We've grown class-conscious."

A Catholic priest in the precinct confessed, "If I ever attacked Roosevelt from the pulpit, it would be the end of me here.". . .

Other unions went down the line for the President with perhaps less bitterness, but no less efficiency. In Cleveland, heavily industrialized, heavily unionized, Roosevelt swept every ward. His city-wide majority was better than two to one, his plurality 150,000. Alexander F. Whitney, of the Railroad Brotherhoods, boasted, "You can go through all Cleveland and I'll bet you won't find a railroad man who voted against Roosevelt."

Many Brotherhood members live in the Collinwood section near the New York Central yards and roundhouse. In economic status, Collinwood ranks just above average for Cleveland. It consists chiefly of one-family frame houses worth around $5000, with garages in the rear, trees along the sidewalk, and lawn space in front. Through seniority ratings, the older Brotherhood men work steadily; their incomes run between $2000 and $3500 a year.

They remember Hoover as imposing a 10 per cent wage cut; Roosevelt for not only restoring that cut but adding a wage increase, and for the Railroad Retirement Act. Since the railroads have not been hiring young men until recently, these railway workers tend to fall into older age groups. Many are working to clear the mortgages off their homes, so that they will be able to retire on pensions in a few years. In one block, six railroad men have bought homes since 1936. . . .

As in every city sampled, Minneapolis' vote broke primarily along economic lines. In the seven lowest-income wards, with rentals averaging under thirty dollars a month, Roosevelt won by better than two and a half to one. In the four wards with rentals from thirty to forty dollars a month, it was Roosevelt by seven to six. In the three wards where the rental average topped forty dollars, Willkie won by five to three. Roosevelt managed to squeeze through in one of these three wards by 8251 to 8066. In the highest-income ward, Willkie's margin fell just under three to one. . . .

How great has been the impact of this urban revolt upon the traditional Republican line-up can be seen in the Negro vote. Only in St. Louis, which continues to draw them from the South, do the Negroes still seem divided in their allegiances between the party of Lincoln and the party of Roosevelt. Harlem's Seventeenth Assembly District went better than seven to one for the New Deal.

Probably 50 per cent of Harlem's Negroes are getting relief of some kind. Older Negroes—they're most likely to be Republican—shake their graying heads ruefully and mutter, "Our people are selling their birthrights for a mess of pottage."

To the younger Negroes the WPA and relief mean not only material aid but a guaranty that no longer must they work at any salary given them, that they are entitled—they emphasize the word—to a living wage. Through the WPA, Harlem's Negroes have had opened to them white-collar opportunities which before had been shut, such as the music and art and writers' projects. Negroes, too, remember that Mrs. Roosevelt visited Harlem personally, that President Roosevelt has appointed more Negroes to administrative positions paying around $5000 a year than any President before him. Each time Roosevelt makes such an appointment, the Amsterdam News, Harlem's leading newspaper, headlines it in 72-point type. Every young Negro gets a vicarious thrill thinking, "There may be a chance up there for me."

Harlem definitely has grown class as well as race conscious. Last year the Seventeenth for the first time got a Negro installed as Democratic leader of the district. Under the warming hand of the great white father in Washington a flock of unions has sprung up. They include garment workers, janitors, bartenders, waitresses, waiters, Pullman porters, laundry workers, newspapermen, retail clerks and redcaps.

Consumer and tenant leagues have arisen to battle with Harlem's disgraceful housing problem. All sorts of groups are pressing campaigns to force neighborhood stores, once manned entirely by whites, to hire Negroes. Initiated after a race riot a few years ago, the drive has met with astonishing success.

Today, Negroes work in hundreds of establishments as behind-the-counter salesmen, as movie cashiers, as meat cutters, as salesgirls in department stores. Some labor groups hold daily classes to teach Negroes selling, typing and stenography. This is done so that the unions will be able to rebuff employers who protest, "I can't hire Negroes; they're not experienced." The proportion of Negro-owned stores is growing.

Whether or not Roosevelt is responsible, he gets the credit. In many a Harlem home hangs a rotogravure photograph of the new emancipator; some families have spent fifty cents to have it framed.

A young police reporter on the News summed it up when he remarked, "Negroes feel Roosevelt started something."

"Something" certainly has been started. In 1932 Roosevelt became President in a popular recoil against the depression. His third-term victory, however, is the result of an upsurging of the urban masses. In the New Deal they have found their leveling philosophy; under it they have been given recognition through patronage, benefits and new opportunities; they have been awakened to the consciousness of the power of their numbers.

From the GOP viewpoint, the harshest fact this post-mortem reveals is that the Republicans are on the wrong side of the birth rate, not so much the current rate as the birth rates of 1890, 1900, 1910 and 1920, which are beyond their rectifying. Grade-school enrollments have begun to fall, but not high-school enrollments as yet. For another two or three presidential elections the elements which re-elected Roosevelt will continue to grow in voting strength, actually and relatively.

Thus far, these elements are united behind Roosevelt personally. Can the Democratic Party hold them, apart from Roosevelt? If it can, then it may become the normal majority party, with the Republicans occupying the unenviable position of the Democrats after the Civil War.

VII
THUNDER ON THE LEFT

Selection 36 refers to William Woodin, Roosevelt's first Secretary of the Treasury, and to Harold Ickes, who, in addition to being Secretary of the Interior, served as Administrator of the Public Works Administration (PWA). Langston Hughes, author of Selection 37, emerged from the Harlem Renaissance of the 1920's to play an active role in the social protest movement of the 1930's. Lincoln Steffens' letter in Selection 38 represents an attack not only on the two major parties but on the EPIC (End Poverty in California) movement of the novelist Upton Sinclair, who won the Democratic nomination for governor in California in 1934. Later in the 1930's, John Dewey, who states his response to communism in Selection 39, would head the "Dewey Commission" which would conclude that Moscow had falsely charged Leon Trotsky with being a counter-revolutionary. Huey Long, who in Selection 40 fantasies his victory in 1936, did not live to see that campaign; he was assassinated in September 1935. His "cabinet" includes William E. Borah, independent Republican senator from Idaho; James Couzens, a pro-New Deal Republican senator from Michigan; Smedley Butler, a retired major general of the Marines who stirred up a tempest in 1933 by charging that he had been approached by financial interests to lead a fascist movement; Major General Lytle Brown, who had served as chief of Army Engineers; and Edward Keating, a former Colorado congressman who edited the railway brotherhood newspaper, Labor. Among the magnates named to his National Share Our Wealth Committee, Pierre du Pont, a founder of the arch-conservative American Liberty League, was an especially droll choice. Long derived his sobriquet of "Kingfish" from a character in the radio serial, Amos 'n' Andy. Selection 41 comes from a unique document. Since detailed proceedings of cabinet meetings have not been kept, historians have no records of actual verbal exchanges between a President and his aides. In November 1933, however, Roosevelt created the National Emergency Council, a coordinating agency whose spontaneous exchanges were transcribed, word by word. Among those present at this White House session on February 5, 1935, were Secretary of State Cordell Hull, Vice President John Nance Garner, and Joseph P. Kennedy, chairman of the Securities and Exchange Commission. In Selection 42, Coughlin denounces "the immoral Tugwellism of destruction." Typically, opponents of the Administration lashed out less at the President than at the men around him and Rexford G. Tugwell, the most conspicuous of the New Deal planners, was a favorite whipping boy for both right and left.

36

The Failure of
Liberal Democracy

THE economic consequences of the New Deal have been exactly what might have been foreseen by a competent Brain Trust. Capitalist recovery, on the classic lines of laissez-faire, has not only been impeded but arrested. And its only economic alternative, social planning on socialist lines, has been sedulously avoided.

The New Deal is trying to right the unbalance of our economic life by strengthening all its contradictions. For Big Ownership it tries to safeguard profits and to keep intact the instruments of its financial domination. For the middle classes it tries to safeguard their small investments, which only serves to reintrench Big Ownership. For labor it tries to raise wages, increase employment, and assure some minimum of economic safety, while at the same time it opposes labor's real interests through its scarcity program. In trying to move in every direction at once the New Deal betrays the fact that it has no policy.

And it has no policy because as a liberal democracy it must ignore the overwhelming fact of our epoch, the irreconcilable conflict between capital and labor. The result is that we are today neither an economy of balanced scarcity, nor an economy of progressive abundance, nor in transit from one to the other. We are today in an economy of stalemate.

During the last year of Mr. Hoover's régime this country was in a state of complete economic disintegration. There was no confidence, there was no hope. Our business structure was collapsing all about us. Finally the banks closed.

When Mr. Roosevelt took office confidence surged back. During its

SOURCE: Benjamin Stolberg and Warren Jay Vinton, The Economic Consequences of the New Deal (New York, 1935), pp. 81–5.

first few months the New Deal staged an inflationary boom. As soon as the bankers returned from their Holiday, Mr. Woodin, then Secretary of the Treasury, sold the public on the idea that the very same credit structure which had collapsed two weeks before had miraculously become sound again. The Administration announced that prices were going to rise, and invited the public to buy while the buying was good. We went off the gold standard, the dollar went down, prices went up, and the public started to buy. Retailers replenished their stocks. Manufacturers laid in raw materials and began to produce in a hurry before the Blue Eagle could "crack down" on them.

As a result the index of business activity was pumped up in four months from 58 in March, 1933, to 89 in July. There it was punctured abruptly and business activity fell off as rapidly as it had risen. By November it was down to 68. During the first five months of 1934 there was a slow improvement, but by June the increased margins of profits and higher prices of the N.R.A., applied to our anemic purchasing power, began to show their inevitable effects. Business fell off again, and by October, 1934, it was back to 70.

Of course business conditions are somewhat better than they were in the moribund year of 1932. But since June, 1933, there has been no forward progress. Indeed, there has been regression. In October, 1934, which is the last month for which we have available figures, business activity was 2.6 per cent less than a twelvemonth before. Industrial production had declined 6.4 per cent. The steel, lumber, automobile, and textile industries were all less active. Freight car loadings, a sound index of distribution, were 6.1 per cent less. Building construction, measured by value of contracts awarded, was 6.7 per cent lower, despite the heroic efforts of Mr. Ickes to stimulate public works.

When production dropped labor's position naturally worsened. During the same period—from October, 1933, to October, 1934—unemployment increased by 5.4 per cent, while the real weekly wages of industrial workers who still had jobs decreased 2.0 per cent. The number of those on relief increased 33 per cent and the cost of relief almost doubled.

Yet Big Business, with the aid of the N.R.A., has been extracting greatly enlarged profits from our stricken society. Our great industrial corporations increased their profits during the first nine months of 1934 by 76 per cent as against the same period in 1933. According to the New York Times, "the chemical companies reported a 45 per cent increase; the mines and metals group, 360 per cent; office equipment, 157 per cent; and tobacco, 166 per cent." And dividends rose 17 per cent in the twelve months ending October, 1934.

When profits rise while wages lag it means but one thing. It means that behind the vivid confusion of the New Deal, the redistribution of the national income is stealthily and fatally progressing upwards, and that the power of Big Ownership is steadily enlarging. And unless the government succeeds in reversing this disastrous process, Big Ownership is bound to intensify the crisis in the long run.

There is nothing the New Deal has so far done that could not have been done better by an earthquake. A first-rate earthquake, from coast to coast, could have reestablished scarcity much more effectively, and put all the survivors to work for the greater glory of Big Business—with far more speed and far less noise than the New Deal.

37

Ballad of Roosevelt

The pot was empty,
The cupboard was bare.
I said, Papa,
What's the matter here?
    I'm waitin' on Roosevelt, son,
    Roosevelt, Roosevelt,
    Waitin' on Roosevelt, son.

The rent was due,
And the lights was out.
I said, Tell me, Mama,
What's it all about?
    We're waitin' on Roosevelt, son,
    Roosevelt, Roosevelt,
    Just waitin' on Roosevelt.

Sister got sick
And the doctor wouldn't come
Cause we couldn't pay him
The proper sum—
    A-waitin' on Roosevelt,
    Roosevelt, Roosevelt,
    A-waitin' on Roosevelt.

Then one day
They put us out o' the house.
Ma and Pa was
Meek as a mouse
    Still waitin' on Roosevelt,
    Roosevelt, Roosevelt.

SOURCE: Langston Hughes, "Ballad of Roosevelt," *New Republic*, LXXXI (Nov. 14, 1934), 9.

But when they felt those
Cold winds blow
And didn't have no
Place to go
    Pa said, I'm tired
    O'waitin' on Roosevelt,
    Roosevelt, Roosevelt.
    Damn tired o' waitin' on Roosevelt.

I can't git a job
And I can't git no grub.
Backbone and navel's
Doin' the belly-rub—
    A-waitin' on Roosevelt,
    Roosevelt, Roosevelt.

And a lot o' other folks
What's hungry and cold
Done stopped believin'
What they been told
    By Roosevelt,
    Roosevelt, Roosevelt—

Cause the pot's still empty,
And the cupboard's still bare,
And you can't build a bungalow
Out o' air—
    Mr. Roosevelt, listen!
    What's the matter here?

38

A Muckraker's Proclamation

To Sam Darcy,
Nominee of the Communist Party for Governor of California
Chairman of the Communist Party Rally
San Francisco, California.

The Getaway,
Carmel, Cal. [*1934*]

Comrades:

All my long life—too long—I have been following the stink of the trail of our so-called political corruption back up from the bad politics we deplored to the good business that bought and owns our bad government: to its war and its peace; to our riches, to our poverty, vice, to our college-bred ignorance on down to the world-wide collapse from within of the whole stupid, crooked, mean economic system that we call civilization today. When the panic came in 1929, I struck the trail again to see and listen to some of the big bosses of this big business, the men who had jeered at us muckrakers and—I found that they did not know what had happened to them and us, they did not know what was wrong, what to do about it! They DID not know, they DO not know. Our rulers and masters do not understand the machinery of their business or of our civilization; nor what to do about it; and our schools and colleges—our culture does not know what else to do than to go on and rise and collapse again, and again, and again.

And they want you and me to be patient—they in their comfortable riches, want you and me in our distress to stand still and take poverty and wretchedness on the chin—

Now, all this lifetime of mine when they jeered at me and my colleagues of the muckrake—these makers of the muck in high jest bade me report to them if I came to the end of my trail when, if ever, I found a cause and a cure for us and for them and our evils— And I promised

SOURCE: Ella Winter and Granville Hicks (eds.), *The Letters of Lincoln Steffens* (2 vols., New York, 1938), II, 1050–1.

many of them and myself that when that day came I would indeed—report.

Well, that day has come.

I can come down to earth, here, on this carefully chosen spot—before this crowd of willing listeners, to the only crowd that *must act*—I can come here and point out to you and to them and to all my fellow-American citizens a scientific cure for all our troubles.

It is Communism. For these United States. I mean *especially* for this great and successful country, at this very time of its distress and confusion, now, when we are shocked to discover that in our dumb blindness we have hit upon machinery and methods by which we can produce so much food, shelter and clothing, that we cannot distribute our abundance at a private profit— Now here, where seventeen million hungry people are creating a fierce demand for all we can produce and more —exactly for America, the American Communist Party proposes a program which meets all our social problems—*all*—graft, ignorance, poverty and over-production, vice and an impending war—exactly.

Communism can solve our problem. Communism does solve our problem—in Soviet Russia— That's my muckraker's proclamation; that the American Communist Party program meets our American capitalist situation precisely and it is the only American party that meets it—head on: all of it: the political corruption, the poverty and plenty, the periodic depressions of business—all our troubles; and proposes to solve them at any cost. The Communist Party offers to do that in California, in the United States; it offered to do it in Germany and it has done it in Soviet Russia, where you can go and see—as I have—where anyone can go and see our horrid old uncivilized economic system lying upside down on its back out on the steppes with its rusty wheels in the air.

There, before our eyes, our searching, unbelieving eyes, there, a leading part of the human race has done the job, brown, that we still have to do. And need to do, and must do. We cannot do it as Upton Sinclair proposes. We cannot any of us go out "as one good man for governor" and do it individually. We must do it as the American Communist Party, taught, fortunately, by the Russian pioneers, proposes to do it, by the building of a trained, highly-disciplined party, all of whose members —*all*—want—at any cost—to do the same one, agreed-upon, fundamental thing.

[Lincoln Steffens]

39

Why I Am Not a Communist

. . . I write with reference to being a Communist in the Western world, especially here and now in the United States, and a Communist after the pattern set in the U.S.S.R.

1. *Such* Communism rests upon an almost entire neglect of the specific historical backgrounds and traditions which have operated to shape the patterns of thought and action in America. The autocratic background of the Russian Church and State, the fact that every progressive movement in Russia had its origin in some foreign source and has been imposed from above upon the Russian people, explain much about the form Communism has taken in that country. It is therefore nothing short of fantastic to transfer the ideology of Russian Communism to a country which is so profoundly different in its economic, political, and cultural history. Were this fact acknowledged by Communists and reflected in their daily activities and general program, were it admitted that many of the practical and theoretical features of Russian Communism (like belief in the plenary and verbal inspiration of Marx, the implicit or explicit domination of the Communist party in every field of culture, the ruthless extermination of minority opinion in its own ranks, the verbal glorification of the mass and the actual cult of the infallibility of leadership) are due to local causes, the character of Communism in other countries might undergo a radical change. But it is extremely unlikely that this will take place. For official Communism has made the practical traits of the dictatorship of the proletariat and over the proletariat, the suppression of the civil liberties of all non-proletarian elements as well as of dissenting proletarian minorities, integral parts of the standard Communist faith and dogma. It has imposed and not argued the theory of dialectic materialism (which in the U.S.S.R. itself has to undergo frequent restatement in accordance with the exigencies of party factional controversy) upon all its followers. Its cultural phi-

SOURCE: John Dewey, "Why I Am Not a Communist," *The Modern Monthly*, VIII (1934), 135-7.

losophy, which has many commendable features, is vitiated by the absurd attempt to make a single and uniform entity out of the "proletariat."

2. Particularly unacceptable to me in the ideology of official Communism is its monistic and one-way philosophy of history. This is akin to the point made above. The thesis that all societies must exhibit a uniform, even if uneven, social development from primitive communism to slavery, from slavery to feudalism, from feudalism to capitalism, and from capitalism to socialism, and that the transition from capitalism to socialism must be achieved by the same way in all countries, can be accepted only by those who are either ignorant of history or who are so steeped in dogma that they cannot look at a fact without changing it to suit their special purposes. From this monistic philosophy of history, there follows a uniform political practice and a uniform theory of revolutionary strategy and tactics. But where differences in historic background, national psychology, religious profession and practice are taken into account—and they must be considered in every scientific theory— there will be corresponding differences in political methods, differences that may extend to general policies as well as to the strategy of their execution. For example, as far as the historic experience of America is concerned, two things among many others are overlooked by official Communists whose philosophy has been projected on the basis of special European conditions. We in the United States have no background of a dominant and overshadowing feudalism. Our troubles flow from the oppressive exercise of power by financial over-lords and from the failure to introduce new forms of democratic control in industry and government consonant with the shift from individual to corporate economy. It is a possibility overlooked by official Communists that important social changes in the direction of democratization of industry may be accomplished by groups working with the working-class although, strictly speaking, not of them. The other point ignored by the Communists is our deeply-rooted belief in the importance of individuality, a belief that is almost absent in the Oriental world from which Russia has drawn so much. Not to see that this attitude, so engrained in our habitual ways of thought and action, demands a very different set of policies and methods from those embodied in official Communism, verges to my mind on political insanity.

3. While I recognize the existence of class-conflicts as one of the fundamental facts of social life to-day, I am profoundly skeptical of class war as the means by which such conflicts can be eliminated and genuine social advance made. And yet this is a basic point in Communist theory and is more and more identified with the meaning of dialectic

materialism as applied to the social process. Historically speaking, it may have been necessary for Russia in order to achieve peace for her war-weary soldiers, and land for her hungry peasants, to convert incipient class-war into open civil war culminating in the so-called dictatorship of the proletariat. But nonetheless Fascism in Germany and Italy cannot be understood except with reference to the lesson those countries learned from the U.S.S.R. How Communism can continue to advocate the kind of economic change it desires by means of civil war, armed insurrection and iron dictatorship in face of what has happened in Italy and Germany I cannot at all understand. Reliable observers have contended that the communist ideology of dictatorship and violence together with the belief that the communist party was the foreign arm of a foreign power constituted one of the factors which aided the growth of Fascism in Germany. I am firmly convinced that imminent civil war, or even the overt threat of such a war, in any western nation, will bring Fascism with its terrible engines of repression to power. Communism, then, with its doctrine of the necessity of the forcible overthrow of the state by armed insurrection, with its doctrine of the dictatorship of the proletariat, with its threats to exclude all other classes from civil rights, to smash their political parties, and to deprive them of the rights of freedom of speech, press and assembly—which Communists now claim for themselves under capitalism—Communism is itself, an unwitting, but nonetheless, powerful factor in bringing about Fascism. As an unalterable opponent of Fascism in every form, I cannot be a Communist.

4. It is not irrelevant to add that one of the reasons I am not a Communist is that the emotional tone and methods of discussion and dispute which seem to accompany Communism at present are extremely repugnant to me. Fair-play, elementary honesty in the representation of facts and especially of the opinions of others, are something more than "bourgeois virtues." They are traits that have been won only after long struggle. They are not deep-seated in human nature even now—witness the methods that brought Hitlerism to power. The systematic, persistent and seemingly intentional disregard of these things by Communist spokesmen in speech and press, the hysteria of their denunciations, their attempts at character assassination of their opponents, their misrepresentation of the views of the "liberals" to whom they also appeal for aid in their defense campaigns, their policy of "rule or ruin" in their so-called united front activities, their apparent conviction that what they take to be the end justifies the use of any means if only those means promise to be successful—all these, in my judgment, are fatal to the very end which official Communists profess to have at heart. And if I read the temper of the American people aright, especially so in this country.

5. A revolution effected solely or chiefly by violence can in a modernized society like our own result only in chaos. Not only would civilization be destroyed but the things necessary for bare life. There are some, I am sure, now holding and preaching Communism who would be the first to react against it, if in this country Communism were much more than a weak protest or an avocation of literary men. Few communists are really aware of the far-reaching implications of the doctrine that civil war is the *only* method by which revolutionary economic and political changes can be brought about. A comparatively simple social structure, such as that which Russia had, may be able to recover from the effects of violent, internal disturbance. And Russia, it must be remembered, had the weakest middle class of any major nation. Were a large scale revolution to break out in highly industrialized America, where the middle class is stronger, more militant and better prepared than anywhere else in the world, it would either be abortive, drowned in a blood bath, or if it were victorious, would win only a Pyrrhic victory. The two sides would destroy the country and each other. For this reason, too, I am not a Communist.

I have been considering the position, as I understand it, of the orthodox and official Communism. I cannot blind myself, however, to the perceptible difference between communism with a small c, and Communism, official Communism, spelt with a capital letter.

40

Huey Long's "First Days in the White House"

IT had happened. The people had endorsed my plan for the redistribution of wealth and I was President of the United States. I had just sworn upon the Bible from which my father read to us as children to uphold the Constitution and to defend my country against all enemies, foreign and domestic.

Yet standing there on the flag-draped platform erected above the East portico of the Capitol, delivering my inaugural address, it all seemed unreal. I felt that I was dreaming. The great campaign which was destined to save America from Communism and Fascism was history. Other politicians had promised to re-make America; I had promised to sustain it. . . .

As my eyes swept the throng before me, I paused in my inaugural address and looked into the face of the retiring president. He seemed worn and tired. He wore the same expression of resigned fatigue that I had observed in the face of President Hoover on Inauguration Day in 1933 when Mr. Roosevelt declared so confidently that: "The only thing we have to fear is fear itself."

And with all humility, fully conscious of the solemnity of the promise I was making, I laid aside my prepared speech and closed my inaugural address extemporaneously with these words:

I promise life to the guaranties of our immortal document, the Declaration of Independence, which has decreed that all shall be born equal, and by this I mean that children shall not come into this life burdened with debt, but on the contrary, shall inherit the right to life, liberty and such education and training as qualifies them and equips them to take their proper rank in the pursuance

SOURCE: Huey Pierce Long, My First Days in the White House (Harrisburg, Pa., 1935), pp. 3–11, 18–20, 88–90.

of the occupation and vocation wherein they are worth most to themselves and to this country. And now I must be about my work.

The former president arose and seized my hands. He shouted something in my ear but his words were drowned by the roar from the crowd.

I left the platform immediately. The secret service men hurried me into an open car. On the twelve-minute ride to the White House we went down historic Pennsylvania Avenue, where hundreds of thousands of people lined the curb. When I reached the White House, into which so many Presidents had entered in confusion and from which they had departed in bewilderment, I sensed anew the tremendous responsibilities I had assumed as President of the United States.

My family and intimate friends soon arrived from the Capitol. We ate lunch, and then went out to the sheltered grandstand on the Avenue in front of the White House to review the inaugural parade. Two hours later, as the parade ended, I went to the executive offices of the White House, and there sought seclusion.

I was alone. The mass of tasks confronting me was bewildering. I was aware that I would have to disengage myself from the detailed functions of administering the government. I decided to delegate authority to hands not only wholly competent, but generally recognized to be honest and courageous as well.

Installed as the Chief Executive of the United States, and officially acting as such, I drafted a message to the Senate of the United States, as follows:

To the Senate of the United States:

I have the honor to nominate, and by and with your consent will appoint the following members of my cabinet, viz:—

For Secretary of State: William E. Borah of Idaho.
For Secretary of the Treasury: James Couzens of Michigan.
For Secretary of War: Smedley D. Butler of Pennsylvania.
For Secretary of the Navy: Franklin D. Roosevelt of New York.
For Secretary of the Interior: Major General Lytle Brown of Tennessee.
For Secretary of Commerce: Herbert Hoover of California.
For Attorney General: Frank Murphy of Michigan.
For Secretary of Labor: Edward Keating of Colorado. . . .

Soon after I had sent the cabinet names to the Senate, my secretary informed me that Mr. Hoover was trying to get me on the telephone from Palo Alto, California. I had the call transferred to my study and after I had identified myself I heard the voice of that Quaker gentleman say:

"Er-r-r-r, Mr. President—er-r-r, this is Hoover. Is it true that you have tendered me the position of Secretary of Commerce?"

I said I had sent his name to the Senate.

"But, Mr. President, I should have been consulted," the former President said. "This has placed me in a very embarrassing position."

"In what way, Mr. Hoover?" I inquired.

"Why, I am a former President of the United States, and it's a terrible step down for me to be asked to serve in your cabinet," he replied.

"Now let me put you straight," I said. "You say you are being embarrassed because, as a former President of the United States, it would be a step down for you to serve as a cabinet officer under another President. Just what is your position in public life today, Mr. Hoover?"

He hesitated and then:

"Well, suppose I decline any appointment upon the ground that I do not care to be associated with you?" came the now steady tones of the Quaker gentleman.

"All right, Mr. Hoover," I replied. "That is something for you to decide in your own conscience. I shall not attempt to influence you. It is something between you and the American people. You will have to explain to them why you will not serve your country again in its hour of need."

Mr. Hoover's voice lost its angry tone.

"All right, Mr. President," he replied. "I will consider it.". . .

I had been told that former President Franklin D. Roosevelt would leave after the inaugural ceremonies to take a rest on an estate just outside Washington. Some minutes after ten o'clock that night I was called to the telephone.

I heard a voice:

"Hello, Kingfish!"

It was Franklin D. Roosevelt. The last time he called me by that title was in greeting me in a telephone conversation the day before he was nominated for the Presidency by the Democratic convention at Chicago in 1932.

"Yes, Mr. President," I answered.

"What in the world do you mean by offering me a cabinet post, after all the things you have said about me as President?" he demanded.

"I only offered you a position which I thought you were qualified to fill."

"Well, I thank you for the gesture, Huey, but I can't feel that you have complimented me very much."

"Why not, Frank?"

"Well, it's a terrible fall from the Presidency to the Secretaryship of the Navy," he replied.

"You sound just like Hoover," I said, "but he couldn't call to mind any position he held just now."

"Well, Huey, I'll have to give this more consideration," the former President told me. "I had a statement all prepared here, declining, but I'll destroy it. Say, suppose I accept and fail to become the best Secretary? What's the penalty then?"

"In that case," I replied, "people will hold me responsible, and they may punish me for your failure."

The former President chuckled:

"Well, Huey, that's almost reason enough to accept the position. You'll hear from me later."

It soon became practically certain that all members of the cabinet, as selected, would accept.

My worries about the completion of my cabinet being almost over, I undertook to set in motion my plan for a redistribution of the nation's wealth.

My plan was outlined in my first legislative message to the Congress, which I delivered orally on the second day of my Presidency. In it I recommended the creation of a giant national organization for a survey of all wealth and poverty. It was the first step in carrying out the Share Our Wealth program. . . .

After they departed, I said to those remaining:

"Now, gentlemen, I appoint John D. Rockefeller, Jr. chairman of a National Share Our Wealth Committee, and I appoint as additional members Andrew W. Mellon, Winthrop W. Aldrich, Pierre S. du Pont, Irenée du Pont, Owen D. Young, Charles M. Schwab, and Bernard M. Baruch. I further empower Mr. Rockefeller as chairman to name such additional members as he may desire, upon sole condition that he shall name no member from the firm of J. P. Morgan or its Philadelphia ally, Drexel and Company. You, Mr. Aldrich, will communicate that authority to Mr. Rockefeller.

"Now, gentlemen, will you join me at dinner?"

They did. To my surprise, it turned out to be a friendly dinner. Mr. Pierre du Pont rather startled his associates by saying he was heartily in favor of the Share Our Wealth program. He said he felt that five million dollars was a trifle low for a limit on a fortune, because some individuals, by their genius, might create a business, as had he and his brother and cousins, the value of which might be increased by wise management from a few million dollars to hundreds of millions of dollars. He expressed fear that future government seizure of fortunes in excess of five million dollars a year would disrupt the operation of an industry.

I was surprised, too, by the views of old Andy Mellon. He told us that his fortune had become a tremendous bother and nuisance. It was apparent to me that he was an unhappy man, and that he wanted above all to have the affection of the American people, which he believed he had lost through no fault of his own. He appeared willing to assume a role in the Share Our Wealth program. Before the dinner ended, I named him Vice-Chairman of the Committee, and his face lighted with real pleasure when I made the appointment.

After dinner I said:

"Now, gentlemen, you will be called together, I presume, by Mr. Rockefeller, and undoubtedly you will meet in New York City. When you are ready, bring your plan to me."

41

The Administration
Strikes Back at Long

PRESIDENT ROOSEVELT:
There is only one other thing that I want to talk about, somewhat informally, but rather firmly. You have probably read in the press that I had a visit—I should say visitation—from some gentlemen of the lower House, who came down to say that they were being badly treated, and tomorrow they are having a meeting that should not be described as an indignation meeting though it will probably result that way. They came down and made two speeches which were to the general effect that nobody loves them, nobody pays any attention to them. I said, "Don't make speeches; get specific."
Well, some of them have been specific, and they brought out certain things that I think everybody around this table and in this room should keep very closely in the front of their brain all the time. . . .
The complaint from the Congressmen is that in a great many of these appointments by these new agencies, especially, they are not Civil Service people and they are working against the Congressmen. They are not asking that these people work for the Congressmen, but they are asking that they be prevented from working against them, either for other Democrats or for Republicans, and they are entitled to that.
I think it is extremely important that everyone of you, when you get complaints from Congressmen in any specific case—you can tell them to be specific, that is all right; but when they are specific, don't turn it off by saying in a perfunctory manner that some field agent solemnly says he knows this man has never done anything like that. But you should get a thorough investigation of it and if the evidence is 50–50, don't assume that your field agent is right and the Congressman is wrong. There

SOURCE: Lester Seligman and Elmer E. Cornwell, Jr. (eds.), New Deal Mosaic (Eugene, Ore., 1965), pp. 434–7.

is too much tendency along that line. Nobody wants to put all these agencies into Administration politics, but we must prevent them from being anti-Administration. If they are not in sympathy with what we are doing, we do not need to use them. And there are a lot of people employed by these emergency agencies who are not in sympathy.

MR. KENNEDY:

That has been called to our attention, Mr. President, but what are we going to do about it?

PRESIDENT ROOSEVELT:

Fire the fellow! A few good examples of firing people for not living up to these principles would be an awfully good thing.

I am telling these Congressmen that if they do not get satisfaction along these lines to let me know. When you get word from me on the thing, you can know I mean it. These things I mention will—inevitably— eventually get up to me.

SECRETARY WALLACE:

In a delicate situation like Louisiana we may have to ask your advice.

PRESIDENT ROOSEVELT:

You won't have to do that. Don't put anybody in and don't keep anybody that is working for Huey Long or his crowd! That is a hundred per cent!

VICE-PRESIDENT GARNER:

That goes for everybody!

PRESIDENT ROOSEVELT:

Everybody and every agency. Anybody working for Huey Long is not working for us.

SECRETARY HULL:

It can't be corrected too soon.

PRESIDENT ROOSEVELT:

You will get a definite ruling any time you want it.

42

Father Coughlin's Union Party

BY 1932 a new era of production had come into full bloom. It was represented by the motor car, the tractor and the power lathe, which enabled the laborer to produce wealth ten times more rapidly than was possible for his ancestors. Within the short expanse of 150 years the problem of production had been solved, due to the ingenuity of men like Arkwright and his loom, Fulton and his steam engine, and Edison and his dynamo. These and a thousand other benefactors of mankind made it possible for the teeming millions of people throughout the world to transfer speedily the raw materials into the thousand necessities and conveniences which fall under the common name of wealth.

Thus, with the advent of our scientific era, with its far-flung fields, its spacious factories, its humming motors, its thundering locomotives, its highly trained mechanics, it is inconceivable how such a thing as a so-called depression should blight the lives of an entire nation when there was a plenitude of everything surrounding us, only to be withheld from us because the so-called leaders of high finance persisted in clinging to an outworn theory of privately issued money, the medium through which wealth is distributed.

I challenged this private control and creation of money because it was alien to our Constitution, which says "Congress shall have the right to coin and regulate the value of money." I challenged this system of permitting a small group of private citizens to create money and credit out of nothing, to issue it into circulation through loans and to demand that borrowers repay them with money which represented real goods, real labor and real service. I advocated that it be replaced by the American system—namely, that the creation and control of money and credit are the rights of the people through their democratic government.

Has this American system of money creation and control been our practice?

SOURCE: Father Charles E. Coughlin, "A Third Party," *Vital Speeches,* II (1936), 613–16.

Unfortunately, no. Our governments, through a policy of perversion and subterfuge, established, step by step, the Federal Reserve Banking System. Power was given to a handful of our fellow-citizens to create and control more than 90 per cent of all our money mostly by a mere stroke of the fountain pen; to issue it into circulation as real legal tender; and to exact of the hundred and twenty-five million citizens the obligation of paying it back with interest, not through a stroke of the fountain pen but through arduous hours of toil, of sweat and of heartaches. Before the year 1932 very few persons fully realized the existence of this financial bondage.

Millions of citizens began asking the obvious questions: "Why should the farmer be forced to follow his plow at a loss?" "Why should the citizens—at least 90 per cent of them—be imprisoned behind the cruel bars of want when, within their grasp, there are plenty of shoes, of clothing, of motor cars, of refrigerators, to which they are entitled?". . .

At last, when the most brilliant minds amongst the industrialists, bankers and their kept politicians had failed to solve the cause of the needless depression, there appeared upon the scene of our national life a new champion of the people, Franklin Delano Roosevelt! He spoke golden words of hope. He intimated to the American people that the system of permitting a group of private citizens to create money, then to issue it to the government as if it were real money, then to exact payment from the entire nation through a system of taxation earned by real labor and service, was immoral. With the whip of his scorn he castigated these usurers who exploited the poor. With his eloquent tongue he lashed their financial system which devoured the homes of widows and orphans.

No man in modern times received such plaudits from the poor as did Franklin Roosevelt when he promised to drive the money changers from the temple—the money changers who had clipped the coins of wages, who had manufactured spurious money and who had brought proud America to her knees.

March 4, 1933! I shall never forget the inaugural address, which seemed to re-echo the very words employed by Christ Himself as He actually drove the money changers from the temple.

The thrill that was mine was yours. Through dim clouds of the depression this man Roosevelt was, as it were, a new savior of his people!

Oh, just a little longer shall there be needless poverty! Just another year shall there be naked backs! Just another moment shall there be dark thoughts of revolution! Never again will the chains of economic poverty bite into the hearts of simple folks, as they did in the past days of the Old Deal!

Such were our hopes in the springtime of 1933.

My friends, what have we witnessed as the finger of time turned the pages of the calendar? Nineteen hundred and thirty-three and the National Recovery Act which multiplied profits for the monopolists; 1934 and the AAA which raised the price of foodstuffs by throwing back God's best gifts into His face; 1935 and the Banking Act which rewarded the exploiters of the poor, the Federal Reserve bankers and their associates, by handing over to them the temple from which they were to have been cast!

In 1936, when our disillusionment is complete, we pause to take inventory of our predicament. You citizens have shackled about your limbs a tax bill of $35,000,000,000, most of which, I repeat, was created by a flourish of a fountain pen. Your erstwhile savior, whose golden promises ring upon the counter of performance with the cheapness of tin, bargained with the money changers that, with seventy billion laboring hours in the ditch, or in the factory, or behind the plow, you and your children shall repay the debt which was created with a drop of ink in less than ten seconds.

Is that driving the money changers out of the temple?

Every crumb you eat, every stitch of clothing you wear, every menial purchase which you make is weighted down with an unseen tax as you work and slave for the debt merchants of America. But the $55,000,000,-000 of debt bonds, held mostly by the debt merchants and the well circumstanced of this country, have been ably safeguarded from taxation by this peerless leader who sham battles his way along the avenue of popularity with his smile for the poor and his blindness for their plight. Is that driving the money changers from the temple?

You laborers of America who work no more than an average of 200 days a year at $5 a day are forced to contribute at least fifty days of your labor—to steal it from your wives and your children, to deprive them of the conveniences and the luxuries advertised in every paper and magazine—as tribute for the benefit of the sacrosanct bondholders.

Is that driving the money changers from the temple?

You farmers of America, of whom 3,000 every week are driven over the hill to the poorhouse through the ruthless confiscation which is still protected under the guise of friendship, are forced to bear the burden of $8,000,000,000 of mortgage debt on farms at 6 per cent—farms which have depreciated 50 per cent during these last five years, farms which cannot be operated at a profit except temporarily through the immoral Tugwellism of destruction.

Is that driving the money changers from the temple, or is it driving Americans from their homes?

For God's command of "increase and multiply," spoken to our first parents, the satanic principles of "decrease and devastate" has been substituted.

It is not pleasant for me who coined the phrase "Roosevelt or ruin" —a phrase fashioned upon promises—to voice such passionate words. But I am constrained to admit that "Roosevelt and ruin" is the order of the day because the money changers have not been driven from the temple. . . .

Alas! The temple still remains the private property of the money changers. The golden key has been handed over to them for safekeeping —the key which now is fashioned in the shape of a double cross.

Oh, would that another Milton could write the story of "Paradise Lost" to the people. Would that the blind bard could reconstruct the theme of "Paradise Regained" by the bankers!

Neither Old Dealer nor New Dealer, it appears, has courage to assail the international bankers, the Federal Reserve bankers. In common, both the leaders of the Republicans and the Democrats uphold the old money philosophy. Today in America there is only one political party— the banker's party. In common, both old parties are determined to sham battle their way through this November election with the hope that millions of American citizens will be driven into the no-man's land of financial bondage.

My friends, there is a way out, a way to freedom! There is an escape from the dole standard of Roosevelt, the gold standard of Landon. No longer need you be targets in "no-man's land" for the financial crossfire of the sham-battlers! . . .

This is a new day for America with its new "Union Party." Lemke has raised a banner of liberty for you to follow as you carry it unsullied into the ranks of the money changers' servants now occupying the White House and the halls of Congress.

Behind it will rally agriculture, labor, the disappointed Republicans and the outraged Democrats, the independent merchant and industrialist and every lover of liberty who desires to eradicate the cancerous growths from decadent capitalism and avoid the treacherous pitfalls of red communism.

VIII
THE CONSERVATIVE
OPPOSITION

In Selection 43, Senator Hastings claims that the Securities Act of 1933, which established government regulation of stock issues, "prevented new industries from developing"; but the slow pace of new financing probably resulted more from the reluctance of shell-shocked investors to take new risks. Hastings' article also exploits national indignation about the Roosevelt Administration's decision to cancel air mail contracts with private companies; when the Army Air Corps flew the mail in February 1934, savage winter weather caused crashes which took the lives of several pilots; within three months the Administration had capitulated to the private carriers. In Selection 44, Mencken writes of Thomas J. Walsh, Democratic senator from Montana; Roosevelt chose him to be Attorney General, but he died shortly before Inauguration Day. James A. Farley was Postmaster-General and chairman of the Democratic National Committee. The "British professor" Hoover alludes to in Selection 45 was John Maynard Keynes. In Selection 46, Frank Sullivan mentions Governor Philip La Follette of Wisconsin, who headed an abortive third party movement in 1938 which combined prescriptions for more radical action with rebukes to the Administration for coddling the unemployed. The "Six Dwarfs" refers to the popular Walt Disney movie, Snow White and the Seven Dwarfs. When the columnist Raymond Clapper read the report of the Senate Judiciary Committee (Selection 47), he wrote in his diary: "Bitter document, extremely rough. . . . It reads almost like a bill of impeachment." Of the ten names signed to the report, the first seven came from the President's own party, including such hitherto Administration stalwarts as Joseph O'Mahoney of Wyoming.

43

The Republican Creed

I DO not here propose to try to state the issues to which every candidate will subscribe, but shall undertake, in a general way, to state the issues in which the people of the nation are greatly interested.

In 1932, the Democratic party in its platform emphasized the importance of its promises by stating that it made a covenant, an agreement, with the people. Notwithstanding this statement, the Administration has been guilty of the most flagrant violation of party pledges, the like of which is nowhere recorded in our political history. No responsible Democrat, anywhere, undertakes to defend his party upon this point. It is very important, however, from the voter's point of view.

The voter dare not trust again one who has violated pledges so shamefully. The promises were important. There was the promise to reduce Federal expenses by 25 per cent. It was stated that this could be done by consolidating and eliminating bureaus, and avoiding extravagance. The budget was to be balanced. Republicans were condemned for permitting deficits to exist. Sound money was to be maintained, at all hazards. The Hawley-Smoot Tariff bill was condemned, including all Executive authority in the matter of tariff making; the tariff, they said, had destroyed our foreign trade. The anti-trust laws were to be strengthened and enforced. Government in business was to be eliminated, and so on. The failure in all these things makes an important issue.

The turning over to the President, by a subservient Congress, of the powers which, under the Constitution, could only be exercised properly by Congress, upon the plea of the President that the emergency made it necessary, is of such vital importance to the nation that the voters must pass upon it. This is an issue that strikes at the very foundation of our government. The abuse of the power thus given emphasizes its danger, but makes a separate and distinct issue. Many Republicans in Congress voted to give the President these extraordinary powers, and they did it

SOURCE: Daniel O. Hastings, "Battle of November," *Today*, II (1934), 3-4, 19.

from a purely patriotic motive, but there are few, if any, who believe the powers given have been wisely used.

As an illustration, who could have foreseen what use would be made of the powers given in the National Industrial Recovery Act? Did any-one suppose that every little business of the nation was to be controlled, thereafter, by a bureau in Washington? Did anyone suppose he could not sell his services or his wares, thereafter, for an amount that was sat-isfactory to himself? Was it supposed that, thereafter, no one could go into business or extend his business without the consent of the Presi-dent's representative? Was it believed that from this Act of a few pages the bureaus in Washington, by themselves, could write more than 10,-000 pages of new laws, laws creating new crimes, and setting punish-ment by fine and imprisonment? The bureau administering this Act also has taken upon itself the right to levy a tax, to cover its expense, not only upon the person signing a code, but on all persons who come within the code definition. If the Democrats depend upon this Act, and its ad-ministration, as their outstanding accomplishment, they ought to be defeated.

Does anybody in America agree with the administration of the Agri-cultural Adjustment Act? Perhaps those who have received large sums of money for not doing something may agree, but most of those have found it necessary to sign unconscionable agreements in order to get the Federal money; they have agreed to abide by all the rules and regula-tions laid down by the Department, and these rules include many things the farmer knows nothing about.

But the worst of all this is found in the processing tax upon the food we eat and the clothes we wear, thus imposing a tax upon one class of persons for the benefit of another, a tax upon people in one territory for the benefit of people in another territory. And the significant thing about this is that the farmers for whom the benefits are intended are, because of its regimental characteristics, as much opposed to it as other people who bear the burdens. This makes a very important issue.

The foolish policy of destroying cotton, wheat, pigs and other essen-tials is an important matter to be considered. This policy, together with the distressing drouth in the Middle-West, has left it uncertain whether we shall not have to import foodstuffs this Winter. It has increased the cost of living to such a point that those persons whose wages have not been increased find it almost impossible to make both ends meet. The Democrats ask that this be approved.

The taking of the gold coins of American citizens, with payment at an arbitrary price, fixed by a government official, and the making of posses-sion of such coins, after a certain date, a crime, are against the average person's idea of a free democracy. This is made more offensive when it is remembered that, at that very time, we were paying something like 50 per cent more for gold in the foreign market.

The cancellation of the air mail contracts, which were valid contracts between American corporations and the Federal government, without hearing and without evidence of fraud, was such a violation of the American principle of justice and fair play that it was almost universally condemned at the time, and is not likely to be forgotten on election day. This cannot be answered merely by saying these contracts were fraudulently made. Even if that were true, and I do not admit it, it does not excuse the Postmaster General from following the American plan of a hearing, a fair trial, before conviction is announced and sentence imposed.

The most serious situation confronting the nation at the beginning of the present Administration was the great number of unemployed. This was the outstanding problem, but today there are at least 10,000,-000 people out of work and about one-sixth of our population is deriving its sole support from the Federal government. Relief payments total $86,000,000 a month. In the meantime, we have spent billions of dollars for the sole purpose of remedying these conditions. The passing of the Securities Act prevented new industries from developing; the industries already existing have been coerced into cooperation, and labor has been used as a political weapon, tempted by promises that have proved to be entirely empty. The country has been torn with industrial strife from coast to coast; many lives have been sacrificed and hundreds of millions of dollars have been lost beyond any hope of recovery. The confidence which is so necessary to recovery lasted but a few months. The voter who seriously considers these questions will hold the Administration responsible.

The Democratic party always has been outspoken in its approval of the Civil Service plan for Federal employes. Notwithstanding this fact, the Democratic Congress insisted that every emergency measure that was passed should leave the person administering the law entirely free to select his own employes, without regard to the Civil Service requirements. It is generally conceded that practically all appointments must receive the approval of the chairman of the Democratic National Committee. There are approximately 200,000 of these employes, at the present time, and the sole qualification for the selection of most of them has been their political value. These non-Civil Service employes are the individuals who spy upon the storekeeper, the merchant and the manufacturer, the farmer and the herder, to see if they are living up to the daily orders which are issued from Washington to regulate the regimentation of our goose-stepping nation. This effort to put the nation in the same position as the Tammany-controlled City of New York is disgusting, and will be resented by many people at the polls.

The huge sums of money that have been spent, directly or indirectly, for relief, have been made a political football by the Administration. Positive proof of it is to be found in the recent election in the State of Maine, as well as the bold bid for votes made by Mr. Farley in his political speeches in the Middle-West, where he specifically used this argument. It is no credit to the person who makes the argument that his influence is necessary to get relief, and it is a disgrace to an Administration that permits it to be made and fosters it. The Democrat party cannot escape this issue.

The Democrats complain of Republican criticism, urging that, in distressing times like these, criticism is unpatriotic, but I would remind them that free speech and a free press were the demands successfully made by the fathers who were responsible for this Republic. Criticism ought not to distress the government official who is sure he is following the right course; if he is not sure, he ought to welcome it.

The Democrats, in answer to the Republican criticism, challenge them to propose a plan of their own. This is no adequate answer to well-directed criticism. When they propound the question, they realize that they have a Democrat President and that there is no hope of the Republicans having a Senate majority in the next Congress, and they know that no plan of the Republicans can be put in operation over their opposition. The only hope the Republicans can offer the voter is that, if enough Democrats are thrown out of Congress, we thus shall be able to prevent the Administration from going any further toward socialism or communism.

I do not hesitate, however, to say what I think the program of the next Congress ought to be. Speaking generally, I would say that we ought to undo, as quickly as possible, many of the things that the Administration has done in the past eighteen months. I would withdraw from the President any right to modify or change the gold content of the American dollar; I would withdraw the right to print $3,000,000,000 in greenbacks; I would withdraw the right to change the relation of gold to silver; I would repeal the authority given to the President to change the tariff law now protecting American industry, except upon recommendation of the Tariff Commission as heretofore; I would instantly repeal the authority given the President under the NRA and the AAA; I would repeal the Bankhead Cotton Control Act; I would modify the Securities Act and make it comparable to the British Act upon the same subject; I would promote the relations between capital and labor with an attitude of impartiality; I would put all Federal employes under the Civil Service Act; I would abolish at least 90 per cent of the bureaucracies now existing in Washington; I would stop spending billions of dollars on non-liquidating public works, and undertake to create such confidence in the business world that private capital would ultimately provide work for the unemployed; I would spend the money for relief where it would do the greatest good; I would systematize the spending of the relief money so that it could not be improperly used; I would map out some definite plan for balancing the Federal budget; I would see that all forms of social legislation avoided a tendency toward communism; and, finally, I would restore American liberty to American people, with only such restrictions upon it as a safe and sound social order might require.

44

Dr. Roosevelt Is a Quack

QUACKS are always friendly and ingratiating fellows, and not infrequently their antics are very amusing. The Hon. Franklin D. Roosevelt, LL.D., is typical of the species. There has never been a more amiable President, not even excepting the Martyr Harding, and there has never been a better showman, not even excepting Roosevelt I. He likes to have confident, merry people about him, and to turn the light of a Christian Science smile upon the snares and ambuscades of his job. . . .

There is some reason for believing that Dr. Roosevelt, at the time of his nomination, had a leaning toward what may be called ethical practice. He had done plenty of quacking to get that nomination, but now that he had it, he talked in highly orthodox terms. The budget would have to be balanced. There would have to be a cleaning out of useless jobholders—by moral suasion, if possible, but if not, then with lengths of hose filled with BB shot. Above all, the dollar would have to be protected, that Uncle Sam might go shaving in the morning without blushing at his own face. . . .

His mood actually lasted over election day, and even beyond the end of the year. How else are you to account for his choice of the Hon. Thomas J. Walsh as his Attorney-General? Walsh, to be sure, passed publicly as a liberal, but he was certainly anything but a radical. On Sundays he served Yahweh as a pious Catholic puritan, but his weekday fetish was the Constitution, and he could no more brook contempt of it than he could brook contempt of the Holy Saints. It is impossible to imagine him conniving at any of the non-constitutional chicaneries that were so soon to be brought to Washington by the young professors. The very thought of them would have set him to yelling murder, and he'd have combatted them with all the horrible ferocity of an Irish-

SOURCE: H. L. Mencken, "Three Years of Dr. Roosevelt," *The American Mercury*, XXXVII (1936), 257–65.

man in a shindy, and all the learning and eloquence of a really great advocate.

If Walsh had lived for another year or two, the Supreme Court would never have had to swim ashore through those greasy rollers of alphabetical soup. He would have heaved every tureen of it out of the window as fast as the pedagogues and non-constitutional lawyers brought it in, and if the Führer had sought to stay him he would have resigned his portfolio, taken to the stump, and either intimidated the Administration into common sense and common decency or wrecked it out of hand. But Walsh's Sunday God, for reasons that must remain inscrutable, had business for him in Havana, Cuba, and on his way back from that insalubrious port he departed this life. His exitus released the furies. Roosevelt reverted instantly to his natural and more comfortable quackery, and soon was shining before the world as the boldest and most preposterous practitioner of modern times.

But here, I think, we had better be charitable again. Isn't it possible to argue that, as things stood on March 4, 1933, no other course was feasible? I am willing to say so. The dying agonies of the Republican Administration had got the country into a really dreadful state of mind, and it was probably beyond help from the pharmacopoeia. . . . The plain people, when social and economic bellyaches of unusual severity seize them, sometimes fall into hysteria and panic, and get out of hand. There is, commonly, no cure for their distress save time, and they refuse to wait, so the wise statesman resorts to quackery, thus putting them at their ease until nature can do its work. Abraham Lincoln was not above this trick, and I see no reason why we should burn Dr. Roosevelt at the stake because, in those first phrenetic days of his Administration, he made use of it.

It both worked and didn't work. The bank holiday, when its assets and liabilities are counted up at last, will probably turn out to have paid expenses and no more. There is no reason to believe that the net loss of the bank depositors of the country would have been either larger or smaller if the wobbly banks had been allowed to bust, and the good ones had been let alone. There were banks that were able to pull themselves out of insolvency during the moratorium, and there were others that were shoved into insolvency by its attending rumors and alarms. The NRA, I incline to think, was clearly more successful, at least in its early stages. The theory behind it, though unsound, nevertheless had a considerable plausibility, and to its execution there was brought a degree of demagogic talent seldom available to a Christian government on this earth. Part of that talent was Dr. Roosevelt's own: he reached, in the spring of 1933, his professional apogee, his apex as a virtuoso. But a great deal more of it was supplied by Brigadier-General Hugh S. Johnson, J.D.—in private life only Barney Baruch's stooge, but in his public capacity a rabble-rouser of magnificent and indeed almost incomparable gifts. . . .

The first success of the NRA had been so vast, at least to outward appearance, that it set the whole tone of the Roosevelt Administration. Almost overnight all rational plans for dealing with the depression were abandoned, and recourse was had to the dizzy devices of pure and unadulterated quackery. Nothing more was heard about such homely enterprises as balancing the budget, getting rid of supernumerary job-holders, and protecting the dollar. Instead, we began to hear of grandiose projects for wiping out every ache and blemish of civilization at one herculean swoop. Wizards of the highest amperage, it appeared, were at hand to do the job, and they were armed with new and infallible arcana. They knew more about everything under the sun than anybody else under the sun; they were masters of all the orthodox arts and sciences, and of a dozen new ones that they had invented themselves; their minds moved majestic and imperturbed in the face of chaos, like that of Omnipotence Itself. These wizards, we were told, would solve all the problems that harassed the country. They would give us a Planned Economy, scientific in every detail, and out of it would flow the More Abundant Life, with everyone rich and happy, and the very birds in the trees singing hallelujah.

Well, what did these wizards turn out to be, once they had got into the ring? They turned out to be the sorriest mob of mountebanks ever gathered together at one time, even in Washington. The best of them were seen to be only professional uplifters and do-gooders, trained in no craft more respectable than that of cadging and spending other people's money. And from this maximum they ranged quickly downward to a miscellaneous rabble of vapid young pedagogues, out-of-work Y.M.C.A. secretaries, third-rate journalists, briefless lawyers, and soaring chicken-farmers. In the whole outfit there was hardly a man who had ever reached solid distinction in any recognized profession or trade. They were, at the top, poor dubs; at the bottom, they were blatant and intolerable idiots. Their arcana were stale mixtures of all the quackeries vended in the backwaters of the country since the Civil War, from Free Silver to the Single Tax, and their methods were those of wart-removers at county fairs since the time when the memory of man runneth not to the contrary. . . .

Of such sort are the "trained experts" who were to have brought in the More Abundant Life. Their pretensions are as utterly bogus as those of Lydia Pinkham or Dr. Munyon. They possess no useful talent of any kind, and seem to be quite incapable of anything colorably describable as sober judgment. To hand over to such incandescent vacuums the immensely difficult and complicated problems which now confront the country is as insane as it would be to hand over a laparotomy to a traffic cop. They are completely incompetent, not only for public affairs of the first magnitude, but also for all save the most trivial of private affairs. Hopkins, before his apotheosis, was a collector for the Red Cross, and after that a ballyhoo man for other such noisy organizations—jobs calling only for the statistical fervor of a life insurance solicitor and the evangelical smile of a Y.M.C.A. secretary. How the Salvation Army missed him I do not know. Wallace, another great star in the troop of jitney Marxes, was the unsuccessful editor of a farm paper. Ickes was a professional public nuisance in Chicago. La Perkins was a lady uplifter, and a shining ornament of that appalling clan. Tugwell, as to one half of him, was a member of the order of inferior pedagogues, and, as to the other, one of the kept idealists of the New Republic. Descend to the lower ranks and you come upon a truly astounding rabble of impudent nobodies, with a huge swarm of Jim Farley's deserving Democrats filling the background. . . . The blame for this dreadful burlesque of civilized government is to be laid at the door of the Hon. Mr. Roosevelt, and at his door alone. He is directly and solely responsible for every dollar that has been wasted, for every piece of highfalutin rubbish that has been put upon the statute books, and for the operations of every mountebank on the public payroll, from the highest to the lowest. He was elected to the Presidency on his solemn promise to carry on the government in a careful and sensible manner, and to put only competent men in office. He has repudiated that promise openly, deliberately, and in the most cynical manner. Instead of safeguarding the hard-earned money of the people and relieving them from their appalling burden of taxation, he has thrown away billions to no useful end or purpose, and has piled up a debt that it will take generations to discharge. And instead of appointing conscientious and intelligent officials, he has saddled the country with a camorra of quarrelling crackpots, each bent only upon prospering his own brand of quackery and augmenting his own power. There has never been a moment when he showed any serious regard for the high obligations lying upon him. The greatest President since Hoover has carried on his job with an ingratiating grin upon his face, like that of a snake-oil vendor at a village carnival, and he has exhibited precisely the same sense of responsibility in morals and honor; no more.

If signs count for anything, the jig is now nearly up. There has been a tremendous shift in public sentiment during the past year, and it begins to look probable that not all the billions of the late AAA, the WPA, and the rest of them, and not all the nefarious science of Jim Farley, by Tammany out of the Anti-Saloon League, will suffice to save the More Abundant Life next November. Whether Dr. Roosevelt himself is aware of this I do not know. If a realization of it seizes him he may be trusted to turn his coat with great precipitancy, as he did on the issues of Prohibition, sound money, and government expenditure. There is, to give it a polite name, a fine resilience in him; he keeps his principles fluid, like the assets of a well-managed bank. If he became convinced tomorrow that coming out for cannibalism would get him the votes he so sorely needs, he would begin fattening a missionary in the White House backyard come Wednesday. Having made the mess, he will volunteer heroically for the job of cleaning it up. But my guess, strongly supported by a far from subconscious wish, is that the great masses of American freemen, including even multitudes now on the innumerable doles, will decide by November that some other scavenger—indeed, any other scavenger—will be safer. There was a time when the Republicans were scouring the country for a behemoth to pit against him. Now they begin to grasp the fact that, if they can beat him at all, which seems most likely, they can beat him with a Chinaman, or even a Republican.

The only issue is Roosevelt. Is he a hero, as his parasites allege, or a quack, as I have argued here? The answer will be heard on election day. Every vote will be cast either for him or against him. His opponent will be only the residuary legatee, the innocent bystander.

45

Herbert Hoover Indicts
the New Deal

THROUGH four years of experience this New Deal attack upon
free institutions has emerged as the transcendent issue in America.
All the men who are seeking for mastery in the world today are using
the same weapons. They sing the same songs. They all promise the joys
of Elysium without effort.

But their philosophy is founded on the coercion and compulsory
organization of men. True liberal government is founded on the emanci-
pation of men. This is the issue upon which men are imprisoned and
dying in Europe right now. . . .

I gave the warning against this philosophy of government four years
ago from a heart heavy with anxiety for the future of our country. It
was born from many years' experience of the forces moving in the world
which would weaken the vitality of American freedom. It grew in four
years of battle as President to uphold the banner of free men.

And that warning was based on sure ground from my knowledge of
the ideas that Mr. Roosevelt and his bosom colleagues had covertly
embraced despite the Democratic platform.

Those ideas were not new. Most of them had been urged upon me.

During my four years powerful groups thundered at the White House
with these same ideas. Some were honest, some promising votes, most
of them threatening reprisals, and all of them yelling "reactionary"
at us.

I rejected the notion of great trade monopolies and price-fixing
through codes. That could only stifle the little business man by regi-
menting him under the big brother. That idea was born of certain
American Big Business and grew up to be the NRA.

SOURCE: Herbert Hoover, Address, October 30, 1936, *The New York Times*, October 31, 1936.

I rejected the schemes of "economic planning" to regiment and coerce the farmer. That was born of a Roman despot 1,400 years ago and grew up into the AAA.

I refused national plans to put the government into business in competition with its citizens. That was born of Karl Marx.

I vetoed the idea of recovery through stupendous spending to prime the pump. That was born of a British professor.

I threw out attempts to centralize relief in Washington for politics and social experimentation. I defeated other plans to invade States' rights, to centralize power in Washington. Those ideas were born of American radicals.

I stopped attempts at currency inflation and repudiation of government obligation. That was robbery of insurance policy holders, savings bank depositors and wage-earners. That was born of the early Brain Trusters.

I rejected all these things because they would not only delay recovery but because I knew that in the end they would shackle free men. . . .

Our people did not recognize the gravity of the issue when I stated it four years ago. That is no wonder, for the day Mr. Roosevelt was elected recovery was in progress, the Constitution was untrampled, the integrity of the government and the institutions of freedom were intact.

It was not until after the election that the people began to awake. Then the realization of intended tinkering with the currency drove bank depositors into the panic that greeted Mr. Roosevelt's inauguration.

Recovery was set back for two years, and hysteria was used as the bridge to reach the goal of personal government.

I am proud to have carried the banner of free men to the last hour of the term my countrymen entrusted it to me. It matters nothing in the history of a race what happens to those who in their time have carried the banner of free men. What matters is that the battle shall go on.

The people know now the aims of this New Deal philosophy of government.

We propose instead leadership and authority in government within the moral and economic framework of the American System.

We propose to hold to the Constitutional safeguards of free men.

We propose to relieve men from fear, coercion and spite that are inevitable in personal government.

We propose to demobilize and decentralize all this spending upon which vast personal power is being built. We proposed to amend the tax laws so as not to defeat free men and free enterprise.

We propose to turn the whole direction of this country toward liberty, not away from it.

The New Dealers say that all this that we propose is a worn-out system; that this machine age requires new measures for which we must sacrifice some part of the freedom of men. Men have lost their way with a confused idea that governments should run machines.

Man-made machines cannot be of more worth than men themselves. Free men made these machines. Only free spirits can master them to their proper use.

The relation of our government with all these questions is complicated and difficult. They rise into the very highest ranges of economics, statesmanship and morals.

And do not mistake. Free government is the most difficult of all government. But it is everlastingly true that the plain people will make fewer mistakes than any group of men no matter how powerful. But free government implies vigilant thinking and courageous living and self-reliance in a people.

Let me say to you that any measure which breaks our dikes of freedom will flood the land with misery.

46

The Cliché Expert Testifies as a Roosevelt Hater

MR. ARBUTHNOT: No sir! Nobody is going to tell me how to run my business.

Q: Mr. Arbuthnot, you sound like a Roosevelt hater.

A: I certainly am.

Q: In that case, perhaps you could give us an idea of some of the clichés your set is in the habit of using in speaking of Mr. Roosevelt.

A: S-s-s-s-s-s!

Q: I beg your pardon?

A: I was hissing. Our set always hisses whenever Roosevelt's name is mentioned or his picture shown.

Q: Oh, to be sure. I forgot. Well now, to return to Mr. Roosevelt—

A: S-s-s-s-s-s!

Q: Mr. Arbuthnot, it might simplify matters if we took the hissing for granted from now on. I mean to say, whenever I mention Mr. Roosevelt's name we'll just assume that you have countered with a hiss. Is that agreeable to you?

A: Certainly, if you insist.

Q: I think it would expedite matters, if you don't mind. Now then, what I want to know first is what you Roosevelt haters call the President.

A: Why, the—!

Q: Oh, I don't mean that kind, Mr. Arbuthnot.

A: Well, we call him That Madman in the White House, or That Fellow Down in Washington. Sometimes we call him Mister Roosevelt, or Your Friend, Franklin D.—just like that.

Q: Sort of sarcastic, eh?

SOURCE: Frank Sullivan, "The Cliché Expert Testifies as a Roosevelt Hater," in A Pearl in Every Oyster (Boston, 1938), pp. 88–96.

A: And how!

Q: I see. Please proceed and give me your frank opinion of the President.

A: Well, I voted for him in 1932. I think he did a good job when the banks were closed, but . . .

Q: Yes. Go on.

A: Now don't misunderstand me. I'm a liberal. I'm in favor of a lot of these reforms Roosevelt has been trying to put over, but I don't like the way he's going about it.

Q: Why?

A: Because he's trying to destroy the American way of life.

Q: For instance?

A: Well, you take the Supreme Court. Where Roosevelt made his big mistake was in attacking the Court.

Q: I see.

A: And where Roosevelt made his big mistake was in arousing all this class hatred. You know, all this forgotten-man stuff.

Q: Yes.

A: And where Roosevelt made his big mistake was in starting all this pump priming. You can't spend your way out of a depression.

Q: Really?

A: Certainly not. Where's the money coming from to pay for all this —this—

Q: Do you mean "orgy of spending"?

A: That's just the phrase I was searching for. You know how it's all going to wind up?

Q: How?

A: Inflation. We're going to have the worst inflation in this country you ever saw. These taxes. Twenty-five cents out of every dollar goes for taxes. Why, our children and our children's children will be paying for all this long after you and I are dead and gone. Now, you take relief. I certainly think it's all right to help people who deserve help, but I don't believe in all this coddling, as Governor La Follette says. The trouble with half the people on relief is they don't *want* to work. You can't tell me that most of these people can't find work. If a man wants a job bad enough he'll find one all right. Half these people on relief are foreigners, anyhow.

Q: And what is it these foreigners do, Mr. Arbuthnot?

A: They come over here and take the bread out of our own people's mouths. Let 'em go on back home where they came from. We haven't got enough jobs to go around as it is. And you take the C.I.O.

Q: Yes?

A: A bunch of Communists. In my opinion, no man should be forced to join a labor union against his will. I think Henry Ford has got the right idea. And I certainly object to a radical like that John L. Lewis running this country.

Q: Does John L. Lewis run this country?

A: Why certainly he runs it. He's got Roosevelt so scared he don't dare say his soul's his own. They say Lewis has a key to a back door of the White House.

Q: What about the WPA, Mr. Arbuthnot?

A: Oh, the shovel brigade. I'm against the WPA and the PWA and all this alphabet-soup stuff. Say, speaking of the WPA, did you hear the one about the WPA worker and King Solomon? Why is a WPA worker like King Solomon?

Q: I heard it. Now then—

A: Because he takes his pick and goes to bed.

Q: Is that the funniest New Deal joke you know, Mr. Arbuthnot?

A: Oh, no. Here's the funniest. Have you heard there's only Six Dwarfs now?

Q: Only six?

A: Yeah. Dopey's in the White House.

Q: Mr. Arbuthnot, you slay me. Well, go on. Tell us more. Why don't you like Mr. Roosevelt? What's the matter with him?

A: Well, the trouble with Roosevelt is he's an idealist.

Q: Yes?

A: And the trouble with Roosevelt is he's destroyed individual initiative.

Q: Do tell.

A: And the trouble with Roosevelt is he's a Communist.

Q: I see. Go on.

A: The trouble with Roosevelt is he's a Fascist.

Q: A Fascist, too?

A: Certainly. He wants to be dictator. Don't tell me he hasn't got his eye on a third term.

Q: Sakes alive! Has he?

A: And the trouble with Roosevelt is his vanity. That's what makes him so stubborn. He just won't listen to reason. And the trouble with Roosevelt is he's got no right to spend the taxpayers' money to build up his own personal political machine. Even at that, the trouble with Roosevelt isn't so much Roosevelt himself, it's that bunch he's got himself surrounded with down there in Washington.

Q: What bunch?

A: Oh, this fellow Corcoran. This fellow Cohen. This fellow Frankfurter. This fellow Arnold. This fellow Tugwell.

Q: But this fellow Tugwell isn't there any more.

A: Well, you know who I mean. This bunch of college professors he's got down there. Brain Trusters. I'd rather have Farley, at that. Poor Farley.

Q: Why "poor Farley"?

A: Poor Farley, he takes the rap for all Roosevelt's mistakes. He's the goat. By the way, they're all washed up, you know.

Q: Who's all washed up?

A: Roosevelt and Farley. I have it on good authority that they aren't friends any more. Roosevelt fights with all his old friends sooner or later, just like Wilson did. But can you imagine—a lot of crackpot college professors telling businessmen how to run their business. This country would be all right if Roosevelt would let it alone.

Q: You mean the country is—

A: Basically sound. Right. The trouble with this country is too much government interference in business. A businessman never can tell what That Fellow in the White House is going to do next. All your profits go for taxes, anyhow.

Q: And I suppose you discount the statistics showing a rise in national income because . . .

A: Because those figures are based on the fifty-cent Roosevelt dollar.

Q: What is it business needs, Mr. Arbuthnot?

A: Business needs a breathing spell.

Q: Thus far Mr. Arbuthnot, your comments have been confined to Mr. Roosevelt's policies. Have you, as an expert in the jargon of the Roosevelt haters, anything to say about his private, personal life?

A: Have I? Oh boy! Why, he's a rich man's son. He never did a tap of work in his life. Where does *he* get off, posing as a champion of the people?

Q: A traitor to his class, eh?

A: Oh, we don't use that chestnut any more. It's out of date. What Roosevelt wants to do is set up a dynasty. He's got most of his family on the public payroll down there in Washington now. Don't worry, they're feathering the old nest.

Q: I believe you boys refer to James Roosevelt as the Crown Prince, do you not?

A: Well, yes, only we add a little twist to that and call him the Clown Prince.

Q: Mr. Arbuthnot, I know that you Roosevelt haters have quite a collection of spicy stories about the Roosevelt family. Could you summarize all these in one cliché?

A: Certainly. How can you expect Roosevelt to run the country when he can't even control his own family?

Q: What about Mrs. Roosevelt?

A: She ought to stay home and tend to her own business instead of gallivanting around the country making a holy show of herself. I should think the First Lady would have a little dignity.

Q: What about the President's fishing trips?

A: Fishing trips! Look at the country, the shape it's in, and he goes fishing. On a battleship, too. You know who pays for those junkets, don't you!

Q: Who?

A: The taxpayers, that's who. Oh well, it won't be long now.

Q: What do you mean?

A: I mean Franklin D. is on his way out. He's finally overreached himself. You know what the voters are going to deliver Franklin Delano Roosevelt this fall?

Q: What?

A: A stinging rebuke, that's what. He's lost his hold on the people. He's been sitting down there in his ivory tower too long, listening to these college professors and forgetting his campaign promises. He's lost touch. He don't know what's going on throughout the country.

Q: You think so?

A: Sure do. The old Roosevelt charm won't work this time. The old Roosevelt smile and that "my friends" baloney won't get him anywhere this fall. The people are onto him at last.

Q: You're quite sure of this?

A: Well, in a way I am and in a way I ain't. Look at how he's spending the taxpayers' money to further his own personal ambition. After all, you can't beat Santa Claus.

47

The Supreme Court Is
the Shield of Liberty

THE Committee on the Judiciary, to whom was referred the bill
(S. 1392) to reorganize the judicial branch of the Government,
after full consideration, having unanimously amended the measure,
hereby report the bill adversely with the recommendation that it do
not pass. . . .

The bill before us does not with certainty provide for increasing the
personnel of the Federal judiciary, does not remedy the law's delay,
does not serve the interest of the "poorer litigant" and does not provide for the "constant" or "persistent infusion of new blood" into
the judiciary. What, then, does it do?

The answer is clear. It applies force to the judiciary. It is an attempt
to impose upon the courts a course of action, a line of decision which,
without that force, without that imposition, the judiciary might not
adopt. . . .

Can reasonable men by any possibility differ about the constitutional
impropriety of such a course?

Those of us who hold office in this Government, however humble
or exalted it may be, are creatures of the Constitution. To it we
owe all the power and authority we possess. Outside of it we have none.
We are bound by it in every official act.

We know that this instrument, without which we would not be able
to call ourselves presidents, judges, or legislators, was carefully planned
and deliberately framed to establish three coordinate branches of government, every one of them to be independent of the others. For the
protection of the people, for the preservation of the rights of the in-

SOURCE: "Reorganization of the Federal Judiciary," Senate Report No.
711, 75th Cong., 1st Sess. (1937).

dividual, for the maintenance of the liberties of minorities, for maintaining the checks and balances of our dual system, the three branches of the Government were so constituted that the independent expression of honest difference of opinion could never be restrained in the people's servants and no one branch could overawe or subjugate the others. That is the American system. It is immeasurably more important, immeasurably more sacred to the people of America, indeed, to the people of all the world than the immediate adoption of any legislation however beneficial.

That judges should hold office during good behavior is the prescription. It is founded upon historic experience of the utmost significance. Compensation at stated times, which compensation was not to be diminished during their tenure, was also ordained. Those comprehensible terms were the outgrowths of experience which was deepseated. Of the 55 men in the Constitutional Convention, nearly onehalf had actually fought in the War for Independence. Eight of the men present had signed the Declaration of Independence, in which, giving their reasons for the act, they had said of their king: "He has made judges dependent upon his will alone for their tenure of office and the amount and payment of their salaries." They sought to correct an abuse and to prevent its recurrence. When these men wrote the Constitution of their new Government, they still sought to avoid such an abuse as had led to such a bloody war as the one through which they had just passed. So they created a judicial branch of government consisting of courts not conditionally but absolutely independent in the discharge of their functions, and they intended that entire and impartial independence should prevail. Interference with this independence was prohibited, not partially but totally. Behavior other than good was the sole and only cause for interference. This judicial system is the priceless heritage of every American. . . .

Let us, for the purpose of the argument, grant that the Court has been wrong, wrong not only in that it has rendered mistaken opinions but wrong in the far more serious sense that it has substituted its will for the congressional will in the matter of legislation. May we nevertheless safely punish the Court?

Today it may be the Court which is charged with forgetting its constitutional duties. Tomorrow it may be the Congress. The next day it may be the Executive. If we yield to temptation now to lay the lash upon the Court, we are only teaching others how to apply it to ourselves and to the people when the occasion seems to warrant. Manifestly, if we may force the hand of the Court to secure our interpretation of the Constitution, then some succeeding Congress may repeat the process to secure another and a different interpretation and one which may not sound so pleasant in our ears as that for which we now contend. . . .

This bill is an invasion of judicial power such as has never before been attempted in this country. . . .

Shall we now, after 150 years of loyalty to the constitutional ideal of an untrammeled judiciary, duty bound to protect the constitutional rights of the humblest citizen even against the Government itself, create the vicious precedent which must necessarily undermine our system? The only argument for the increase which survives analysis is that Congress should enlarge the Court so as to make the policies of this administration effective.

We are told that a reactionary oligarchy defies the will of the majority, that this is a bill to "unpack" the Court and give effect to the desires of the majority; that is to say, a bill to increase the number of Justices for the express purpose of neutralizing the views of some of the present members. In justification we are told, but without authority, by those who would rationalize this program, that Congress was given the power to determine the size of the Court so that the legislative branch would be able to impose its will upon the judiciary. This amounts to nothing more than the declaration that when the Court stands in the way of a legislative enactment, the Congress may reverse the ruling by enlarging the Court. When such a principle is adopted, our constitutional system is overthrown!

This, then, is the dangerous precedent we are asked to establish. When proponents of the bill assert, as they have done, that Congress in the past has altered the number of Justices upon the Supreme Court and that this is reason enough for our doing it now, they show how important precedents are and prove that we should now refrain from any action that would seem to establish one which could be followed hereafter whenever a Congress and an executive should become dissatisfied with the decisions of the Supreme Court.

This is the first time in the history of our country that a proposal to alter the decisions of the court by enlarging its personnel has been so boldly made. Let us meet it. Let us now set a salutary precedent that will never be violated. Let us, of the Seventy-fifth Congress, in words that will never be disregarded by any succeeding Congress, declare that we would rather have an independent Court, a fearless Court, a Court that will dare to announce its honest opinions in what it believes to be the defense of the liberties of the people, than a Court that, out of fear or sense of obligation to the appointing power, or factional passion, approves any measure we may enact. We are not the judges of the judges. We are not above the Constitution.

Even if every charge brought against the so-called "reactionary" members of this Court be true, it is far better that we await orderly but inevitable change of personnel than that we impatiently overwhelm them with new members. Exhibiting this restraint, thus demonstrating our faith in the American system, we shall set an example that will protect the independent American judiciary from attack as long as this Government stands. . . .

We recommend the rejection of this bill as a needless, futile, and utterly dangerous abandonment of constitutional principle.

It was presented to the Congress in a most intricate form and for reasons that obscured its real purpose.

It would not banish age from the bench nor abolish divided decisions.

It would not affect the power of any court to hold laws unconstitutional nor withdraw from any judge the authority to issue injunctions.

It would not reduce the expense of litigation nor speed the decision of cases.

It is a proposal without precedent and without justification.

It would subjugate the courts to the will of Congress and the President and thereby destroy the independence of the judiciary, the only certain shield of individual rights.

It contains the germ of a system of centralized, administration of law that would enable an executive so minded to send his judges into every judicial district in the land to sit in judgment on controversies between the Government and the citizen.

It points the way to the evasion of the Constitution and establishes the method whereby the people may be deprived of their right to pass upon all amendments of the fundamental law.

It stands now before the country, acknowledged by its proponents as a plan to force judicial interpretation of the Constitution, a proposal that violates every sacred tradition of American democracy.

Under the form of the Constitution it seeks to do that which is unconstitutional.

Its ultimate operation would be to make this Government one of men rather than one of law, and its practical operation would be to make the Constitution what the executive or legislative branches of the Government choose to say it is—an interpretation to be changed with each change of administration.

It is a measure which should be so emphatically rejected that its parallel will never again be presented to the free representatives of the free people of America.

WILLIAM H. KING
FREDERICK VAN NUYS
PATRICK McCARRAN
CARL A. HATCH
EDWARD R. BURKE
TOM CONNALLY
JOSEPH C. O'MAHONEY
WILLIAM E. BORAH
WARREN R. AUSTIN
FREDERICK STEIWER

IX
THE APPROACH OF WAR

Roosevelt's attack on the "old fetishes of so-called international bankers" in Selection 48 reflects the fact that he distrusted financiers more than industrialists. In Selection 49, he recalls his personal experience with war. As Assistant Secretary of the Navy, he toured the Western Front in the summer of 1918, but, as Frank Freidel has pointed out, he was "fascinated rather than repelled" by the experience. In this same speech, the President speaks of "the trade agreements which we are making"; in 1934, the Senate had authorized him to negotiate tariff pacts with other countries in return for reciprocal concessions. "The fighting newspaper publisher" in Selection 50 was Frank Knox, Republican vice-presidential nominee in 1936 and publisher of the Chicago Daily News; Walter Winchell was a gossip columnist and radio commentator. Bliven also refers to the Ludlow referendum proposal which would have required that, except in case of invasion, a majority vote in a national poll must be secured before the United States could declare war; it met defeat in January 1938. During the 1930's, a small number of the refugees mentioned by Benét in Selection 51 came to the United States; the influx increased after the Nazi pogrom of 1938. Irwin Shaw's story in Selection 52 first appeared in the New Yorker. Roosevelt gave his Charlottesville speech in Selection 53 as a commencement address at the University of Virginia. Italian-Americans deeply resented his "dagger" ad lib as an ethnic slur. In Selection 54, John Cudahy was ambassador to Belgium; William C. Bullitt, ambassador to France; Marshal Henri Pétain, head of the French government in Vichy; William Phillips, ambassador to Italy; and Count Galeazzo Ciano, Italian foreign minister. The request for credits that Kennedy anticipated the British would make eventually resulted in the Lend-Lease Act of 1941. The "Dutchess County farmer" in Selection 55 is probably another of Roosevelt's imaginary figures. Grew later called his telegram (Selection 56) "perhaps the most significant message sent to Washington in all the eight years of my mission to Japan." Roosevelt's letter in Selection 57 came in response to a communication from Sayre, who expressed "the feeling that any day Japan may start moving southwards," but warned against being lured into a war with Japan. Robinson Jeffers, whose poem appears as Selection 57, was preoccupied with violence and destruction in a pitiless universe.

48

Roosevelt's Bombshell Message

I would regard it as a catastrophe amounting to a world tragedy if the great Conference of Nations, called to bring about a more real and permanent financial stability and a greater prosperity to the masses of all Nations, should, in advance of any serious effort to consider these broader problems, allow itself to be diverted by the proposal of a purely artificial and temporary experiment affecting the monetary exchange of a few Nations only. Such action, such diversion, shows a singular lack of proportion and a failure to remember the larger purposes for which the Economic Conference originally was called together.

I do not relish the thought that insistence on such action should be made an excuse for the continuance of the basic economic errors that underlie so much of the present world-wide depression.

The world will not long be lulled by the specious fallacy of achieving a temporary and probably an artificial stability in foreign exchange on the part of a few large countries only.

The sound internal economic system of a Nation is a greater factor in its well-being than the price of its currency in changing terms of the currencies of other Nations.

It is for this reason that reduced cost of Government, adequate Government income, and ability to service Government debts are all so important to ultimate stability. So too, old fetishes of so-called international bankers are being replaced by efforts to plan national currencies with the objective of giving to those currencies a continuing purchasing power which does not greatly vary in terms of the commodities and need of modern civilization. Let me be frank in saying that the United States seeks the kind of dollar which a generation hence will have the same purchasing and debt-paying power as the

SOURCE: Franklin D. Roosevelt, wireless to the London Conference, July 3, 1933, in Samuel Rosenman (ed.), *The Public Papers and Addresses of Franklin D. Roosevelt*, II, 264–5.

dollar value we hope to attain in the near future. That objective means more to the good of other Nations than a fixed ratio for a month or two in terms of the pound or franc.

Our broad purpose is the permanent stabilization of every Nation's currency. Gold or gold and silver can well continue to be a metallic reserve behind currencies, but this is not the time to dissipate gold reserves. When the world works out concerted policies in the majority of Nations to produce balanced budgets and living within their means, then we can properly discuss a better distribution of the world's gold and silver supply to act as a reserve base of national currencies. Restoration of world trade is an important factor, both in the means and in the result. Here also temporary exchange fixing is not the true answer. We must rather mitigate existing embargoes to make easier the exchange of products which one Nation has and the other Nation has not.

The Conference was called to better and perhaps to cure fundamental economic ills. It must not be diverted from that effort.

49

"I Hate War"

M ANY who have visited me in Washington in the past few months may have been surprised when I have told them that personally and because of my own daily contacts with all manner of difficult situations I am more concerned and less cheerful about international world conditions than about our immediate domestic prospects. . . .

It is a bitter experience to us when the spirit of agreements to which we are a party is not lived up to. It is an even more bitter experience for the whole company of Nations to witness not only the spirit but the letter of international agreements violated with impunity and without regard to the simple principles of honor. Permanent friendships between Nations as between men can be sustained only by scrupulous respect for the pledged word.

In spite of all this we have sought steadfastly to assist international movements to prevent war. We cooperated to the bitter end—and it was a bitter end—in the work of the General Disarmament Conference. When it failed we sought a separate treaty to deal with the manufacture of arms and the international traffic in arms. That proposal also came to nothing. We participated—again to the bitter end—in a conference to continue naval limitations, and when it became evident that no general treaty could be signed because of the objections of other Nations, we concluded with Great Britain and France a conditional treaty of qualitative limitation which, much to my regret, already shows signs of ineffectiveness.

We shun political commitments which might entangle us in foreign wars; we avoid connection with the political activities of the League of Nations; but I am glad to say that we have cooperated whole-heartedly in the social and humanitarian work at Geneva. Thus we are a part of the world effort to control traffic in narcotics, to improve international

SOURCE: Franklin D. Roosevelt, Address at Chautauqua, N.Y., August 14, 1936, in Samuel Rosenman (ed.), *The Public Papers and Addresses of Franklin D. Roosevelt*, V, 285–92.

health, to help child welfare, to eliminate double taxation and to better working conditions and laboring hours throughout the world.

We are not isolationists except in so far as we seek to isolate ourselves completely from war. Yet we must remember that so long as war exists on earth there will be some danger that even the Nation which most ardently desires peace may be drawn into war.

I have seen war. I have seen war on land and sea. I have seen blood running from the wounded. I have seen men coughing out their gassed lungs. I have seen the dead in the mud. I have seen cities destroyed. I have seen two hundred limping, exhausted men come out of line—the survivors of a regiment of one thousand that went forward forty-eight hours before. I have seen children starving. I have seen the agony of mothers and wives. I hate war.

I have passed unnumbered hours, I shall pass unnumbered hours, thinking and planning how war may be kept from this Nation.

I wish I could keep war from all Nations; but that is beyond my power. I can at least make certain that no act of the United States helps to produce or to promote war. I can at least make clear that the conscience of America revolts against war and that any Nation which provokes war forfeits the sympathy of the people of the United States.

Many causes produce war. There are ancient hatreds, turbulent frontiers, the "legacy of old forgotten, far-off things, and battles long ago." There are new-born fanaticisms, convictions on the part of certain peoples that they have become the unique depositories of ultimate truth and right.

A dark old world was devastated by wars between conflicting religions. A dark modern world faces wars between conflicting economic and political fanaticisms in which are intertwined race hatreds. To bring it home, it is as if within the territorial limits of the United States, forty-eight Nations with forty-eight forms of government, forty-eight customs barriers, forty-eight languages, and forty-eight eternal and different verities, were spending their time and their substance in a frenzy of effort to make themselves strong enough to conquer their neighbors or strong enough to defend themselves against their neighbors.

In one field, that of economic barriers, the American policy may be, I hope, of some assistance in discouraging the economic source of war and therefore a contribution toward the peace of the world. The trade agreements which we are making are not only finding outlets for the products of American fields and American factories but are also pointing the way to the elimination of embargoes, quotas and other devices which place such pressure on Nations not possessing great natural resources that to them the price of peace seems less terrible than the price of war.

We do not maintain that a more liberal international trade will stop war; but we fear that without a more liberal international trade, war is a natural sequence.

The Congress of the United States has given me certain authority to provide safeguards of American neutrality in case of war.

The President of the United States, who, under our Constitution, is vested with primary authority to conduct our international relations, thus has been given new weapons with which to maintain our neutrality.

Nevertheless—and I speak from a long experience—the effective maintenance of American neutrality depends today, as in the past, on the wisdom and determination of whoever at the moment occupy the offices of President and Secretary of State.

It is clear that our present policy and the measures passed by the Congress would, in the event of a war on some other continent, reduce war profits which would otherwise accrue to American citizens. Industrial and agricultural production for a war market may give immense fortunes to a few men; for the Nation as a whole it produces disaster. It was the prospect of war profits that made our farmers in the West plow up prairie land that should never have been plowed, but should have been left for grazing cattle. Today we are reaping the harvest of those war profits in the dust storms which have devastated those war-plowed areas.

It was the prospect of war profits that caused the extension of monopoly and unjustified expansion of industry and a price level so high that the normal relationship between debtor and creditor was destroyed.

Nevertheless, if war should break out again in another continent, let us not blink the fact that we would find in this country thousands of Americans who, seeking immediate riches—fools' gold—would attempt to break down or evade our neutrality.

They would tell you—and, unfortunately, their views would get wide publicity—that if they could produce and ship this and that and the other article to belligerent Nations, the unemployed of America would all find work. They would tell you that if they could extend credit to warring Nations that credit would be used in the United States to build homes and factories and pay our debts. They would tell you that America once more would capture the trade of the world.

It would be hard to resist that clamor; it would be hard for many

Americans, I fear, to look beyond—to realize the inevitable penalties, the inevitable day of reckoning, that come from a false prosperity. To resist the clamor of that greed, if war should come, would require the unswerving support of all Americans who love peace.

If we face the choice of profits or peace, the Nation will answer— must answer—"We choose peace." It is the duty of all of us to encourage such a body of public opinion in this country that the answer will be clear and for all practical purposes unanimous.

With that wise and experienced man who is our Secretary of State, whose statemanship has met with such wide approval, I have thought and worked long and hard on the problem of keeping the United States at peace. But all the wisdom of America is not to be found in the White House or in the Department of State; we need the meditation, the prayer, and the positive support of the people of America who go along with us in seeking peace.

No matter how well we are supported by neutrality legislation, we must remember that no laws can be provided to cover every contingency, for it is impossible to imagine how every future event may shape itself. In spite of every possible forethought, international relations involve of necessity a vast uncharted area. In that area safe sailing will depend on the knowledge and the experience and the wisdom of those who direct our foreign policy. Peace will depend on their day-to-day decisions.

At this late date, with the wisdom which is so easy after the event and so difficult before the event, we find it possible to trace the tragic series of small decisions which led Europe into the Great War in 1914 and eventually engulfed us and many other Nations.

We can keep out of war if those who watch and decide have a sufficiently detailed understanding of international affairs to make certain that the small decisions of each day do not lead toward war and if, at the same time, they possess the courage to say "no" to those who selfishly or unwisely would let us go to war. . . .

50

History Repeats Itself

READING the newspapers, the past few days, I have had a nightmare feeling. It is as though I were watching for the second time
the early reels of a motion picture whose story ends in tragedy. As I
see the actors on the screen make again the same mistakes I have seen
before, knowing what the unhappy outcome will be I am sickened by
the realization of how history does in fact repeat itself—how literally
true it is that we learn nothing from experience.

I remember vividly the days before April, 1917, when a country that
did not want to go to war was tricked and bullied and persuaded into
doing so. That war was a useless and unholy enterprise; not only this
country but the world would have been far better off if we had stayed
out of it and permitted the European conflict to end, as it probably
would have ended, with a negotiated peace. Today, I see signs that the
same sort of pressure is being applied, for reasons which have as little
merit, to push us into the Far Eastern struggle. I see a sudden tension
where a few weeks ago there was none—a tension wholly unjustified by
any events of which I am aware. Old moorings have suddenly been
slipped. People are beginning to spout magnificent but meaningless
phrases concerning "our national honor." Even more than usual, such
phrases are substituted for thinking. Day by day, items fling themselves across the headlines that make me feel some sort of madness is
descending upon my familiar solid world.

President Roosevelt says we must not "close our eyes to the fact
that we are part of a large world of other nations and peoples." He
feels we "owe some measure of cooperation and even leadership in maintaining standards of conduct helpful to the goal of ultimate peace." But
no one has suggested, Mr. President, that we should close our eyes to
this obvious fact and obligation. No one is opposed to doing what we
can in maintaining "standards of conduct helpful to the goal of ul-

SOURCE: Bruce Bliven, "This Is Where I Came In," New Republic, XCIII
(1938), 245–6.

timate peace." But what are those standards? Do we live up to them
when we permit Americans to get in front of an advancing Japanese
army, remain there for many months, and then, some of them, get
killed? Are these standards honored when we insist that Tokyo must—
or take the consequences—control the young hotheads in the Japanese
army whom the government is plainly unable to control? Do we maintain these standards when we seize this moment of grave tension,
general apprehension, to demand a sudden and staggering increase of
half a billion dollars in our military establishment, whose efforts to
cope properly with the next war are already costing us a billion a year
and more?

I admit I am terrified when Alfred M. Landon suddenly emerges from
his obscurity to announce that in this deep national crisis he is standing behind President Roosevelt. There isn't any deep national crisis,
Mr. Landon: the best way to produce one is for people like you to go
around saying that it is here.

I am terrified when Colonel Knox, the fighting newspaper publisher,
announces that he too is standing behind the President. Nobody has
asked Colonel Knox to stand anywhere at all. No one, so far as I know,
has the faintest desire to do so.

It alarms me to see that most of the daily press, having announced
in huge black type that ninety-six were killed when the *Panay* sank,
printed obscurely with no headlines at all the final fact that the number
of Americans who died was three. The death of three men, or even
one man, is a tragic happening; but I seem to detect in the editors a
desire—unconscious, of course: all our most mischievous desires are
unconscious—to leave with the public the original impression, so much
more exciting and dramatic, so much better as a basis for jingoism.

I am dismayed when Secretary Hull says that our 7,000 soldiers,
sailors and Marines will be kept in China indefinitely and that American citizens will not be asked to leave. The good gray Secretary says
that in the Far East we have developed during a century "certain rights,
certain interests, certain obligations and certain practices." The government cannot, he says, "suddenly disavow its obligations and responsibilities." Our citizens "cannot suddenly disavow or suddenly cut
themselves off from the past." Secretary Hull is talking extremely
dangerous nonsense. When he says "the American government cannot" what he means is "I won't." A fair translation of his statement
would be: "We have quite a lot of money invested in China. We have
already taken the risk of sacrificing some lives in protection of that
money, and lost. We propose to continue that gamble, including the
danger of getting into a war."

I am perturbed when Henry L. Stimson, former Secretary of State, chooses this moment to come forward with a very long letter in *The New York Times* upholding the right of the President to make war and opposing the plan for a popular referendum in all cases except one of actual invasion. Colonel Stimson, like others, seems to feel a tension in the air, to believe we have suddenly and somehow arrived at a tremendous American crisis. . . .

I am alarmed when Walter Winchell quotes "a big man in Wall Street" as saying the United States will be at war inside of three weeks. I am reasonably sure that the big man in Wall Street knows no more about it than Walter does, or I do. What frightens me out of my boots is the development in the American climate of opinion that permits such a bit of gossip to be idly uttered, cheerfully printed, casually read. Nothing like that could have happened three months ago. No more could we, then, have had the Washington columnists reporting that our belligerence toward Japan, our piling note on note, our demanding fresh apologies while earlier ones still linger in the air—that all these things are a deliberate plan to take popular attention away from the "recession" which, in a few weeks, has recapitulated the whole economic history of 1930 and 1931.

Finally, I am terrified when word comes from the White House after a press conference that the President knows (I paraphrase) that he can count upon the patriotism of the American people to stand behind him in whatever action he takes in this grave hour. When you put it in those terms, Mr. President, the country will always and automatically say Yes. We have been conditioned through lifetimes to make a positive response to such a positive demand. But my point is that no situation exists which requires any such response. It is possible to argue that we ought to take collective action with the "democracies" against the aggressor nations—through even this is a far oversimplified statement of what seems to me a highly dubious course. But what is being said and done in Washington today bears little relation to any such proposal. The flag is being waved as though the past twenty years of world history had never taken place. The challenge that is being hurled is from the United States alone to Japan alone. I am well aware that naval warfare across 6,000 miles of the Pacific is technically very difficult. But I am aware, also, that even if we never invaded Japan, and Japan never invaded us, such a war would be a world calamity. It would, in all human probability, set the match to Europe. It would destroy our democracy and that of every other country, including the socialist regime of Soviet Russia. When it comes to lighting matches in a powder mine, I am an advocate of good, hearty cowardice. I wouldn't even light matches in the doorway. In fact, I would keep well away from the place.

In 1917 there was also that strange tension in the air, that feeling of an approaching storm. Then, as now, we were writing notes to a foreign power that was interfering with the "right" of our citizens to walk in the path of the avalanche. Then, as now, all sorts of queer people popped up announcing that they would never, never desert the President. Then as now, apologies were made and were instantly denounced as unsatisfactory. And so I feel, as I watch the motion picture of events unreeling on the screen of time, that I have seen it all before. This is where I came in. Must I experience the whole drama once again?

51

Litany for Dictatorships

For all those beaten, for the broken heads,
The fosterless, the simple, the oppressed,
The ghosts in the burning city of our time . . .

For those taken in rapid cars to the house and beaten
By the skilful boys, the boys with the rubber fists,
—Held down and beaten, the table cutting their loins,
Or kicked in the groin and left, with the muscles jerking
Like a headless hen's on the floor of the slaughter-house
While they brought the next man in with his white eyes staring.
For those who still said "Red Front!" or "God Save the Crown!"
And for those who were not courageous
But were beaten nevertheless.
For those who spit out the bloody stumps of their teeth
Quietly in the hall,
Sleep well on stone or iron, watch for the time
And kill the guard in the privy before they die,
Those with the deep-socketed eyes and the lamp burning.

For those who carry the scars, who walk lame—for those
Whose nameless graves are made in the prison-yard
And the earth smoothed back before morning and the lime scat-
tered.

For those slain at once. For those living through months and years
Enduring, watching, hoping, going each day
To the work or the queue for meat or the secret club,
Living meanwhile, begetting children, smuggling guns,
And found and killed at the end like rats in a drain.

SOURCE: Stephen Vincent Benét, "Litany for Dictatorships," in *The
Selected Works of Stephen Vincent Benét* (New York, 1942), pp. 429–32.

For those escaping
Incredibly into exile and wandering there.
For those who live in the small rooms of foreign cities
And who yet think of the country, the long green grass,
The childhood voices, the language, the way wind smelt then,
The shape of rooms, the coffee drunk at the table,
The talk with friends, the loved city, the waiter's face,
The gravestones, with the name, where they will not lie
Nor in any of that earth. Their children are strangers.

For those who planned and were leaders and were beaten
And for those, humble and stupid, who had no plan
But were denounced, but grew angry, but told a joke,
But could not explain, but were sent away to the camp,
But had their bodies shipped back in the sealed coffins,
"Died of pneumonia." "Died trying to escape."

For those growers of wheat who were shot by their own wheat-
     stacks,
For those growers of bread who were sent to the ice-locked wastes,
And their flesh remembers their fields.

For those denounced by their smug, horrible children
For a peppermint-star and the praise of the Perfect State,
For all those strangled or gelded or merely starved
To make perfect states; for the priest hanged in his cassock,
The Jew with his chest crushed in and his eyes dying,
The revolutionist lynched by the private guards
To make perfect states, in the names of the perfect states.

For those betrayed by the neighbors they shook hands with
And for the traitors, sitting in the hard chair
With the loose sweat crawling their hair and their fingers restless
As they tell the street and the house and the man's name.

And for those sitting at table in the house
With the lamp lit and the plates and the smell of food,
Talking so quietly; when they hear the cars
And the knock at the door, and they look at each other quickly
And the woman goes to the door with a stiff face,
Smoothing her dress.
                    "We are all good citizens here.

We believe in the Perfect State."
And that was the last
Time Tony or Karl or Shorty came to the house
And the family was liquidated later.
It was the last time.
We heard the shots in the night
But nobody knew next day what the trouble was
And a man must go to his work. So I didn't see him
For three days, then, and me near out of my mind
And all the patrols on the streets with their dirty guns
And when he came back, he looked drunk, and the blood was on
    him.

For the women who mourn their dead in the secret night,
For the children taught to keep quiet, the old children,
The children spat-on at school.
For the wrecked laboratory,
The gutted house, the dunged picture, the pissed-in well,
The naked corpse of Knowledge flung in the square
And no man lifting a hand and no man speaking.

For the cold of the pistol-butt and the bullet's heat,
For the rope that chokes, the manacles that bind,
The huge voice, metal, that lies from a thousand tubes
And the stuttering machine-gun that answers all.

For the man crucified on the crossed machine-guns
Without name, without resurrection, without stars,
His dark head heavy with death and his flesh long sour
With the smell of his many prisons—John Smith, John Doe,
John Nobody—oh, crack your mind for his name!
Faceless as water, naked as the dust,
Dishonored as the earth the gas-shells poison
And barbarous with portent.
This is he.
This is the man they ate at the green table
Putting their gloves on ere they touched the meat.
This is the fruit of war, the fruit of peace,
The ripeness of invention, the new lamb,
The answer to the wisdom of the wise.
And still he hangs, and still he will not die,
And still, on the steel city of our years

The light fails and the terrible blood streams down.
We thought we were done with these things but we were wrong.
We thought, because we had power, we had wisdom.
We thought the long train would run to the end of Time.
We thought the light would increase.
Now the long train stands derailed and the bandits loot it.
Now the boar and the asp have power in our time.
Now the night rolls back on the West and the night is solid.
Our fathers and ourselves sowed dragon's teeth.
Our children know and suffer the armed men.

52

Weep in Years to Come

THEY came out of the movie house and started slowly eastward in the direction of Fifth Avenue. "Hitler!" a newsboy called. "Hitler!"

"That Fletcher," Dora said, "the one that played her father. Remember him?"

"Uh huh," Paul said, holding her hand as they walked slowly up the dark street.

"He's got stones in his kidney."

"That's the way he acts," Paul said. "Now I know how to describe the way that man acts—he acts like a man who has stones in his kidney."

Dora laughed. "I X-rayed him last winter. He's one of Dr. Thayer's best patients. He's always got something wrong with him. He's going to try to pass the stones out of his kidney this summer."

"Good luck, Fletcher, old man," Paul said.

"I used to massage his shoulder. He had neuritis. He makes fifteen hundred dollars a week."

"No wonder he has neuritis."

"He asked me to come to his house for dinner." Dora pulled her hand out of Paul's and slipped it up to his elbow and held on, hard. "He likes me."

"I bet he does."

"What about you?"

"What about me what?" Paul asked.

"Do you like me?"

They stopped at Rockefeller Plaza and leaned over the marble wall and looked down at the fountain and the statue and the people sitting out at the tables, drinking, and the waiters standing around, listening to the sound of the fountain.

"I can't stand you," Paul said. He kissed her hair.

"That's what I thought," Dora said. They both laughed.

SOURCE: Irwin Shaw, "Weep in Years to Come," *Mixed Company* (New York, 1950), pp. 310–17.

They looked down at the Plaza, at the thin trees with the light-green leaves rustling in the wind that came down between the buildings. There were pansies, yellow and tight, along the borders of the small pools with the bronze sea statues, and hydrangeas, and little full trees, all shaking in the wind and the diffuse, clear light of the flood lamps above. Couples strolled slowly down from Fifth Avenue, talking amiably in low, calm, week-end voices, appreciating the Rockefeller frivolity and extravagance which had carved a place for hydrangeas and water and saplings and spring and sea-gods riding bronze dolphins out of these austere buildings, out of the bleak side of Business.

Paul and Dora walked up the promenade, looking in the windows. They stopped at a window filled with men's sports clothes—gabardine slacks and bright-colored shirts with short sleeves and brilliant handkerchiefs to tie around the throat.

"I had visions," Paul said, "of sitting in my garden, with two Great Danes, dressed like that, like a Hollywood actor in the country."

"Have you got a garden?" Dora asked.

"No."

"Those're nice pants," Dora said.

They went on to the next window. "On the other hand," Paul said, "there are days when I want to look like that. A derby hat and a stiff blue shirt with a pleated bosom and a little starched white collar and a five-dollar neat little necktie and a Burberry overcoat. Leave the office at five o'clock every day to go to a cocktail party."

"You go to a cocktail party almost every afternoon anyway," Dora said. "Without a derby hat."

"A different kind of cocktail party," Paul said. He started her across Fifth Avenue. "The kind attended by men with starched blue pleated bosoms. Some day."

"Oh, Lord," Dora said as they ran to escape a bus, "look at those dresses."

They stood in front of Saks.

"Fifth Avenue," Paul said. "Street of dreams."

"It's nice to know things like that exist," Dora murmured, looking into the stage-lit window at the yellow dress and the sign that said "Tropical Nights in Manhattan" and the little carved-stone fish that for some reason was in the same window. "Even if you can't have them."

"Uptown?" Paul asked. "Or to my house?"

"I feel like walking." Dora looked up at Paul and grinned. "For the moment." She squeezed his arm. "Only for the moment. Uptown."

They started uptown.

"I love those models," Paul said. "Each and every one of them. They're superior, yet warm; inviting, yet polite. Their breasts are always tipped at the correct angle for the season."

"Sure," Dora said, "papier-mâché. It's easy with papier-mâché. Look. Aluminum suitcases. Travel by air."

"They look like my mother's kitchen pots."

"Wouldn't you like to own a few of them?"

"Yes." Paul peered at them. "Fly away. Buy luggage and depart. Leave for the ends of the earth."

"They got a little case just for books. A whole separate little traveling bookcase."

"That's just what I need," Paul said, "for my trips on the Fifth Avenue bus every morning."

They passed St. Patrick's, dark and huge, with the moon sailing over it.

"Do you think God walks up Fifth Avenue?" Paul asked.

"Sure," said Dora. "Why not?"

"We are princes of the earth," Paul said. "All over the world men slave to bring riches to these few blocks for us to look at and say 'Yes, very nice' or 'Take it away, it stinks.' I feel very important when I walk up Fifth Avenue."

They stopped at the window of the Hamburg-American Line. Little dolls in native costumes danced endlessly around a pole while other dolls in native costume looked on. All the dolls had wide smiles on their faces. "Harvest Festival in Buckeburg, Germany," a small sign said.

A private policeman turned the corner and stood and watched them. They moved to the next window.

" 'A suggestion to passengers to promote carefree travel,' " Paul read off a booklet. "Also, Hapag-Lloyd announces a twenty-per-cent reduction for all educators on sabbatical leave. They are 'Masters in the Art of Travel,' they say."

"I used to want to go to see Germany," Dora said. "I know a lot of Germans and they're nice."

"I'll be there soon," Paul said as they passed the private policeman.

"You're going to visit it?"

"Uh huh. At the expense of the government. In a well-tailored khaki uniform. I'm going to see glamorous Europe, seat of culture, at last. From a bombing plane. To our left we have the Stork Club, seat of culture for East Fifty-third Street. Look at the pretty girls. A lot of them have breasts at the correct angle, too. See how nature mimics art. New York is a wonderful city."

Dora didn't say anything. She hung onto him tightly as they went down the street. They turned at the corner and walked down Madison

Avenue. After a while they stopped at a shop that had phonographs and radios in the window. "That's what I want." Paul pointed at a machine. "A Capehart. It plays two symphonies at a time. You just lie on your back and out come Brahms and Beethoven and Prokofieff. That's the way life should be. Lie on your back and be surrounded by great music, automatically."

Dora looked at the phonograph, all mahogany and doors and machinery. "Do you really think there's going to be a war?" she said.

"Sure. They're warming up the pitchers now. They're waiting to see if the other side has right-handed or left-handed batters before they nominate their starting pitchers."

They continued walking downtown.

"But it's in Europe," Dora said. "Do you think we'll get into it?"

"Sure. Read the papers." He glanced at the window they were passing. "Look at those nice tables. Informal luncheons on your terrace. Metal and glass for outdoor feeding. That would be nice, eating out on a terrace off those wonderful colored plates, rich food with green salads. With a view of mountains and a lake, and, inside, the phonograph."

"That sounds good," Dora said quietly.

"I could get an extra speaker," Paul said, "and wire it out to the terrace, so we could listen as we ate. I like Mozart with dinner." He laughed and drew her to a bookstore window.

"I always get sad," Dora said, "when I look in a bookshop window and see all the books I'm never going to have time to read."

Paul kissed her. "What did you think the first time you saw me?" he asked.

"What did you think?"

"I thought, 'I must get that girl!' "

Dora laughed, close to him.

"What did you think?" Paul asked.

"I thought"—she giggled—"I thought, 'I must get that man!' "

"Isn't New York marvelous?" Paul said. "Where did you say you come from?"

"Seattle," Dora said. "Seattle, Washington."

"Here we are on Madison Avenue, holding hands, shopping for the future. . . ."

"Even if there was a war," Dora said after a while, "why would you have to get mixed up in it? Why would the United States have to get mixed up in it?"

"They got into the last one, didn't they?" Paul said. "They'll get into this one."

"They were gypped the last time," Dora said. "The guys who were killed were gypped."

"That's right," said Paul. "They were killed for six-per-cent interest on bonds, for oil wells, for spheres of influence. I wish I had a sphere of influence."

"Still," said Dora, "you'd enlist this time?"

"Yop. The first day. I'd walk right up to the recruiting office and say, 'Paul Triplett, twenty-six years old, hard as nails, good eyes, good teeth, good feet; give me a gun. Put me in a plane, so I can do a lot of damage.'"

They walked a whole block in silence.

"Don't you think you'd be gypped this time, too?" Dora said. "Don't you think they'd have you fighting for bonds and oil wells all over again?"

"Uh huh."

"And even so, you'd sign up?"

"The first day."

Dora pulled her hand away from him. "Do you *like* the idea of killing people?"

"I hate the idea," Paul said slowly. "I don't want to hurt anybody. I think the idea of war is ridiculous. I want to live in a world in which everybody sits on a terrace and eats off a metal-and-glass table off colored plates and the phonograph inside turns Mozart over automatically and the music is piped out to an extra loud-speaker on the terrace. Only Hitler isn't interested in that kind of world. He's interested in another kind of world. I couldn't stand to live in his kind of world, German or home-made."

"You wouldn't kill Hitler," Dora said. "You'd just kill young boys like yourself."

"That's right."

"Do you like that?"

"I'm really not interested in killing Hitler, either," Paul said. "I want to kill the idea he represents for so many people. In years to come I'll cry over the young boys I've killed and maybe if they kill me, they'll cry over me."

"They're probably just like you." They were walking fast now.

"Sure," Paul said. "I'm sure they'd love to go to bed with you tonight. I bet they'd love to walk along the fountains with the bronze statues in Rockefeller Plaza, holding hands with you on a spring Saturday evening and looking at the sports clothes in the windows. I bet a lot of them like Mozart, too, but still I'll kill them. Gladly."

"Gladly?"

"Yes, gladly." Paul wiped his eyes with his hands, suddenly tired. "Gladly today. I'll weep for them in years to come. Today they're guns aimed at me and the world I want. Their bodies protect an idea I have to kill to live. Hey!" He stretched out his hands and caught hers. "What's the sense talking about things like this tonight?"

"But it's all a big fraud," Dora cried. "You're being used and you know it."

"That's right," Paul said. "It's all a big fraud, the whole business. Even so, I got to fight. I'll be gypped, but by a little bit I'll do something for my side, for Mozart on a terrace at dinner. What the hell, it's not even heroism. I'll be dragged in, whatever I say."

"That's too bad," Dora said softly, walking by herself. "It's too bad."

"Sure," Paul said. "Some day maybe it'll be better. Maybe some day the world'll be run for people who like Mozart. Not today."

They stopped. They were in front of a little art store. There was a reproduction of the Renoir painting of a boating party on the river. There was the woman kissing the Pekinese, and the man in his underwear with a straw hat and his red beard, solid as earth, and the wit with his cocked derby hat whispering to the woman with her hands to her ears, and there was the great still life in the foreground, of wine and bottles and glasses and grapes and food.

"I saw it in Washington," Paul said. "They had it in Washington. You can't tell why it's a great picture from the print. There's an air of pink immortality hanging over it. They got it in New York now and I go look at it three times a week. It's settled, happy, solid. It's a picture of a summertime that vanished a long time ago." Paul kissed her hand. "It's getting late, darling, the hours're dwindling. Let's go home."

They got into a cab and went downtown to his apartment.

53

The Charlottesville Program

I NOTICE by the program that I am asked to address the classes of 1940. I avail myself of that privilege, but I also take this very apt occasion to speak to many other classes, classes that have graduated through all the years, classes that are still in the period of study, classes not alone of the schools of learning of the Nation but classes that have come up through the great schools of experience; in other words a cross section, a cross section just as you who graduate today are a cross section of the Nation as a whole. . . .

Some . . . still hold to the now somewhat obvious delusion that we of the United States can safely permit the United States to become a lone island, a lone island in a world dominated by the philosophy of force.

Such an island may be the dream of those who still talk and vote as isolationists. Such an island represents to me and to the overwhelming majority of Americans today a helpless nightmare, the helpless nightmare of a people without freedom; yes, the nightmare of a people lodged in prison, handcuffed, hungry, and fed through the bars from day to day by the contemptuous, unpitying masters of other continents.

It is natural also that we should ask ourselves how now we can prevent the building of that prison and the placing of ourselves in the midst of it.

Let us not hesitate—all of us—to proclaim certain truths. Overwhelmingly we, as a Nation—and this applies to all the other American nations —are convinced that military and naval victory for the gods of force and hate would endanger the institutions of democracy in the western world, and that equally, therefore, the whole of our sympathies lies with those nations that are giving their life blood in combat against these forces.

SOURCE: Franklin D. Roosevelt, Address at Charlottesville, Va., June 10, 1940, in *Department of State Bulletin*, II (1940), 635.

The people and the Government of the United States have seen with the utmost regret and with grave disquiet the decision of the Italian Government to engage in the hostilities now raging in Europe.

More than 3 months ago the Chief of the Italian Government sent me word that because of the determination of Italy to limit, so far as might be possible, the spread of the European conflict, more than 200 millions of people in the region of the Mediterranean had been enabled to escape the suffering and the devastation of war.

I informed the Chief of the Italian Government that this desire on the part of Italy to prevent the war from spreading met with full sympathy and response on the part of the Government and the people of the United States, and I expressed the earnest hope of this Government and of this people that this policy on the part of Italy might be continued. I made it clear that in the opinion of the Government of the United States any extension of hostilities in the region of the Mediterranean might result in a still greater enlargement of the scene of the conflict, the conflict in the Near East and in Africa, and that if this came to pass no one could foretell how much greater the theater of the war eventually might become.

Again on a subsequent occasion, not so long ago, recognizing that certain aspirations of Italy might form the basis of discussions between the powers most specifically concerned, I offered, in a message addressed to the Chief of the Italian Government, to send to the Governments of France and of Great Britain such specific indications of the desires of Italy to obtain readjustments with regard to her position as the Chief of the Italian Government might desire to transmit through me. While making it clear that the Government of the United States in such an event could not and would not assume responsibility for the nature of the proposals submitted nor for agreements which might thereafter be reached, I proposed that if Italy would refrain from entering the war I would be willing to ask assurances from the other powers concerned that they would faithfully execute any agreement so reached and that Italy's voice in any future peace conference would have the same authority as if Italy had actually taken part in the war, as a belligerent.

Unfortunately, unfortunately to the regret of all of us and to the regret of humanity, the Chief of the Italian Government was unwilling to accept the procedure suggested, and he has made no counterproposal.

This Government directed its efforts to doing what it could to work for the preservation of peace in the Mediterranean area, and it likewise expressed its willingness to endeavor to cooperate with the Government of Italy when the appropriate occasion arose for the creation of a more stable world order, through the reduction of armaments and through the construction of a more liberal international economic system which would assure to all powers equality of opportunity in the world's markets and in the securing of raw materials on equal terms.

I have likewise, of course, felt it necessary in my communications to Signor Mussolini to express the concern of the Government of the United States because of the fact that any extension of the war in the region of the Mediterranean would inevitably result in great prejudice to the ways of life and government and to the trade and commerce of all of the American republics.

The Government of Italy has now chosen to preserve what it terms its "freedom of action" and to fulfill what it states are its promises to Germany. In so doing it has manifested disregard for the rights and security of other nations, disregard for the lives of the peoples of those nations which are directly threatened by this spread of the war; and has evidenced its unwillingness to find the means through pacific negotiations for the satisfaction of what it believes are its legitimate aspirations.

On this tenth day of June 1940, the hand that held the dagger has struck it into the back of its neighbor.

On this tenth day of June 1940, in this University founded by the first great American teacher of democracy, we send forth our prayers and our hopes to those beyond the seas who are maintaining with magnificent valor their battle for freedom.

In our, in our unity, in our American unity, we will pursue two obvious and simultaneous courses; we will extend to the opponents of force the material resources of this Nation and, at the same time, we will harness and speed up the use of those resources in order that we ourselves in the Americas may have equipment and training equal to the task of any emergency and every defense.

All roads leading to the accomplishment of these objectives must be kept clear of obstructions. We will not slow down or detour. Signs and signals call for speed—full speed ahead.

Yes, it is right that each new generation should ask questions. But in recent months the principal question has been somewhat simplified. Once more the future of the Nation, the future of the American people is at stake.

We need not and we will not, in any way, abandon our continuing effort to make democracy work within our borders. Yes, we still insist on the need for vast improvements in our own social and economic life.

But that, that is a component part of national defense itself.

The program unfolds swiftly, and into that program will fit the responsibility and the opportunity of every man and woman in the land to preserve his and her heritage in days of peril.

I call for effort, courage, sacrifice, devotion. Granting the love of freedom, all of these are possible.

And—and the love of freedom is still fierce, still steady in the Nation today.

54

The Cry for Appeasement

June 13, 1940

L UNCHED with Anne O'Hare McCormick and listened to her
views, which are rather blue. I told her, and subsequently told the
Secretary, a matter which has been disturbing my mind for some days,
ever since the President used the phrase of the "hand that holds the
dagger" in his Charlottesville speech. Incidentally the phrase first read
"Brutus' attack on Caesar"—or words to that effect. It was cut out and
the copy prepared without it, and this other phrase was interjected over
the air. In my opinion we have gone a little farther than we should go—
not only in attacking the heads of other Governments but in making
gestures to the Allies. If we are not very careful we are going to find ourselves the champions of a defeated cause. Today Paris is occupied by the
Germans, the French army disorganized and in retreat, and millions of
refugees along the roads of southern France in various states of despair
and destitution. France has utterly collapsed. It may not be but a few
weeks before England collapses and Hitler stands rampant across the
continent of Europe. The United States must not put herself in a position of antagonizing that military power until it is ready to meet it. It
will take us two years to be ready to meet it. To oppose it today is not
only rash, but seems to be oblivious to the fact that it only takes one
power to make a war. We may have war thrust upon us if we antago-
nize the military machine which is about to assume control of the whole
continent of Europe.

But further than that, there are implications of a political nature
which are pregnant with infinite possibilities. The Democratic Convention is scheduled to meet in just about a month—July 15—and this
is June 13. Suppose England collapses within thirty days and Roosevelt

SOURCE: Fred L. Israel (ed.), *The War Diary of Breckinridge Long*
(Lincoln, Nebr.), pp. 104-5, 107-8, 115-16, 122-3, 146-8.

appears as a candidate for renomination before the Convention as an individual who has antagonized the only two powers in Europe and as the champion of the lost cause. It is quite possible that there might be serious opposition to his nomination. If he should be nominated, as he probably would anyhow, there would probably be raised by the Republicans the cry that we had tried to put the country into the war; that we had jeopardized the neutrality of the United States by supplying arms and ammunition to the losing belligerents; and that we had by personal invective antagonized the two powers to be supreme on the continent of Europe. It is quite conceivable that the country would rally to the Republican cause. It is certain that all the German elements, the Italian elements, and many of the foreign elements, and every subversive agent and every Russian activist and all the Communists, and all the Socialists, and most assuredly all the Republicans, and there are a lot of them, would be aligned against us, and we would probably be defeated in November. . . .

June 17, 1940

This morning the French have practically surrendered. They have ceased fighting and asked for an armistice. . . . A conference in the Secretary's office this morning. The Military Liaison reported the demoralization of the French and the probable invasion of England from Ireland with parachute troops and an intensive extension of warfare against England. But that of course does not need a military expert to predict. The fate of the British fleet will be next. After all, it is not the fleet of the British Empire but the fleet of little England. It is the people of England itself that own it, pay for it, maintain it, man it and control it. It is controlled in the interests of the people of England. They look down upon the Canadians and Australians and South Africans. They call them "colonials," and assume that they are in a different scale of life and belong to a different scheme of things. Only England is foremost in their minds, and if the sacrificing of the fleet will save England, they will sacrifice it. They will be so mad at us for not having come to their assistance that when they sacrifice it they will probably hope the Germans will come after us with it and will wish them bon voyage. By all that I mean simply that the fleet is theirs, for their own protection, and for their own use, and if they can sacrifice it to save themselves, they will do it irrespective of what happens to Canada, Australia and other things.

At the moment it looks like 30 or 60 days as a lease of life for England. She will fight, and there will be a scrap, and if she can delay it,

Germany will be eventually licked, but anybody who would predict that today would have to draw a long bow to his imagination. . . .

June 28, 1940

Events follow one another so fast in this world it is hard to really appreciate the rate of speed at which we are proceeding. The known world has been overrun a few times in history, but it took years and years and years. Alexander did it in his world, small as it was, and he had an army of a stupendous size of a million men on foot. Caesar did it two thousand years ago. Genghis Khan overran his world, which was another one from the one our ancestors had lived in. Napoleon did a good job in Europe but failed to conquer all of Europe. But those all were processes of years. Today Hitler has placed himself more or less supreme in continental Europe outside of Russia. Yesterday Russia started again, and it looks as if she would occupy Finland, and she has been conceded the right to occupy Bessarabia. Rumania loses Bessarabia, and she is now afraid she will lose the Dobrudja to Hungary. Turkey is afraid she will lose her strip in continental Europe, and it looks as if she was about to have a movement made against it. England is preparing against the onslaught by Germany to defeat her own island. The British navy has deserted Hong Kong and left it undefended. The French are about to lose Indo China to Japan. The islands of the seas are wondering which of them will be taken next. The colonial possessions in Africa are in a quandary, and South Africa is showing distinct signs of rebelling against the rule of England. In South America, Argentina and Uruguay and Chile are showing other signs of having within their midst strong adherents to the Nazi cause. The whole world seems to be in movement. It is kaleidoscopic. The picture is never the same for more than a few minutes. As I sit at my desk and read the telegrams that come through the day from every part of the world I am conscious of the astonishing fact that when I have digested a situation as reported from one part of the world before the day goes by a development will upset the concept upon which that information was based. No one knows what will happen next. Of all the epochs of history to be alive this seems to be the most exciting and the most conducive to an appalled interest. . . .

August 8, 1940

Cudahy went to London recently and has unburdened himself of a highly questionable press interview in which he advocates feeding the starving Belgians and the starving people of Europe, generally praising the Germans and comparing them most generously with the American troops. We ordered him home immediately, but the reverberations of his indiscretion will be rumbling around for some time. . . .

August 13, 1940

. . . Lunched with Bullitt. He says Pétain is not Fascist or Nazi but simply the administrator of an estate in bankruptcy—trying to save what he can. He thinks France will continue long under German influence if not control because of the fear of further punishment. He thinks this country alarmingly calm and disinterested about its fate; that Hitler will be here through South America "before Christmas"; that sentiment should be aroused; that the President told him to get movements started and he is doing it. He quoted the President as saying he himself could not be alarming because the people would think he was playing politics—with which I quite agree. . . .

England is experiencing a serious bombardment. It looks like the beginning of the long expected drive. There are many losses on each side but the British cannot replace their lost men. That is the neck of the bottle. The implications are serious for us. If England is forced to submit—which I easily envisage and somewhat expect—though I see a hard struggle with possible victory—we may look for the British fleet to get to German hands—or at least what may be left of it. In that case we have a fight on our hands—with the Atlantic and Pacific to guard—and South America not only to protect but to prevent the establishment there of even local armies armed and trained by Germans. They would have air bases there as a matter of course—and refuelling ports—and we could not permit that. If we did it would be our turn next. . . .

August 16, 1940

Phillips was in yesterday. I did not ask him whether he is resigning—though I know he wants to. He has family difficulties. He looks very well—says all his information is Germany will win—control all Central, Western, Eastern Europe, let Italy run Balkans, North Africa, Mediterranean. Ciano confident. He (Phillips) thinks there should be no more provocative statements. Wants to rest in Maine woods.

Cudahy was in today. He is sure Germany will win—if by a miracle England can hold out it will be a "30 years war" and Europe destroyed—all to our own disadvantage—and Communism win—more or less my own thesis. He sees no disadvantage to us if Germany wins. . . .

November 6, 1940

. . . I was up late last night, so slept somewhat late this morning and arrived late at the Department. Kennedy came down, and I sat in for a long talk with him, the Secretary and Welles. He is quite a realist, and he sees England gone. I think he is probably somewhat influenced by the situation he has been in. It could hardly be otherwise. Bombs dropping around, industry paralyzed and communication lines being gradually disrupted must bring with them a sense of defeatism.

Anyway, Kennedy thinks that England is broke; that she will have about two hundred million dollars in gold; that she can spend that here but if she does she will have to go off the gold standard; that if she goes off the gold standard her obligation to us cannot be met; that in any case she cannot continue to buy from us for cash and that she must have money. He said that they were just waiting until the present moment, after the election, to present to us their requests for credits. Without credits they cannot continue. He warned them that changing our system was a question of changing our laws and that change could not be easily done and would require a great deal of consideration and possible delay in action, if there was to be any action.

He thinks we ought to be realists in our policy; that we ought to realize that the British Empire is gone; that the British Navy may be gone. Even with the British Navy afloat they have won only one victory and that at Montevideo. Every time they have gone in range of a shore battery or an air field on land they have been defeated. They are unable to clear the seas of raiders. If Italy is successful in Greece and Germany goes on into Turkey, the British bases in the Mediterranean will have to be abandoned, and they will be forced out of the Mediterranean, if they can get out. He sees the Empire crumbling.

On the other hand, he sees Hitler rampant on European soil, dominant even over England. He sees a new philosophy, both political and economic, with the United States excluded from European markets and from Far Eastern markets and from South American markets, for he feels that we are not able to absorb the products of South America except for gold and that we would soon be transferring our gold to South America and that the process could not last very long.

Consequently he thinks that we ought to sake some steps to implement a realistic policy and make some approach to Germany and to Japan which would result in an economic collaboration. He does not see how or what. He has no suggestion to make. He only feels that what we are doing is wrong but does not know how to do it right.

He says we are sending Generals and Admirals to England and instead we ought also to be sending economic experts. He says England is just as much of a socialistic state today as is Germany or Italy. He is sure that England cannot hold out unless America will just take over the airplane production and furnish England thousands and thousands and thousands of planes. She will not be able to make planes much longer. Even when she does receive them from America she has to put them in the factories and supplement them with armor. He said she had not received from the United States, up to the time he left, one single fighting plane. English planes were superior to the Germans and the English fighting flying men were superior to the Germans. He has seen three English fighting planes drive off and bring down twenty Germans, but the Germans have now adopted a new technique in maneuvers, and now they do get through to London, and they have very great explosives. He has seen twenty houses collapsed by one. They now do penetrate, and they allow seven minutes to get from the coast to London. He thinks the English will soon be battered into a desire for some understanding with Germany and that Churchill will go and that Lloyd George will take his place.

Furthermore, he thinks that the spirit and the morale of the world is broken; that people have lost their faith in God. He cited an example of a little church in Horta which was holding a vesper service and that there was a crowd of men on the other side of the street. Upon being approached the men said there was no use in going to church, that men could no longer believe in God, that the situations which were developing in the world could never happen if there was a God; that they were disillusioned; they were without hope.

He is going to take a short vacation and use up his leave for a month or more and then he is going to return to Washington and see the President. He is going to say that if there is something real to be done in England and if a policy can be worked out that will insure the winning of this war that he will go back to England, but if there is not that he will tell the President that there is nothing for him to do in England and that he will resign. He does not believe in our present policy. He does not believe in the continuing of democracy. He thinks that we will have to assume a Fascist form of government here or something similar to it if we are to survive in a world of concentrated and centralized power.

55

The Destroyer-Base Deal

The White House,
August 22, 1940

Dear Dave:

Here is the real meat in the coconut as expressed to me by a Dutchess County farmer yesterday morning. I told him the gist of the proposal which is, in effect, to buy ninety-nine year leases from Great Britain for at least seven naval and air bases in British Colonial possessions—not including the Dominion of Canada, which is a separate study on my part. The farmer replied somewhat as follows:

"Say, ain't you the Commander-in-Chief? If you are and own fifty muzzle-loadin' rifles of the Civil War period, you would be a chump if you declined to exchange them for seven modern machine guns—wouldn't you?"

Frankly, my difficulty is that as President and as Commander-in-Chief I have no right to think of politics in the sense of being a candidate or desiring votes. You and I know that our weakness in the past has lain in the fact that from Newfoundland to Trinidad our sole protection OFFSHORE lies in the three contiguous Islands of Porto Rico, St. Thomas and St. Croix. That, in the nature of modern warfare, is a definite operating handicap. If for fifty ships, which are on their last legs anyway, we can get the right to put in naval and air bases in Newfoundland, Bermuda, the Bahamas, Jamaica, St. Lucia, Trinidad and British Guiana, then our operating deficiency is largely cured.

Naturally, knowing the situation in all of these places intimately, I do not want the United States to assume control over the civilian populations on these Islands. In the first place, they do not want to live under the American Flag, and, in the second place, the civilian populations would be a drain on the national treasury, would create all kinds of

SOURCE: Franklin D. Roosevelt to David I. Walsh, August 22, 1940, in Elliott Roosevelt (ed.), *F.D.R.: His Personal Letters* (2 vols., New York, 1950), II, 1056–7.

tariff involvements in the Senate and House, and give future generations of Americans a headache.

Honestly, Dave, these Islands are of the utmost importance to our national defense as naval and air operating bases.

In regard to German retaliation, I think you can rest quietly on that score. If Germany, at the conclusion of this war or before that, wants to fight us, Germany will do so on any number of trumped-up charges.

Finally, I hope you will not forget that the founder of the Democratic Party purchased Louisiana from a belligerent nation, France, while France was at war with England. He did this without even consulting the Congress. He put the deal through and later on he asked the House Committee on Appropriations to put $15,000,000 into the appropriation bill.

By the way, the fifty destroyers are the same type of ship which we have been from time to time striking from the naval list and selling for scrap for, I think, $4,000 or $5,000 per destroyer. On that basis, the cost of the right to at least seven naval and air bases is an extremely low one from the point of view of the United States Government—i.e., about $250,000!

I do hope you will not oppose the deal which, from the point of view of the United States, I regard as being the finest thing for the nation that has been done in your lifetime and mine. I am absolutely certain that this particular deal will not get us into war and, incidentally, that we are not going into war anyway unless Germany wishes to attack us.

I hope to see you very soon.

Always sincerely,
[FRANKLIN D. ROOSEVELT]

56

The "Green-Light" Telegram

. . . 3. Whatever the intentions of the present Japanese Government may be there cannot be any doubt that the military and other elements in Japan see in the present world situation a "golden opportunity" to carry their dreams of expansion into effect; the German victories, like strong wine, have gone to their heads; they have believed implicitly until recently in Great Britain's defeat; they have argued that the war will probably be ended in a quick German victory and that Japan's position in Greater East Asia should be consolidated while Germany is still agreeable and before Japan might be robbed of her far-flung control in the Far East by the eventual hypothetical strengthening of the German naval power; although carefully watching the attitude of the United States they have discounted effective opposition on our part. It has been and is doubtful that the saner heads in and out of the government will be able to control these elements.

4. However, now a gradual change can be sensed in the outburst of exhilaration which greeted the inception of the new government. It is beginning to be seen by the Japanese Government, the army, the navy, and the public, that Germany may not defeat Great Britain after all, a possibility which I have constantly emphasized in the plainest language to my Japanese contacts and now, in addition to that dawning realization, they see that Britain and the United States are steadily drawing closer together in mutual defense measures with the American support of the British fleet by the transfer of fifty destroyers and with our acquisition of naval bases in British Atlantic possessions. Reports are being heard of our rapid construction of a two-ocean Navy and of our consideration of strengthening our Pacific naval bases and they even hear rumors that we will eventually use Singapore. Japanese consciousness is logically

SOURCE: Joseph Grew, telegram to the Secretary of State, September 12, 1940, in U. S. Department of State, *Peace and War* (Washington, 1943), pp. 569–72.

being affected by these rumors and developments. They tend on the one hand to emphasize the potential danger facing Japan from the United States and Great Britain eventually acting together in positive action (Japan has long appreciated the danger of combined Anglo-American measures as evidenced by the efforts to avoid the simultaneous irritation of these two countries) or from the United States acting alone. They furnish cogent arguments on the other hand for those Japanese elements who seek political and economic security by securing raw material sources and markets entirely within Japanese control. In regard to Germany, it is beginning to be questioned by the Japanese whether even a victorious Germany would not furnish a new hazard to their program of expansion both in China and in their advance to the south. Meanwhile, an uncertain factor in their calculations is always the future attitude and position of Russia. They are beginning to be concerned by these various considerations. High-powered diplomacy, particularly in the Dutch East Indies, will continue. But the fact that the Japanese military forces could be restrained even temporarily by the government from their plans for a headlong invasion of Indo-China denotes a degree of caution which I have no doubt was influenced partially at least by the American attitude. Until the world situation, particularly the position of the United States, becomes clearer the "nibbling policy" appears likely to continue.

5. I have expressed the opinion in previous communications that American-Japanese relations would be set on a downward curve if sanctions were applied by the United States. It is true that measures are now justified by our new program of national preparedness which need not fall within the category of outright sanctions. On the other hand, the probability must be contemplated that drastic embargoes on such important products as oil, of which a super-abundance is known to be possessed by the United States, would be interpreted by the people and government of Japan as actual sanctions and some form of retaliation might and probably would follow. The risks would depend not so much upon the careful calculations of the Japanese Government as upon the uncalculating "do or die" temper of the army and navy should they impute to the United States the responsibility for the failure of their plans for expansion. It may be that such retaliation would take the form of counter-measures by the government but it would be more likely that it would be some sudden stroke by the navy or army without the prior authorization or knowledge of the government. These dangers constitute an imponderable element which cannot be weighed with assurance at any given moment. However, it would be short sighted to deny their existence or to formulate policy and adopt

measures without fully considering these potential risks and determining the wisdom of facing them squarely.

6. . . . Since I have set forth carefully the inevitable hazards which a strong policy involves, I now turn respectfully to the hazards involved in the policy of *laissez faire*.

7. It is impossible in a discussion of the specific question of relations between the United States and Japan to view that problem in its proper perspective unless it is considered part and parcel of the world problem which presents in brief the following aspects: (a) Britain and America are the leaders of a large world-wide group of English-speaking peoples which stand for a "way of life" which today is being threatened appallingly by Italy, Germany, and Japan. . . . The avowed purpose of these powers is the imposition of their will upon conquered peoples by force of arms. In general, the uses of diplomacy are bankrupt in attempting to deal with such powers. Occasionally diplomacy may retard, but it cannot stem the tide effectively. Only by force or the display of force can these powers be prevented from attaining their objectives. Japan is today one of the predatory powers; having submerged all ethical and moral sense she has become unashamedly and frankly opportunist, at every turn seeking to profit through the weakness of others. American interests in the Pacific are definitely threatened by her policy of southward expansion, which is a thrust at the British Empire in the east. (b) Admittedly America's security has depended in a measure upon the British fleet, which has been in turn and could only have been supported by the British Empire. (c) If the support of the British Empire in this her hour of travail is conceived to be in our interest, and most emphatically do I so conceive it, we must strive by every means to preserve the status quo in the Pacific, at least until the war in Europe has been won or lost. This cannot be done, in my opinion, nor can we further protect our interests properly and adequately merely by the expression of disapproval and carefully keeping a record thereof. Clearly, Japan has been deterred from the taking of greater liberties with American interests only because she respects our potential power; equally is it [clear] that she has trampled upon our rights to an extent in exact ratio to the strength of her conviction that the people of the United States would not permit that power to be used. It is possible that once that conviction is shaken the uses of diplomacy may again become accepted. (d) Therefore, if by firmness we can preserve the status quo in the Pacific until and if Great Britain is successful in the European war, a situation will be faced by Japan which will render it impossible for the present opportunist philosophy to keep the upper hand. Then it might be possible at a moment to undertake a readjustment of the whole prob-

lem of the Pacific on a frank, fair, and equitable basis which will be to the lasting benefit of both Japan and America. Until there is in Japan a complete regeneration of thought, a show of force, coupled with the determination that it will be used if necessary, alone can effectively contribute to such an outcome and to our own future security. . . .

57

A World-Wide Conflict

The White House,
December 31, 1940

Dear Frank:

The expression which you give me in your letter of November 13 of your pleasure over my re-election and of your good wishes for the critical four years that lie ahead is naturally most gratifying.

We of course do not want to be drawn into a war with Japan —we do not want to be drawn into any war anywhere. There is, however, very close connection between the hostilities which have been going on for three and a half years in the Far East and those which have been going on for sixteen months in eastern Europe and the Mediterranean. For practical purposes there is going on a world conflict, in which there are aligned on one side Japan, Germany and Italy, and on the other side China, Great Britain and the United States. This country is not involved in the hostilities, but there is no doubt where we stand as regards the issues. Today, Japan and Germany and Italy are allies. Whatever any one of them gains or "wins" is a gain for their side and, conversely, a loss for the other side. Great Britain is on the defensive not alone in and around the British Isles, and not alone in and around the Mediterranean, but wherever there is a British possession or a British ship—and that means all over the world.

You say that you have "the feeling that any day Japan may start moving southwards." As you point out, we are faced with the danger of Japan's continuing her expansion in the Far East, especially toward the south, while the European issue remains in the balance. If Japan, moving further southward, should gain possession of the region of the Netherlands East Indies and the Malay Penninsula, would not the chances of Germany's defeating Great Britain be increased and the chances of England's winning be decreased thereby? I share your view

SOURCE: Franklin D. Roosevelt to Francis B. Sayre, December 31, 1940, in Elliott Roosevelt (ed.), *F.D.R.: His Personal Letters*, II, 1093–5.

that our strategy should be to render every assistance possible to Great Britain without ourselves entering the war, but would we be rendering every assistance possible to Great Britain were we to give our attention wholly and exclusively to the problems of the immediate defense of the British Isles and of Britain's control of the Atlantic? The British Isles, the British in those Isles, have been able to exist and to defend themselves not only because they have prepared strong local defenses but also because as the heart and the nerve center of the British Empire they have been able to draw upon vast resources for their sustenance and to bring into operation against their enemies economic, military and naval pressures on a world-wide scale. They live by importing goods from all parts of the world and by utilizing large overseas financial resources. They are defended not only by measures of defense carried out locally but also by distant and wide-spread economic, military, and naval activities which both diminish the vital strength of their enemies and at the same time prevent those enemies from concentrating the full force of their armed power against the heart and the nerve center of the Empire.

The British need assistance along the lines of our generally established policies at many points, assistance which in the case of the Far East is certainly well within the realm of "possibility" so far as the capacity of the United States is concerned. Their defense strategy must in the nature of things be global. Our strategy of giving them assistance toward ensuring our own security must envisage both sending of supplies to England and helping to prevent a closing of channels of communication to and from various parts of the world, so that other important sources of supply and other theaters of action will not be denied to the British. We have no intention of being "sucked into" a war with Germany. Whether there will come to us war with either or both of those countries will depend far more upon what they do than upon what we deliberately refrain from doing. . . .

With best wishes for a good New Year, I am

Very sincerely yours,

[Franklin D. Roosevelt]

58

"Foreseen for So Many Years"

Foreseen for so many years: these evils, this monstrous violence,
  these massive agonies: no easier to bear.
We saw them with slow stone strides approach, everyone saw them;
  we closed our eyes against them, we looked
And they had come nearer. We ate and drank and slept, they came
  nearer. Sometimes we laughed, they were nearer. Now
They are here. And now a blind man foresees what follows them:
  degradation, famine, despair and so forth, and the
Epidemic manias: but not enough death to serve us, not enough
  death. It would be better for men
To be few and live far apart, where none could infect another;
  then slowly the sanity of field and mountain
And the cold ocean and glittering stars might enter their minds.

                                                        Another
       dream, another dream.
We shall have to accept certain limitations
In future, and abandon some humane dreams; only hard-minded,
  sleepless and realist can ride this rock-slide
To new fields down the dark mountain; and we shall have to per-
  ceive that these insanities are normal;
We shall have to perceive that battle is a burning flower or like a
  huge music, and the dive-bomber's screaming orgasm
As beautiful as other passions; and that death and life are not
  serious alternatives. One has known all these things
For many years: there is greater and darker to know
In the next hundred.
                        And why do you cry, my dear, why do you cry?
It is all in the whirling circles of time.

SOURCE: Robinson Jeffers, "Battle (May 28, 1940)," in *Be Angry at the Sun* (New York, 1941), pp. 130-2.

If millions are born millions will die;
In bed or in battle is no great matter
In the long orbits of time.
If England goes down and Germany up
The stronger dog will still be on top,
All in the turning of time.
If civilization goes down—that
Would be an event to contemplate.
It will not be in our time, alas, my dear,
It will not be in our time.

Sources and Acknowledgments

Part I: The Crisis
1. "Is it well with these States?" is taken from *Burning City*, by Stephen Vincent Benét (New York: Holt, Rinehart & Winston, 1933). Copyright, 1936, by Stephen Vincent Benét. Copyright renewed, ©, 1963, by Thomas C. Benét, Stephanie B. Mahin and Rachel Benét Lewis. Reprinted by permission of Brandt & Brandt.
2. From "No One Has Starved," *Fortune*, VI (September, 1932). Reprinted courtesy of *Fortune* Magazine.
3. "Hooverville" is taken from Charles R. Walker, "Relief and Revolution," *The Forum*, LXXXVIII (August, 1932). Reprinted by permission of the author.
4. From "Rebellion in the Cornbelt," by Mary Heaton Vorse. Originally published in *Harper's Magazine*, CLXVI (December, 1932).
5. "Beans, Bacon, and Gravy" is taken from *American Folksongs of Protest*, edited by John Greenway (Philadelphia, University of Pennsylvania Press, 1953). Reprinted by permission of University of Pennsylvania Press.
6. "The Bank Crisis" is taken from *Industrial Valley*, by Ruth McKenney (New York: Harcourt, Brace & World, 1939). Copyright © 1939 by Ruth McKenney, copyright renewed 1967 by Ruth McKenney. Reprinted by permission of Curtis Brown, Ltd.

Part II: The New Deal Response
7. "The Hundred Days" is taken from Frederick J. Essary, "The New Deal for Nearly Four Months," *The Literary Digest*, CXVI (July 1, 1933).
8. "The New Deal as Savior of Capitalism" is taken from *The Roosevelt I Knew*, by Frances Perkins (New York: Viking Press, 1946). Copyright 1946 by Frances Perkins. Reprinted by permission of The Viking Press, Inc.
9. "The Theory of the New Deal" is taken from A. A. Berle, Jr., "The Social Economics of the New Deal," *The New York Times Magazine*, October 29, 1933. Copyright © 1933 by The New York Times Company. Reprinted by permission. Also reprinted by permission of the author.
10. "NRA Ballyhoo" is taken from *The Blue Eagle from Egg to Earth*, by Hugh S. Johnson (Garden City, N.Y.: Doubleday, Doran and Co., 1935).
11. "The Brain Trust" is taken from "The Hullabaloo Over the 'Brain Trust,'" *The Literary Digest*, CXVI (June 3, 1933).
12. "The TVA's Mission" is taken from "Letter to Newton Arvin" (February, 1939) in *The Journals of David E. Lilienthal*, Vol. I: The TVA Years, 1939–1945 (New York: Harper & Row 1964). Copyright © 1964 by David E. Lilienthal. Reprinted by permission of Harper & Row, Publishers.

13. "The Revival of Confidence" is taken from Rud Rennie, "Changing the Tune from Gloom to Cheer," *The Literary Digest*, CXVII (June 16, 1934).
14. "Rediscovering America" is taken from *The World at Home*, by Anne O'Hare McCormick, edited by Marion Turner Sheehan (New York: Alfred A. Knopf, 1956). Copyright © 1956 by Alfred A. Knopf, Inc. Reprinted by permission. Also reprinted by permission of McIntosh & Otis, Inc.

Part III: Toward The Welfare State
15. "The Relief Lady Calls" is taken from *The Trouble I've Seen*, by Martha Gellhorn (New York: William Morrow & Co., Inc., 1936). Copyright © 1936 by Martha Gellhorn; copyright renewed 1963 by Martha Gellhorn.
16. "WPA Spending" is taken from *Arena*, by Hallie Flanagan (New York: Duell, Sloan and Pearce, 1940). Copyright 1940 by Hallie Flanagan. Reprinted by permission of Duell, Sloan and Pearce, affiliate of Meredith Press.
17. "NYA on the Campus" is taken from *A New Deal for Youth*, by Ernest K. Lindley (New York: Viking Press, 1938). Copyright 1938, by Ernest K. Lindley. All Rights Reserved. Reprinted by permission of The Viking Press, Inc. Also reprinted by permission of the author.
18. "The President Signs the Social Security Act" is taken from Franklin D. Roosevelt, "Presidential Statement upon Signing the Social Security Act," August 14, 1935, in *The Public Papers and Addresses of Franklin D. Roosevelt*, edited by Samuel Rosenman, Volume IV (New York: Random House, 1938).
19. "The Significance of Social Security" is taken from Frances Perkins, "The Social Security Act," September 2, 1935, in *Vital Speeches of the Day* (Pelham, New York: City News Publishing Co., 1935), Volume I. Reprinted by permission of the publisher.

Part IV: Unionizing Industrial America
20. "The Struggle for Industrial Unionism" is taken from *Report of the Proceedings of the Fifty-fifth Annual Convention of the American Federation of Labor* (Washington, D.C.: Judd & Detweiler, 1936).
21. "Violence at Goodyear" is taken from *Life, Liberty and Property*, by Alfred Winslow Jones (Philadelphia: J. B. Lippincott & Co., 1941).
22. "Sit-down at General Motors" is taken from *Labor's New Millions*, by Mary Heaton Vorse (New York: Modern Age Books, 1938).
23. "The National Labor Relations Act," 49 U.S. Statutes at Large 449 (1935).
24. "The Supreme Court Sustains the Wagner Act" is taken from *NLRB v. Jones and Laughlin Steel Corporation*, 301 U. S. 1 (1937).

Part V: Ill Fares The Land
25. "A New Deal for the Farmer" is taken from Franklin D. Roosevelt, Address to Farmers, May 14, 1935, in *Vital Speeches of the Day*, Volume I (Pelham, New York: City News Publishing Co., 1935).

26. "The Paradox of Scarcity and Abundance" is taken from *New Frontiers*, by Henry A. Wallace (New York: Reynal & Hitchcock, 1934). Reprinted by permission of the publishers, Harcourt, Brace & World, Inc.

27. "Triple A Plowed Under," from *Federal Theatre Plays*, edited by Pierre de Rohan (New York: Random House, 1938). Copyright 1938 and renewed 1966 by Random House, Inc. Reprinted by permission.

28. "Letters from the Dust Bowl," taken from Carolyn Henderson, "Letters from the Dust Bowl," *The Atlantic Monthly*, CLVII (May, 1936). Reprinted by permission of *The Atlantic Monthly*.

29. *The River*, by Pare Lorentz (New York: Stackpole & Sons, 1938). Reprinted by permission of The Stackpole Company.

30. "Tough Babes in the Woods" is taken from *Puzzled America*, by Sherwood Anderson (New York: Charles Scribner's Sons, 1935). Copyright 1935 by Sherwood Anderson; renewed. Reprinted by permission of Harold Ober Associates, Inc.

31. "The Joads Reach a Government Camp" is taken from *The Grapes of Wrath*, by John Steinbeck (New York: Viking Press, 1939). Copyright 1939 by John Steinbeck. Reprinted by permission of The Viking Press, Inc. Also reprinted by permission of McIntosh and Otis, Inc.

Part VI: The Roosevelt Coalition

32. "FDR's Class Coalition" is taken from *Chip off My Shoulder*, by Thomas Stokes (Princeton, New Jersey, 1940). Reprinted by permission of Princeton University Press.

33. "Roosevelt Explains the Box Score" is taken from Franklin D. Roosevelt, Address at Forbes Field, Pittsburgh, Pennsylvania, October 1, 1936, in *The Public Papers and Addresses of Franklin D. Roosevelt*, edited by Samuel Rosenman, Volume V (New York: Random House, 1938).

34. "A Complete Rout" is taken from *The Secret Diary of Harold L. Ickes*, Volume I (New York: Simon & Schuster, 1953). Copyright © 1953 by Simon & Schuster, Inc. Reprinted by permission of the publisher.

35. "Politics of the Deed" is taken from Samuel Lubell, "Post-Mortem: Who Elected Roosevelt?" *The Saturday Evening Post*, CCXIII (January 25, 1941). Reprinted by permission of the author.

Part VII: Thunder on The Left

36. "The Failure of Liberal Democracy" is taken from *The Economic Consequences of the New Deal*, by Benjamin Stolberg and Warren Jay Vinton (New York: Harcourt, Brace, 1935). Copyright, 1935, by Benjamin Stolberg and Warren Jay Vinton; renewed, 1963, by Mary Fox Herling and Warren Jay Vinton. Reprinted by permission of Harcourt, Brace & World, Inc.

37. "The Ballad of Roosevelt," by Langston Hughes, *New Republic*, LXXXI November 14, 1934). Copyright © 1934 by Langston Hughes. Reprinted by permission of Harold Ober Associates, Inc.

38. "A Muckraker's Proclamation" is taken from *The Letters of Lincoln Steffens*, edited by Ella Winter and Granville Hicks, Volume II (New

York: Harcourt, Brace, 1938). Copyright, 1938, by Harcourt, Brace & World, Inc.; renewed, 1966, by Ella Winter and Granville Hicks. Reprinted by permission of the publisher.

39. From "Why I Am Not a Communist," by John Dewey, *The Modern Monthly*, VIII (April, 1934). Reprinted by permission of Mrs. John Dewey and The John Dewey Foundation.

40. "Huey Long's 'First Days in the White House' " is taken from *My First Days in the White House*, by Huey Pierce Long (Harrisburg, Pa.: The Telegraph Press, 1935).

41. "The Administration Strikes Back at Long" is taken from the Transcript of Meeting of February 5, 1935, The White House, in *New Deal Mosaic*, edited by Lester Seligman and Elmer E. Cornwell, Jr. (Eugene, Oregon: University of Oregon Press, 1965). Reprinted by permission of University of Oregon Press.

42. "Father Coughlin's Union Party" is taken from Father Charles E. Coughlin, "A Third Party," in *Vital Speeches of The Day*, Volume II (Pelham, New York: City News Publishing Co., 1936). Reprinted by permission of the publisher.

Part VIII: The Conservative Opposition

43. "The Republican Creed" is taken from Daniel O. Hastings, "Battle of November," *Today*, II (October 13, 1934).

44. "Dr. Roosevelt Is a Quack" is taken from H. L. Mencken, "Three Years of Dr. Roosevelt," *The American Mercury*, XXXVII (March, 1936). Reprinted by permission of *The American Mercury*, Box 7213, Houston, Texas.

45. "Herbert Hoover Indicts the New Deal" is taken from Herbert Hoover, Address of October 30, 1936, in *The New York Times* (October 31, 1936).

46. "The Cliché Expert Testifies as a Roosevelt Hater," from *A Pearl in Every Oyster*, by Frank Sullivan (Boston: Little, Brown & Co., 1938), Copyright 1938 by Frank Sullivan; originally appeared in *The New Yorker*. Reprinted by permission of Little, Brown and Co.

47. "The Supreme Court is the Shield of Liberty" is taken from "Reorganization of the Federal Judiciary," *Senate Report No. 711*, 75th Cong, 1st Sess. (1937).

Part IX: The Approach of War

48. "Roosevelt's Bombshell Message" is taken from Franklin D. Roosevelt, wireless to the London Conference, July 3, 1933, in *The Public Papers and Addresses of Franklin D. Roosevelt*, edited by Samuel Rosenman, Volume II (New York: Random House, 1938).

49. "I Hate War" is taken from Franklin D. Roosevelt, Address at Chautauqua, New York, August 14, 1936, in *The Public Papers and Addresses of Franklin D. Roosevelt*, edited by Samuel Rosenman, Volume V (New York: Random House, 1938).

50. "History Repeats Itself" is taken from Bruce Bliven, "This Is Where I Came In," *The New Republic*, XCIII (January 5, 1938). Reprinted by permission of *The New Republic*, copyright 1966, Harrison-Blaine of New Jersey, Inc.

51. "Litany for Dictatorships," from *The Selected Works of Stephen Vincent Benét*. Published by Holt, Rinehart and Winston, Inc. Copyright, 1935, by Stephen Vincent Benét. Copyright renewed © 1963, by Thomas C. Benét, Stephanie B. Mahin, and Rachel Benét Lewis. Reprinted by permission of Brandt & Brandt.

52. "Weep in Years to Come," reprinted from *Selected Short Stories of Irwin Shaw* by permission of Random House, Inc. Also taken from *Mixed Company*, by Irwin Shaw (New York and London, 1950); reprinted by permission of Johnathan Cape, Ltd. Copyright 1939 by Irwin Shaw. Originally appeared in *The New Yorker*.

53. "The Charlottesville Program," taken from Franklin D. Roosevelt, Address at Charlottesville, Va., June 10, 1940, in *Department of State Bulletin*, II (1940).

54. "The Cry for Appeasement" is reprinted from *The War Diary of Breckinridge Long*, edited by Fred L. Israel, by permission of the University of Nebraska Press. Copyright 1966 by the University of Nebraska Press.

55. "The Destroyer-Base Deal" is taken from the letter of Franklin D. Roosevelt to David I Walsh, August 22, 1940, in *F.D.R.: His Personal Letters*, edited by Elliott Roosevelt (New York: Duell, Sloan and Pearce, 1950). Copyright 1948 by Elliott Roosevelt. Reprinted by permission of Duell, Sloan and Pearce, affiliate of Meredith Press. Also reprinted by permission of George G. Harrap & Co., Ltd., London.

56. "The 'Green-Light' Telegram" is taken from Joseph Grew, telegram to the Secretary of State, September 12, 1940, in U. S. Department of State, *Peace and War* (Washington: U.S. Government Printing Office, 1943).

57. "A World-Wide Conflict" is taken from the letter of Franklin D. Roosevelt to Francis B. Sayre, December 31, 1940, in *F.D.R.: His Personal Letters*, edited by Elliott Roosevelt (New York: Duell, Sloan and Pearce, 1950). Copyright 1948 by Elliott Roosevelt. Reprinted by permission of Duell, Sloan and Pearce, affiliate of Meredith Press. Also reprinted by permission of George G. Harrop & Co., Ltd., London.

58. "Foreseen for So Many Years" is taken from "Battle (May 28, 1940)," by Robinson Jeffers. Copyright 1940 by Robinson Jeffers. Reprinted from *Be Angry at the Sun And Other Poems*, by Robinson Jeffers, by permission of Random House, Inc.